WHO CAN BE EDUCATED?

WHO CAN BE EDUCATED?

by Milton Schwebel, Ph.D.
DEAN, GRADUATE SCHOOL OF EDUCATION
RUTGERS UNIVERSITY

Grove Press, Inc. New York

Second Printing
Library of Congress Catalog Card Number: 68-22002
Manufactured in the United States of America

To Bernice, Andy, and Bob

and all those of youthful
spirit the world around
who will not be prisoners
of the myths we create

PREFATORY NOTE

The roots of this book go back to some distant but uncertain experience in the past, possibly a childhood in an interracial public school or an undergraduate seminar in social and political philosophy. I began to formulate the major ideas in the late 1950's and especially during a sabbatical year abroad in the 1960's. Some of the preliminary work was done in the tranquility of the library of the British Museum and also of the University of London and of Maudsley Hospital, and some of the first outlines were written on a terrace overlooking the Mediterranean at Taormina, Sicily. The first product was a series of papers, and the manuscript for this book was written between 1966 and early 1968.

The period of foreign travel which gave me first-hand knowledge of schools, child-guidance clinics, and educational research centers in Western and Eastern Europe was supported in part by New York University through a sabbatical, supplemented by a grant from the World Federation for Mental Health (United States Committee). I am grateful to my friends Dr. Marion Langer and Professor Bernard Fischman for their encouragement in connection with these and for their help in arranging the travels.

Ideas are social products, and some of mine came from discussion with hundreds of students and many colleagues, especially at New York University but also at the Postgraduate Center for Mental Health and, more recently, at Rutgers University. Shorter periods of time at Antioch, Wisconsin, Oklahoma, Southern California, Prince-

ton, Southern, Hawaii, and City University of New York, among others, were also extremely productive. Among the most fruitful exchanges were those with school people in public and parochial schools around the country. I am also indebted to Professors Harold A. Larrabee, Donald E. Super, Robert Hoppock, and Clifford J. Sager.

Not all the dialogues were with academic people, however; many were with the self-educated and with working people outside the university world. Talking with young people is particularly helpful in preventing premature mental senility, because their fresh view of things protects us from lagging too far behind in our perception of a swiftly changing world. I owe a debt of gratitude to students, sons, nieces and nephews, cousins, friends and neighbors, including among the latter the late Andrew J. Bernstein.

I am grateful to Dr. Walter Z. Schwebel, pediatrician, for his critical reading of Chapter Five, and to the following school people for obtaining the data for one of the studies reported herein: Mr. Harris Buxbaum, Dr. Linda de Bottari, Mrs. Shirley Flug, Mrs. Shirley Garmise, Mrs. Tobie Kessler, Dr. Gerald Murphy, and Mrs. Bernice Schwebel. Two research assistants, Mrs. Carol Richards and Mr. Robert Caruso, were helpful at different stages of the writing. For the typing my thanks go to Mrs. Betty Gilbert, Mrs. Suzanne West, and especially to Miss Elizabeth J. Vessels, who did the bulk of the job. Mrs. Dimmes Bishop reviewed and made editorial comments on an early draft of the manuscript. My friends at Grove Press were generous with their time, and Mrs. Mary Heathcote in particular, more humanist than stylist, made the pressures of the final stages not only bearable but even downright enjoyable.

My wife, to whom with my sons this book is dedicated, helped in countless ways, not least of all by giving the author a first-hand view of the life and problems of a gifted kindergarten teacher.

M.S.

CONTENTS

THE ISSUES, PAST AND PRESENT

PART 1

1

THE THEORIES

Asked how he happened to develop his revolutionary theory of relativity, Albert Einstein said that he had challenged an axiom. Instead of going along with universally accepted scientific laws about the universe, he questioned them, and in doing so he gave us a deeper understanding of our physical environment and greater mastery over it. Education has no axioms about intelligence or educability, but a careful look at any school system in America will show that educators operate the schools as if there were such laws—as if we knew the limits of man's capacity to learn. As a result, when students don't learn, school people look to see what is wrong with the children rather than the school.

This book is about such false thinking, and about the alternatives to it. We will see that it pervades American education, damaging all children, some more than others, and we will examine a more constructive and scientifically valid approach to the understanding of learning ability—not a law, but the kind of frank recognition of ignorance about the real limits of learning that could open the door to basic changes in the school systems, and in the universities that prepare teachers for the schools, and in the thinking of American parents.

Almost twenty-five years ago the sociologists Warner, Havighurst, and Loeb wrote a book called *Who Shall Be Educated?*[1] The time was near the end of the Second World War, when most Americans were full of hope for world peace and domestic prosperity, and when

the progress toward equality stimulated by federal actions taken during the war was expected to continue at the same pace. The authors described the inequities in the schools and, in particular, pointed out that able lower-class children—white as well as black—were not getting the education they deserved. Society was deprived of their talents and was saddled instead with people from the higher classes who with much less ability were holding positions for which they were not equipped.

Years passed, the tempo of progress favoring the lower classes slowed down after the war and then quickened as a result of the Supreme Court decision of 1954 in support of school integration, and especially of the forceful demand for equality made by black Americans. Now there was no longer an issue as to who *should* be educated, for the shift in power in the country had compelled governments to accept the view that everyone should have at least secondary education; that is, *everyone who is educable* should be so educated. The question has now become, Who *can* be educated?

The question has changed at the very time when an article with this title characterizes the situation in the schools: "The Rich Get Richer and the Poor Get Poorer . . . Schools."[2] These days, when the news media report that state and federal governments are pouring millions of dollars into education, few of us are prepared to discover that the gap in expenditures between the public school systems of the lower and the higher classes is steadily increasing. In 1957, annual expenditures per pupil in thirty-five of the largest American metropolitan areas were about equal in the cities and their suburbs. By 1962, the situation had changed to the extent that the middle-class suburbs were spending $145 more per pupil on an average than the cities, whose children are mostly those of the very poor and the very rich (and the rich tend to send their children to private schools). Equally shocking is the fact that state aid, which presumably would be used to offset the financial advantage of suburbia, actually discriminates against the cities; the suburbs receive $40 more in state aid per pupil than the cities. Some of the federal aid is directed specifically to disadvantaged areas, but not all the fanfare nor the dramatic rhetoric from high places can change the plain fact that ". . . while one and a quarter billion dollars per year are a lot of dollars, when they are spread over fifty states, for rural as well as city areas, the

impact on any one city—or any one school—is not massive at all."[3] Reducing the size of the class by one child, raising expenditures for supplies per pupil from $7.25 to $8.50, or adding one social worker to the staff of a slum school is not likely to yield results of any consequence except to lend support to those who declare that "those people" (meaning the slum dwellers) cannot benefit from good education.

The evidence seems clear that to begin to close the gap in the quality of education, the community will have to do more than equalize treatment. Equal educational opportunity requires "the application of unequal resources: more rather than less to the students from poor homes." Yet as a nation we are doing the opposite, "spending much more money to educate the children of the well-off than the children of the poor."[4]

Improvement of the city schools does not necessitate a sacrifice on the part of the suburban schools. In fact the children in the suburbs and in the white city schools will benefit in significant ways from genuine and giant steps to correct the inequality. The necessary funds are available and are now being spent on war, freeways, liquor, cosmetics, advertising, and many other things, for despite all our talk of "excellence" we have not committed ourselves intellectually or financially to the creation of excellence or anything even approaching it in city school systems. And a realistic appraisal of current boards of education—almost all of them "more tax-conscious than expenditure-conscious"[5]—gives no reason to believe that this situation will be changed except by public pressure.

Meanwhile militant groups demanding equality resort to actions that frighten community leaders. What kind of answer do the leaders give? In as standard a reflex as voting for inadequate funds, they raise questions about the ability of the lower classes to profit from the kind of education that has long been the province of the higher classes.

The history of man, and in particular the history of education and theories of educability, is marked by a continuous struggle for more and better education for more people. In the battle between the educational "haves" and the "have-nots" (who are usually identical with the economic "haves" and "have-nots"), every gain is countered by another obstacle to the realization of its full benefits. Once

a society concedes that another stratum has a right to public education, some powerful element within the society challenges the competence of that stratum (social class, ethnic group, race) to make worthwhile use of the opportunities it has won. The challenge always comes before there is realization of the right, and always succeeds in eroding it.

So it is happening today. No sooner has the United States embarked on its most ambitious attempt so far to give the poor and especially Negroes some approximation of equality of educational opportunity—which turns out to be not enough even to maintain the 1957 parity in expenditures per pupil between city and suburban schools—than questions are raised as to whether black people have the intellectual ability of whites. *Science,* the journal of the American Association for the Advancement of Science, recently reprinted a statement from the prestigious National Academy of Sciences on the relative importance of heredity and environment on racial differences in behavior. The introductory remarks written by a *Science* editor included the following: "William Shockley of Stanford, who won the Nobel Prize for work on transistors, has lately been arguing for an expansion of research to evaluate the relative effects of heredity and environment on human intelligence and performance. Implicit in his proposals is at least speculation that inferior genetic inheritance, rather than inferior environment, accounts for the relatively poor performance of some Negroes in various competitive situations."[6] This is but one in a long history of statements made by emperors, politicians, scientists, and scholars to raise doubts about the ability of the lower classes—sometimes English, sometimes German, sometimes white Americans, now black Americans—to make equal use of educational opportunity.

With indecent haste, evidence is adduced to raise suspicions about the alleged inferiority of a people *before* the society has completed even the early stages of correcting the inequities and the consequences of centuries of inequality in every form. Their inferiority is established *before* they have had a chance to prove otherwise.

The theories of ability that prevail in our schools today lend themselves to judgments about the inferiority of a class or a people. Placing major stress on genetic inheritance, they justify evaluations of ability primarily on the basis of children's observable perform-

ance. The psychologists and educators who apply the theories make some allowance for deprivation but then are quite prepared to make estimates of ability on the basis of test scores. The theories and the tests enable the society to engage in a self-fulfilling prophecy with the lives of the lower-class children: The students do poorly on the tests; their schooling is inadequate; their ultimate achievement proves the tests were valid in the first place.

The victims of such theories and of the behavior they justify are almost all of the people. When a society creates a view of man that is built on the wish to maintain the status quo in wealth and power, it creates false doctrine which corrupts a public school system, even one as powerful as ours, which has the potential of helping our country reach unparalleled heights of intelligence, culture, and humanism. As a result, almost everyone—students, teachers, and parents—is dissatisfied.

Education is important to a large number of Americans. More than twenty-five percent of them are directly engaged in it as a full-time occupation, either as students, teachers, principals, custodians, or professors.[7] Many more—especially the parents of the students—are so much involved that it occupies their thoughts during many waking hours and disturbs not a few of their sleeping ones. Employers who hire school graduates or dropouts, and the general public itself, whom these former students serve as mechanics or ministers, policemen or pediatricians, are affected by what goes on in the schools.

Such a vast operation, touching so many lives, is bound to attract the attention of numerous critics, and because of the unique conditions under which the schools function, education critics are even freer than most. Unlike other professional groups, teachers work in a fish-bowl situation: the public schools belong to the people who through their elected or appointed representatives presumably determine the objectives and the policies of the schools. Parents and other interested persons can witness the work of the teacher and are able to, or at least consider themselves qualified to, evaluate the quality of the work, as they could not the effectiveness of a doctor or a lawyer. Other professionals' activities are much less exposed and are also more apt to be clothed in the seeming mysteries of their respective professional languages.

There are critics inside the schools, too, especially teachers and students who do not like things as they are. Taken together, and making allowances for attacks by those who are enemies of education or public education *per se,* the criticisms add up to a serious indictment of the schools as they are now functioning. For the first time in the long history of man's formal education, two great powers, the United States and the Soviet Union, stand at the verge of offering universal education through the secondary level, and our schools, at least, are inadequate to the challenge of preparing many of our children, especially for academic studies.

The schools are getting plenty of criticism, but do they deserve it? They do, but just as much as the other professional and public services in America, not to mention private industry. The failure of the American people to get what they need applies as much to health, justice, social welfare, housing, public transportation, and recreation as to education. A 1967 report by the President's Advisory Commission on Health Manpower called for fundamental change in the nation's health care system because present practices result in high-cost, low-quality care. The commission found a serious quality gap between the latest advances in medical science and technology and the treatment given to patients. In a survey of 430 patients admitted to 98 hospitals in New York City in 1962, only 31 percent of the general medical cases received optimal care. Moreover, according to the report as given in *Science,* "Large segments of the population receive little or no care whatever."[8] Yes, other professional services are seriously deficient, even those as important in American life as education.

Recent books by working teachers give compelling evidence of the severity of the problems in the cities. In the North, the slum school is likely to be in an old section of the city, in an equally old building with signs of disrepair on the ceiling and walls, the windows or the plumbing. In the South the buildings are newer, having been erected in the hope, thus far largely fulfilled, of maintaining separate but equal schools—equal, that is, in terms of recency of construction. The sounds in urban schools vary considerably, ranging from the disruptive noises of a seething, undisciplined crowd to the silence of the police state. Seldom are there the sounds of children eagerly

at work, collectively or individually, on projects that excite them and their teachers.

In *The Schoolchildren,* Mary F. Greene and Orletta Ryan, teachers in Puerto Rican East Harlem and in Harlem itself, report on their experiences and the thoughts and lives of the children.[9] The morning starts with announcements and a pep talk by the principal over the loudspeaker system, and with door-slamming student-messengers come to deliver forms to be filled in for various purposes. The teacher trying to convince a child that she must get her mother to fill in a missing form is interrupted by a fight in another part of the room. Then it is time for reading.

> Reading, the dreary iron portals of ten o'clock, now overhangs the children. It's Monday too, the worst day, so violent and deadening are the week-ends in which these often malnourished and sick children have dribbled away hours of their strength on TV, movies, sitting on curbs. Some are now sucking thumbs, others peeping aloud or talking to themselves. But mostly they're just sitting and staring, mouths dropped open and left there. Heads stay in awkward positions. They are utterly exhausted. You'd think this would be a good day, but they are in a comatose state.[10]

Then there is Luce, pretty and intelligent, who suffers from asthma attacks, and who does not stay out of school though she often sniffles and is sick-looking. She wants to read well, yet here in third grade she still falters over the first-grade reader. She plods and struggles and finally stares as in a trance.

> When her eyes lift, they contain the week-end: eight people in two rooms reeking with fried food, strangled at the end of four flights up. Babies, curses, TV mumbling, the people sitting as if drunk or dead, or else screaming shrill abuse. The stairs have trails of garbage, urine, even excrement.[11]

Change the time and the place, the language and the skin color, and instead of a contemporary teacher describing the American scene there is Dickens a century ago writing about the slums of London or Gorky seventy years ago describing counterparts in Russia. In each instance the author described the victims of social circumstance.

Our American teacher-authors are also sensitive and humane, qualities that seem not to be common in the inner-city schools. Jona-

than Kozol, who had attended private secondary schools, Harvard, and then Oxford as a Rhodes Scholar, taught in a segregated fourth-grade classroom in Boston in 1964–65. From this experience has come an eloquent statement whose content is explained by the title and subtitle: *Death at an Early Age: The Destruction of the Hearts and Minds of Negro Children in the Boston Public Schools.*[12]

He tells of Stephen, an apparently mentally disturbed child whose creative but unorthodox art work maddens the art teacher and drives her to carry out a vendetta against the tiny eight-year-old, humiliating him before the class and forbidding him friendship with Kozol.[13] That this woman's efforts as an art teacher can only crush the creative impulses in children is a relatively minor defect compared with what she does to their spirit and dignity.

Another boy in Kozol's class, Frederick, tells about the large raised scar that protrudes near the end of his finger.

> "It happened in September before you were my teacher. I was talking and I was sent down to the cellar and when I got the stick I was scared and I must have pulled back my hand a little so I got it on the knuckle instead of on the finger part. I already had a bad infection. They said it was my fault for not keeping my hand still."[14]

Children are beaten with thin bamboo whips, at times for the offense of failing "to show respect to the very same teachers who have been describing them as niggers."[15]

Kozol tells of the impact of the system on him. There is, of course, the story of his dismissal for failing "to abide by rules and regulations,"[16] by which is meant his devotion to the children and his determination to make their schooling relate to their lives. More important than the personal aspect is the meaning of his story for other teachers, and its implications for parents who care about the kind of instruction their children get. How had the teachers become the calloused men and women they were? Kozol describes his own struggle to fight the eroding effects of a system in which it is commonplace to speak of the children as "animals" and the school building as "a zoo." It is a too-easy out to attribute the corruption of the schools to the individual teachers, for such reasoning is on the same level as blaming children for their backwardness in learning.

In New York as in Boston some teachers talk of the children as if

they were animals. The condition is not new, not a reaction to the black-power movement or to riots, for those of us acquainted with real life in the schools in the 1940's and 1950's heard the lower-class children described as "beasts."

In the 1960's, the New York City teacher Herbert Kohl, author of *36 Children,* has written a book that is at once a moving human document and an account of masterful teaching. He has this to say about current attitudes:

> I attended to teachers' conversations, listened to them abuse the children until I could no longer go into the teachers' lunchroom. The most frequent epithet they used in describing the children was "animals." After a while the word "animal" came to epitomize for me most teachers' ambiguous relations to ghetto children—the scorn and the fear, the condescension yet the acknowledgment of some imagined power and unpredictability. I recognized some of that in myself, but never reached the sad point of denying my fear and uncertainty by projecting fearsome and unpredictable characteristics on the children and using them in class as some last primitive weapon.[17]

Those who want to go on believing that the problems in the ghetto schools are somehow inherent in the children should not read Kohl's book. He shows the malleability of even the most devastated children when they have reason to trust an adult, and especially when the adult shows respect for their intelligence by challenging them to work and think and by expecting them to succeed. From detestation they can with unexpected speed come to like school, learning, and books, and mainly themselves. Given the opportunity that Kohl gave them to become test-wise like white middle-class children, they can learn to be efficient at test-taking and elevate their reading scores to levels far in excess of their teachers' expectations. His students were able to do this only after he reported to them their IQ and reading test scores with a frankness unknown to them, and after he told them what they could do together to raise their scores if they wanted to. "It was," in Kohl's words, "a matter of their whole future, since in junior high school all but those few students put in the 'top' classes (three out of fourteen on each grade) were considered 'not college material' and treated with the scorn that they merited in their teachers' eyes."[18]

Yes, they could learn, but for what purpose? Kohl wondered whether he had been good for them when the following year he learned of their suffering and despair in the seventh grade with teachers who were typical—or typical victims—of the system. There were, he discovered, a few good teachers, men and women who know, understand, and respect the children and suffer as they watch the brutalizing treatment the students get and the abuse they themselves get for being different. And if, under the difficult circumstances imposed by the adults around them, they keep on liking the children, some at least give up being more than kindly custodians.[19] The system destroys teachers as well as students.

The cloud of deception and hypocrisy that hangs over the slum school casts its shadow over all the schools. Ways of thinking that are used to justify differences in the quality of education become part of the ideology of the entire system, suburban as well as inner city. When students are "not college material," white skin and middle-class status do not protect them from "the scorn that they merited in their teachers' eyes," as many a parent will testify. White or black, rich or poor, they have to learn that "the people who created objective tests believed as an article of faith that all the questions they made up had one and only one correct answer. Over and over, it is striking how rigid teachers tend to be and how difficult it is for children who haven't been clued in on this rigidity to figure out what the teacher expects in the way of suppression of original and clever responses."[20] The objectives of the suburban school are to make college material, to make it test-wise, and to get it into the "iviest" colleges. Kohl's thirty-six slum children at least went into the business of learning to play the game with their eyes wide open. They "agreed to be dull for the sake of their future."[21]

If the slum has become a compound without barbed wire, so has suburbia, as Fred M. Hechinger, education editor of the *New York Times,* says in the foreword to *The Shortchanged Children of Suburbia.*[22] Both enclaves have their inhabitants set off from the "outside" world. The suburban enclaves suffer from "an unhappily competitive and a deadening effect . . . sibling rivalry on a suburb-wide level." The atmosphere makes for sameness, narrowness (this is the best of all possible worlds), self-satisfaction, and limited horizons. In this setting teachers "tend to be more anxious to avoid than to

answer troublesome questions." Some parents know and are troubled by the fact that in their highly touted schools controversy is out, adolescents who raise challenging questions especially about controversial matters are *persona non grata,* and the leadership of the system (school board and superintendent) just doesn't want the boat rocked.

What are the solutions to these varied and complex problems? Journalist Maya Pines reports in popular style on new teaching techniques stemming from the work of educators and psychologists who are pioneers of early-age learning.[23] Her descriptions of the experimental projects in this country are interesting, and her emphasis on the cognitive development of the child rather than his "adjustment" as the chief focus of education is valid. But her expectation that the introduction of the new techniques will mean that "poor children will no longer be crushed before they can learn to learn,"[24] is an example of the naïve but widespread belief that we need only find the right method to correct the ills of the public school system.

Clearly, American education cries out for correction. Yet diagnoses and prescriptions have both suffered from the superficiality of confusing symptoms with causes. True, a lot of teaching is very poor. Many of the curricula and textbooks are outdated or, even worse, give a distorted version of the subjects of study, or an utterly irrelevant one. The physical facilities in some communities should have been replaced years ago with modern buildings and equipment. What is more, in some systems the administration of schools and the supervision of teachers is thoroughly inadequate. Finally, separate and unequal education for the several social classes as well as racial groups is being practiced widely even when the children are under one roof. Some school people hate the children they are suppose to serve, and many do not show the respect children must have if they are to learn.

All this is true, but why does it exist? What lies beneath it all? What are the underlying causes?

When a psychotherapist works with a group, let us say a family, he knows he must be sensitive to more than the spoken words. A mother accuses a father angrily: "You never do your share at home. You come in, eat and sit down at the TV and never get out of your chair except for a bottle of beer." The father grins and raises his

hands to suggest the uselessness of further discussion, which, of course, only infuriates the mother. Speaking tensely, a ten-year-old daughter defends her father with, "But what about . . ." And on it goes, the sides forming and giving testimony pro and con. The naïve therapist gets trapped into a careful weighing of the data to determine whether or not the father is doing his part, whereas the experienced one will look at the underlying relationship. What is really going on between the two adults? What is the basis for the conflict? Is one of the mates (or both, for that matter) so frightened by closeness with another person that to defend against it he or she manages to provoke conflict? Or did their earlier lives in families of different and antithetical sociological backgrounds lead them to acquire conflicting roles for the male and female?

A nation faced with complex problems must engage in the same search for underlying factors on a grand scale. Our present shotgun approach to a scattering of apparently unrelated weaknesses in the schools is a good way of perpetuating conditions. Not all the money in the United States will do the job if the job itself is not clear. And it cannot be clear until the nature of the educational problem is clearly defined. Cities must build new schools to replace the deteriorated schools and to make room for a growing population, but new buildings will not be the answer. More children need free lunches and books, and many more need medical, dental, psychological, and social services, but all these will not suffice if the problems extend beyond these needs, as they do. Most educators agree that improved programs for the education of new teachers and the upgrading of licensed teachers are necessary, but improvements that are to have significant effects must be based on understanding of the underlying defects in the present teacher-training programs. Educational research, which is lately experiencing a renaissance in terms of the number of investigators and the funds for their support, can make a major contribution only if it addresses itself to underlying causes. So far it has not done so.

The right answers cannot be gotten until the right questions are framed, and the questions must grow out of the conditions that give rise to the problems. The first among these is the fact that children who grow up in the ghettos do not achieve as well as others.

An equally important fact is that the quality of education given to lower-class children is inferior to that given the more privileged groups, in terms of teachers, books, and physical facilities. Another fact of contemporary life is that nobody expects these children to do as well as the others—not the teachers, nor the parents, nor the children themselves—and this nonexpectation is fulfilled often enough to reinforce it as a true reflection of their ability as students. Next, the school system changes slowly, and when children are backward in learning the difficulty is attributed to them rather than to the system, which today occupies itself with countless studies and experiments and innovations designed to discover how to correct what is wrong with the children. Furthermore, all this occurs in an atmosphere of struggle in which the educational have-nots are demanding more of those who are resistant to yielding more; and the children and the teachers both know that powerful blocs in the community are giving in grudgingly if at all. Finally, this struggle contaminates more than just the atmosphere for learning; it influences the content of the curriculum as well as the theories of learning and teaching, and especially of educability.

All children are deprived by the suppressions and distortions of knowledge long built up to justify inequalities in the face of contrary espoused values. Authors who want their textbooks sold in the South must not contradict that region's interpretation of history and democracy, and those who want an entrée to the schools of the country as a whole must be sure they say nothing that will upset the apple-cart. The status quo must be maintained even at a cost of critical inquiry and dissent, two essential ingredients in the development of the intellect. Now this kind of aseptic atmosphere carries over to all fields of study, to the sciences and humanities as well as history and civics, and all subjects, as a result, get the real guts squashed out of them with the result that all the schools, including the suburban ones, manage to curb the natural proclivity of children to be curious and to want to understand. In other words, the schools manage to bore the students, and their parents are left to resort to the use of all kinds of carrots and whips to keep them in the competition for a place in one of the better colleges.

Underlying all the conflict is the issue of educability. Many

educators, psychologists, and other behavioral scientists believe the question has been answered. In their view the limits are predetermined by the genes inherited from the parents at the moment of conception, and the approximate level of lifetime ability is measurable in childhood. The American school system is founded upon this belief, and the education of all children is considerably influenced by a theory of intelligence that has demanded the widespread use of intelligence tests, homogeneous ability grouping of children, and concepts like that of "college material."

If this assessment is correct, then we must expect a high proportion of mediocrity and a small but still sizable backward group as part of the spectrum of mankind. The schools should be asked to do better the things they are doing now, but not to change their basic theory about man's capacity to learn. But if the proposition is wrong —if man's capacity is not fixed at conception and is subject to unknown but considerable development as a result of intervention in his life experiences; and if the possibility exists of eradicating much even of backwardness—then the changes in the schools must be very marked, even dramatic. For then the failures of children, privileged as well as deprived, have to be accounted for by the behavior of the school, not the IQ of the child.

The position developed in this book is that the prevailing theory of educability is unfounded. To put it more directly, it is false, and if it persists as a keystone in the ideology of American education it will guarantee failure to convert the schools into effective instruments for the education of all children. The irony of the situation is that this false view of man succeeds in capturing the support of friends of public education who believe it has both scientific validity and consistency with democratic values. On the contrary, it is based more on faith than on fact, and it is anything but favorable to cultivation of the individual differences of all children. In fact, one would be hard put to demonstrate that it is good for any children.

A contemporary study of educability necessarily leads to a careful look at past views of man's capacity and earlier theories of ability. The search opens up a clear perspective on the importance of education throughout the history of man and reveals the basic cause of the problems of our own schools: In the history of the Western

world the powerful and the wealthy have resisted the demand of the lower classes for education of their children, and have yielded reluctantly, and only under great pressure. When the forces of history led to the introduction of democratic theories and processes, the denial began to be rationalized in terms of the limitations of the lower classes. Plato developed a theory of educability, essentially differentiating the social classes, that became a model from which we have hardly deviated. From the contemporary theory of intelligence, which is little different from the Platonic conception of man, have come such modern derivatives as the IQ test. Though not inherently good or bad, it has become, through the use made of it, an instrument of subtle torture that adversely affects the child's self-expectations and self-concept, and his parents' and teachers' expectations and concepts of him. It has falsely given everyone the belief that it measures something immutable and predictive of the child's powers to develop intellectually. It has done this for individuals of all social classes and for groups in the lower classes, and it has served to justify differential education: high-quality academic education for the higher classes and low-quality general or vocational education for the lower classes.

From the Platonic concept of man's educability has come another logical outgrowth, the widely practiced grouping of schoolchildren according to their ability, which means chiefly according to their IQ. This procedure has succeeded in separating the social classes in the same school building and in providing the children of the higher classes with richer curricula and better teachers.

What will become abundantly evident as we examine the key theories and practices of American education in the light of the history of the schools, is this fact: All present efforts are doomed to failure unless the nation takes conscious and far-reaching actions to renounce the prevailing conception of educability and to declare itself unreservedly determined to take all necessary measures to provide quality education universally.

To find new answers to the question "Who can be educated?" we will first turn our attention to the past, to examine theories of educability and the provision of schooling in the history of the Western world, and then specifically in the United States. Then we

will see educational choices that this country has made at crucial times in its history. Next we need to look carefully at the determinants of educability: biological, social, psychological, and educational. Finally, the outlook for the future will be considered in the context of what we know of man's capacity to change, and against a background of necessary changes in the nation, the community, and the schools.

2

THE STRUGGLE FOR EDUCATION

The belief that intellectual potential is largely predetermined by heredity is so general, if not always bluntly acknowledged, that its truth for all time is clearly implied. It may be interesting, therefore, to look at some samples of various beliefs about man's educability during other historical periods. We shall find that cause and effect have been reversed in the course of history. Whereas, in fact, educability theory seems to have been determined by *social* need, it has come to appear as if the limits of educability are really set by the *genes* of the individual members of the society; whereas man's consciousness was heightened as the social need dictated, the level of intellect he achieved was explained in *biological* terms.

Plato holds a position of distinction in the cultural history of the Western world equaled by few other men, particularly in those very nations that pride themselves on their democratic tradition. Yet he was "a thorough aristocrat" with "a profound contempt for the opinions of the masses, and a true aristocrat's dislike of any taint of the shop or of the workman's bench."[1] Democracy was, in his opinion, the worst form of government, and his distrust of people is evident in the kinds of controls he incorporated in the ideal state he created in his *Republic.* Music, poetry, the theater were to be censored, and the minds of people carefully guarded against influences from abroad. Education was to be differential depending upon the quality of the person, whether it be gold, silver, brass or iron,

and so too was his station in life to be determined. The expectation was that gold would procreate children of gold, and iron would procreate iron, but should they not, the child must be placed with his proper group, and his education and place in life would be so determined. The differential system of education had a purpose: to maintain the position of the aristocracy in the declining days of the Athenian city-state, a state founded upon slavery. Platonic idealism as a philosophic system is characterized by the existence of absolute and eternal truths. Both the philosophic system and the educational scheme were based on the conviction of and surely the wish for permanence, for the status quo.

Plato, whom Karl Popper classified as a thoroughgoing totalitarian, and for whom he used the strong terms militarist and racist,[2] has had an enormous influence on human thought. The Greek intellectual tradition helped set the pattern for European education, but Platonic thought in particular provided a blueprint. For it is a fact, as the historians Kazamias and Massialas have put it, that "the concern for the education of the leaders rather than the masses has characterized European education right up to the last couple of centuries, and in some instances pervades educational thinking and practice today."[3]

Controversy about what youth should be taught is probably as old as human society. Some 2500 years ago Aristotle referred to the uncertainty of his own day on this issue in words that are startlingly contemporary:

> . . . people do not agree on the subjects which the young should learn, whether they take virtue in the abstract or the best life as the end to be sought, and it is uncertain whether education should be properly directed rather to the cultivation of the intellect or the moral discipline. The question is complicated, too, if we look at the actual education of our own day; nobody knows whether the young should be trained at such studies as are merely useful as means of livelihood or in such as tend to the promotion of virtue or in the higher studies . . .[4]

The perplexity of Aristotle's time takes on more meaning when seen in the light of contemporary social and political conditions. They were not much different from the conditions that influenced his teacher, Plato. "Desirable" and "necessary" as applied to educa-

tion are relative terms, and the conditioning factors are the needs of the society, not the capabilities of the individuals. It is noteworthy that two and a half millennia ago intellectual leaders were fragmenting education, separating the manual from the mental, and considering the possibility that vocational training in the absence of "the higher studies" or even of "the promotion of virtue" was sufficient education. It is enough, they were saying in effect, for a man to know how to perform his job; knowledge about society and the universe, and the cultivation of intellect, are not essential. This is a point of view repeated time and again, a familiar one that we shall see in the words of a nineteenth-century King of Prussia and later opponents of higher education in the advanced nations of the world. We can be sure that the authors of all these views had no doubt that "the higher education" and not vocational training was the only appropriate schooling for their own children.

There was no formal instruction in ancient Rome until the Greek conquest in the second century B.C. Thereafter educated Greek slaves, brought to Rome as teachers, introduced the Greek methods of instruction. The formal school system, advanced for its day, was available only to the children of the wealthy. This was, in fact, one of the many legacies of ancient Greece: good education available to the upper classes.

The medieval period, dating from the fall of the Roman Empire in 476 until the Renaissance in the fourteenth century, produced a different educational pattern. Nobles were on top of the highly stratified system of feudal society but it was the clergy, a notch or two below them, who composed the educated class. The princes and knights had their own body of knowledge to master but that was limited to the requirements of life as warrior and gentleman. As for the peasants, the largest class of all, the only education they had was what they got in the form of religious instruction.

The two special concerns of the period, in the view of historian R. F. Butts, were the acquisition of subject matter and the inculcation of proper religious attitudes. Notably absent was a concern for the development of the individual as a person in his own right, and for his preparation to engage in any aspect of life outside the church. Though the individual and his secular life had held the interest of

the Greeks and Romans, these were overshadowed by the paramount religious concerns of the Middle Ages.[5]

Social institutions changed very little during seven centuries until developments in commerce and industry in the twelfth, thirteenth, and early fourteenth centuries led to important educational innovations. A new set of factors—the Crusades, expansion of trade, growth of cities—demanded more advanced education. Skilled artisans were needed to perform new occupational roles (for example, to manufacture in large quantities items like shoes that the peasants had made for themselves before they moved to the cities), and the system of apprenticeship was introduced to satisfy these new social needs. Men who were engaged in a particular business or trade organized guilds as a way of establishing and protecting a monopoly. The term first used for those organizations was *universitas,* but this term soon began to be limited to groups of faculties and students. The universities that arose during this period—the forerunners of the Western university—were designed to educate the elite to fill new needs for professionals in teaching, theology, law, and medicine.

The Renaissance, some two millennia after ancient Greece, opened a new and exciting chapter. During the intervening centuries, estimates of man's capacity to learn and to reason had undoubtedly shifted frequently, but not as a chance factor. There were the interminably long periods of stability, not truly "dark," but eras when man advanced very little, when his political and economic needs required the education only of the clergy, and it was through theology and superstition that men found meaning in their universe. A few centuries later, by 1450, modern science was born, and Leonardo da Vinci and other great thinkers of the period demonstrated man's capacity to transform nature. Implicit in this change is a positive view about the great possibilities for man's educability.

Renaissance, or "rebirth," was a turning point in the history of man, during which he broke from blind orthodoxy and heavy reliance on faith, and learned to apply his intellectual resources to the task of comprehending the workings of his universe. He began to free himself as an individual from the highly structured and self-abnegating life that had prevailed through the many centuries of

medievalism, and in a developing spirit of humanism to place a high value on the individual and his self-realization.

Yet with all its benefits and its promise for the future, the Renaissance offered little more in formal education to the children of the common people than other ages had. The fine schools that were created, especially the classical secondary schools in the Italian city-states that served as a model for the *lycée* in France, the *Gymnasium* in Germany, and the Latin grammar schools in England and in early America, were intended for children of the nobility and the wealthy merchants.[6] Nevertheless, men like Copernicus, Galileo, da Vinci—broadly educated, curious, emancipated from many of the centuries-old restrictions on thought—showed by using their intelligence to understand and control the world that man has powers whose limits are unknown, even including his power to change himself.

The class limitations on education that prevailed in ancient Greece and Rome, and during the medieval and Renaissance periods, persisted through the nineteenth century and into the present one; even today societies by direct or indirect means restrict the educational opportunities of the lower social classes. Such explanations as are given have always been couched in terms of inherent differences in the ability of the social classes. Those who are now engaged or simply interested in contemporary discussion of disadvantaged children, in particular the reasons for the schools' problems in educating them, can benefit from debates of the past on the educability of the poor.

Before the end of the seventeenth century the widely held view that men are born with innate ideas which unfold during their lifetime came under attack by John Locke. He stated it as his purpose to prove the falsity that there are "primary notions . . . stamped upon the mind of man, which the soul receives in its very first being, and brings into the world with it." And he attempted to disprove this belief by showing how men, "by the use of their natural faculties, may attain to all the knowledge they have, without the help of any innate impressions."[7] Less than a hundred years later, when the Industrial Revolution had changed the complexion of English life and when great political changes had been brought on by the revolu-

tions in America and France, Joseph Priestley and especially William Godwin attacked the theory of inborn capacity. Godwin wrote:

> How long has the genius of education been disheartened and unnerved by the pretence that man is born all that it is possible for him to become? How long has the jargon imposed upon the world, which would persuade us that in instructing a man you do not add to but unfold his stores?
>
> Education will proceed with a firm step and with a genuine lustre, when those who conduct it shall know what a vast field it embraces; when they shall be made aware that . . . the question whether the pupil shall be a man of perseverance and enterprise or a stupid and inanimate dolt, depends upon the powers of those under whose direction he is placed, and the skill with which those powers shall be applied.[8]

In this period of industrial expansion and social optimism Adam Smith declared that the wide differences between the philosopher and the street porter arise not so much from differences in natural talents as from "habit, custom and education."[9] In 1829, James Mill, philosopher, historian, and a founder of London University, expressed a similar opinion and stated it in terms of the power of education to lift the mass of people to a high order of education and intelligence. But while he favored an "equal degree of intelligence" for all classes (by which he meant equal education), he regarded this as impossible because "a large proportion of mankind" must be engaged in labor and did not have the time to become educated.[10] Robert Owen, a contemporary of Mill, and a successful industrialist who spent much of his wealth on improving the living conditions of the workers and the education of their children, wrote that man's character is formed for him and not by him. Like Godwin before him, Owen preferred to attribute any faults in the development of the child to the conditions of life and the quality of teaching.

These voices calling for change were not, it must be noted, the voices of power and authority. They reflected alterations in the economic and political spheres following both the industrial and the various political revolutions (in the United States, France, Germany, Italy), but there had been no major modification in the locus of control, in the hands that controlled the reins, in the economic and educational status of the peasant and working classes.

The demands for education for more people were met when they coincided with the industrial need for more literacy in the wage-earning class, but each society had its own way of coping with the new challenges and the new needs. Each nation developed its own system of differential education. Schooling designed for various segments of the population was intended to maintain the existent social stratification, and the more autocratic the government the less veiled the policy statement. The class basis of education is evident in the order issued by the King of Prussia, Frederick William IV, in 1854:

> The primary schools have only to work to the end that the common people may grasp and appreciate the Christian Faith . . . may be intelligent in regard to all matters within the narrow sphere to which God has called them . . . may learn to read and write, reckon, and sing . . . may love their rulers and their fatherland, be contented with their social status and live peacefully and happy in their lot . . . I do not think the principles enunciated will raise the common people out of the sphere designated for them by God and Society.[11]

As the American sociologist Dahlke has said, the King thereby formalized the existence of a dual school system, "one part of it designed to keep people in the lower classes in their low status and the other to provide for an elite."[12]

The candor of the Prussian king had been equaled in Britain more than a century before. In the early part of the eighteenth century, the Charity School movement arose in England. Its purpose was "to assure loyalty to the Established Church and to quiet the growing discontent among the poor."[13] The poor had little to hope for because the purpose of the schools was clearly stated as "to make them loyal church members, and to fit them for that station of life in which it had pleased their Heavenly Father to place them."[14] These were not schools designed to develop the mind, to encourage the social and physical sciences, to help individuals improve their society and their lot. Yet despite the inadequacies of the Charity Schools, one English writer, as quoted by the historian I. Doughton, declared:

> There is no Need of any Learning at all for the meanest Ranks of Mankind: Their Business is to Labour, not to Think: Their Duty is to do what they are commanded, to fill up the most servile

> Posts, and to perform the lowest Offices and Drudgeries of Life for the Conveniency of their Superiors, and common Nature gives them Knowledge enough for this Purpose.[15]

It should be noted that this was an Englishman writing about other Englishmen. The problem was not racial or ethnic but clearly that of the struggle between those who demanded education for the socially deprived and those who resisted such demands. By the end of the nineteenth century the clamor for improvements had reached a high peak, but it was then met by a so-called scientific interpretation of human ability, a more sophisticated form of differential or class education.

Sir Francis Galton, cousin of Charles Darwin and sometimes known as the father of British psychology, played a key role in providing a scientific basis for class distinctions in British education by introducing the theory of normal-curve distribution to the study of individual differences. If one were to line up by height a randomly selected group of men, let us say a hundred, very few would be exceedingly short and very few would be exceedingly tall. Somewhat more would be short, somewhat more tall, but the largest number would be the group in the center who are of average height. When this distribution is represented by a curve, with the altitude of the curve representing the numbers of people of a particular height, then it follows that the curve is shaped somewhat like a bell. The curve is low at both ends because there are few very short people and few very tall people, but it is high in the center because most people are of average height. Galton applied this curve theory to mental ability, assuming that nature had set the distribution of intelligence as it had man's height, with most persons of average ability and few of very high or very low intelligence. Since this theory was developed within a social system in which few had the benefit of high-quality British education, it provides a curious example of circular reasoning. The belief is established that intelligence is normally distributed, and the psychologist starts with the assumption that this is so. He then devises a test in which the results will distribute themselves to coincide with a normal curve. He reports the findings, which are, of course, normally distributed, and he and the public conclude that nature has really distributed man's learn-

ing ability in this way. In our time an "intelligence" test like Binet's, whose author never intended it as a measure of something fixed or unchangeable, has been used similarly. If one accepts a static curve theory, IQ tests provide evidence that lower-class children whose scores tend to fall under that portion of the curve that denotes lower IQ's, are less well endowed and can benefit only from limited education. Galton, a brilliant and versatile man, had this to say in a book first published in 1869 and revised in 1892: "It follows from all this, that the average ability of the Athenian race is, on the lowest possible estimate, very nearly two grades higher than our own—that is, about as much as our race is above that of the African Negro."[16] It seems incredible that a man so gifted, and engaged in a science that demanded careful observation and objectivity, should support his views about racial inferiority by the fact that "every book alluding to negro servants in America is full of instances"[17] of half-wittedness. At least it seems incredible except with an understanding of the social forces that impinge upon men at any time in history and that inevitably circumscribe and determine their perceptions of nature and man.

Galton was forty-seven when he published the first edition of *Hereditary Genius*. The British Empire had been at its peak, and it was engaged now in a "holding game," in maintaining the status quo; that is, in being Victorian. Kipling was writing his stories about India while Galton was reporting his observations about Africans, whose mistakes were so stupid, he wrote, that he was made ashamed of his own species. He predicted that a form of moderate civilization would be introduced into Africa by Europeans and thought it possible that the Negroes would fail as completely under these conditions "as they have failed under the old ones, *to submit to the needs of a superior civilization to their own*."[18] Although Boring, the American historian of experimental psychology, thought that scientific objectivity characterized all of Galton's thought,[19] it seems that Galton's brilliant mind was, like that of other men, subject to ideology. Walter Lippmann, in an attack in 1922 on the conclusions drawn from the psychological tests of the First World War, used blunter journalistic style. Of the early-twentieth-century version of Galton's theory, he said, "Obviously this is not a conclusion obtained by research. It is a conclusion planted by the will to believe."[20]

GREAT BRITAIN

The effects of highly differentiated education are clear in Great Britain, where the opportunity for occupational and social class mobility is considerably less than in the United States. There, until very recently, the well-known 11-plus examination—taken by all children shortly after their eleventh birthday—in large measure determined the quality of the child's formal education. If he performed well on the examination, he was assured of a place in one of the publicly supported grammar schools that provide liberal and scientific education of high quality, excellent preparation for university work. If he did not gain such a place, he went to a school of a different caliber, which, with few exceptions, represented terminal education. However, if his parents were wealthy or middle class, he could attend a private preparatory school, one of those called a public school in Great Britain.

It has been national government policy since 1964 to do away with the 11-plus examination and to develop multiple-curricula comprehensive schools. Local communities in Britain have the authority to retain the old system or introduce the new, and some have abandoned the national screening examination and the grammar school in favor of the comprehensive school. Nonetheless, resistance to change is forceful. In London, as the *Times Educational Supplement* of February 2, 1968, reported, forty of the sixty-eight grammar schools will continue to operate in their present form, selecting students by means of the 11-plus, at least until 1975. The comprehensive schools, meanwhile, are using their own tests to separate the children into "streams" or ability groups. The British people have gained by winning the comprehensive schools, but progress will be meager so long as education is still dominated by the same separatist policy.

Sixty percent of the personnel in the British foreign service between 1851 and 1929 were drawn from the eleven most exclusive public schools. In 1926, 71 out of the 80 bishops and deans and 139 of 181 members of the judiciary had attended the exclusive schools. Dahlke presents comparable figures for other leading positions in Britain, all of them convincingly demonstrating the key position of the select schools in British society.[21] The pressure of the ordinary

people during the Second World War led to some marked changes in the educational system, but even today when one visits the town of Eton and sees the well-mannered boys wearing their straw hats, one can be sure that many of the leaders of the British Commonwealth will continue to come from these ranks of upper-class children provided with high-quality education. One English educator reports that "not more than 3 percent of British children" attend the boarding public schools. Yet as recently as 1957 "over 40 percent of the students at Oxford and Cambridge universities (and thus off to a flying start in public life) had been to such schools." These schools have been "the preserve of the governing classes" where boys of privileged families have been able to meet exacting class requirements.[22]

Education in one of the exclusive public schools is still the high road to a high-level position. It is no longer the only one of importance, but without at least grammar-school education as an entrée to a university there is hardly any chance of a first-class public, professional, or scientific career.

Every attempt to democratize the schools stirs strong controversy in Britain. Believing that those who lead the nation—who presumably speak for all social classes—must have the best-developed intelligence and the finest education, conservative elements have opposed the new comprehensive secondary schools that provide, under one roof, varied curricula for youth with varied interests and ability. More liberal groups favor the comprehensive school because it brings the varied classes together and provides more of an opportunity for transfer from one curriculum to another. Their opponents want above all else to preserve the grammar school and to maintain the selection, examination, and the tripartite system whereby on the basis of his test score at age eleven, the student is admitted either to a grammar school, a technical school (like the American vocational training in agriculture, commerce, or industry), or a modern school which offers general non-college-preparatory education. That most children of the lower class will have quality education denied them by this system presumably concerns this group no more than it did the upper classes in previous centuries, probably because the life they know, admire, and want to perpetuate does not require and might even be threatened by educational improvements aimed at raising the intelligence of the lower classes.

Several conditions in Britain have given impetus to change at the level of primary education (ages five to eleven). As recently reported in *Science*,[23] British leaders of government, science, and industry have been compelled to reexamine the early school years, because despite rapidly expanding university capacity there are not enough students in science and engineering, and the proportion of secondary-school students interested in science is declining. This disturbs a nation that spends more on research than its Western European competitors, yet suffers in comparison in economic growth.

The combination of economic motivation and the aspirations of the lower classes for better schools for their children has led the government to encourage a review of many facets of education. The directions of possible change, similar in many respects to those in the United States, are given in a report entitled, "Children and Their Primary Schools," known as the Plowden Report because Lady Bridget Plowden is chairman of the Central Advisory Council for Education in England from which it emanated. This paper asks for what it calls positive discrimination, that is, that schools in areas where children are most handicapped by poor homes and neighborhood conditions be made as good as the best in the country through reduction in class size, use of teacher aides, and a salary supplement to the teachers. Two other major themes in the Plowden Report, besides that of compensatory education, are that the school should be more responsive to the community, and that instruction should be based on results of current research in child development and learning theory.

The author of the *Science* article, John Walsh, who is the journal's news editor in its European office, writes that little has been done or is likely to be done in the near future to carry out the recommended reforms. Weakness in the British economy became apparent with the devaluation of the pound in 1967. Primary schools must compete with the expanding universities for funds earmarked for education, and any further rise in taxes for education would be resisted by the middle and upper classes, which are now opposing the government's program of conversion of secondary schools to the comprehensive system.

Walsh sees parallels between the British and American situation,

where social class in one and race in another "generate variance of the same problem." In both countries educational reformers have gotten some of their principles embodied in government policies but lack effective support from the middle class to pay the stiff costs.

FRANCE

The land of liberty, equality, and fraternity suffers from a great lack of equality in educational opportunity. Since the Revolution of 1789 France has espoused the spirit of equality—the constitutions of 1946 and 1958 reaffirmed the guarantee of equal educational opportunity—but it has failed to deliver the wherewithal for children of the working classes. France has followed the Platonic model more orthodoxly than any other country, and its *lycée* has played a key role in the selection and training of the elite.[24]

The present French educational structure reflects its historical evolution in three different stages. First came the medieval university, which then gave rise to secondary education. Finally, after the French Revolution, free elementary education developed. Public instruction was supposed to be free at each stage, "but during the nineteenth century each of the three stages tended to develop in isolation. The result was a set of superimposed systems, catering for different social classes. The tendency at present is to return to the original idea of progressive stages, but no comprehensive law has yet been passed to bring about the rational grouping of the stages."[25] Because the three stages are isolated, there is the anomalous situation that the elementary schools have their own secondary schools to accommodate the numerous children who finish elementary education successfully and want further study but are not admitted to the separate secondary schools.

Napoleon left his mark on French education as he did on everything French and, in fact, almost everything European. Expressing what Butts calls "the conservative ideal of primary education in France," the Emperor in 1808 called upon the schools to teach the Catholic religion, "inculcate fidelity to the emperor, and produce citizens devoted to the church, the state and their families."[26] The 1833 education law, following Napoleon's statement of purpose,

fixed the curriculum of the primary school at the three R's plus moral and religious instruction. It was nearly fifty years before the Ferry law of 1882 significantly broadened the secular aspect of curriculum and narrowed the religious aspect.[27]

Postwar demands of the French people led to several reforms. For example, the school-leaving age was raised in 1959 from fourteen to sixteen. But a country in which ten years ago only about one in four children went on to secondary education of any kind has a long way to advance. A UNESCO report, referring to reforms in effect by the middle 1950's, states that "the selection of pupils according to their social class is eliminated." The report adds that "pupils' aptitudes and tastes should provide each with an education designed to develop his personality."[28] This sounds modern, objective and democratic, but as the figures in the next paragraph show, it seems to perpetuate the old stratification system under another guise.

Although the classical *lycée* dropped tuition fees in 1930 and admission to it and to the *collège,* a nonclassical, modern secondary school, was in theory open to all with the necessary ability, these institutions continued to recruit from middle and upper social strata. The evidence of a differential system of education is impressive. In 1950, 44 percent of the students in *lycées* and *collèges* were children of civil servants and members of professions, who together numbered little over one and a half million, whereas workers and farmers, who totaled almost fifteen million, provided 22 percent of the school population. In 1956 over 80 percent of the children of upper groups (professionals, executives, and high government officials) were reported to be attending academic secondary schools but only 8 percent of workers' children. In 1959, 31 percent of the students in the first year of these schools came from farmer, worker, and artisan families. This seemed to represent a sizable improvement, since only 9 percent of the same group had been in those schools in 1936, except that most of the children were enrolled in the less prestigious and less academically useful modern schools (no Latin or Greek study) and, furthermore, many of them dropped out. In 1961 agricultural laborers' children had slightly more than one chance in ten of being admitted to the secondary schools, while middle-class children had eight or nine chances in ten.[29]

WEST GERMANY

Early in the eighteenth century Prussia enacted compulsory attendance laws in which parents were responsible for sending their children to school. By 1830 a two-track system was firmly established, so that some 90 percent of the school population attended the *Volksschulen,* eight-year elementary schools, whereas the upper-class children went to the *Vorschulen,* for a three-year course preparatory to entering one of the secondary schools.

The story of German education cannot be separated from the tragic history of the country, but we need not recount that history to see that the pattern already established almost a hundred and fifty years ago—in what was then an advanced system of education—is still very much in force today. At the age of ten, on the basis of a fifteen-hour examination, about 20 percent of the children are selected from the regular eight-year elementary school and admitted to the *Gymnasium.* Parental criticism, more restrained than in Great Britain and France, has not succeeded in modifying this early screening in the highly differentiated German system of education.[30]

SOVIET UNION

In early-nineteenth-century Russia the highly stratified social system had its educational counterpart. The aristocratic schools served the children of the hereditary nobility and the high government and military officers. Next came the *gymnasia* for the children of the middle class and the clergy, and finally the elementary schools for the largest and lowest class, the peasants. There was a trickle from one level to another which was more noticeable after the emancipation of the serfs in 1861, but especially in the decade before the First World War. Even before the Revolution of 1917 the pressures of industrialization and the people's struggles for power and a greater share of the nation's benefits gave the peasants (in 1914) 22 percent of the places in the *gymnasia* for boys, still a small representation considering that the population was so largely rural-farm, but almost double the number of their children in such schools in 1904.[31]

The ideology of the Revolution called for "the abolition of all social class differences and the establishment of a uniform and universal educational system free from any class encumbrances. . . . A campaign was urged against illiteracy, and educational steps were taken to extend opportunities to the working class and the peasants. Indeed there was a conscious attempt to eliminate the opportunities held by the former 'exploiting' classes."[32]

Have these ideals been realized? The question is much debated and remains open. Nobody challenges the Soviets' claim that they have achieved a great expansion in opportunity. Prior to the Revolution less than 10,000,000 were in school, of whom 8,000,000 were in elementary school (that is, only one in every five children of elementary school age attended school). By 1957–58, when the country was completing its reconstruction following the devastation of the Second World War, 30,600,000 were in the system (not counting those in the universities).[33] According to Fred Hechinger, the *New York Times* educational editor, there were 50,000,000 in school in 1967. Enrollment in higher education has increased from 127,400 in about 1915 to 4,000,000 today.[34] Every comparison shows equally dramatic increases.

In the process of growth the Soviet Union has employed many devices to overcome the disadvantages of growing up with uneducated parents or with too little supervision from working parents. One of these is the boarding school, recommended in 1956 and quickly established, so that 1000 were in operation in 1957 with an enrollment of 300,000 pupils. The children live at the school during the week and go home for weekends. The school day is organized to include study, play, and work. In his recent report, Hechinger said that programs in special boarding schools had been set up to help rural youngsters cope with what he termed the "forbidding" competition for college entry. He compared this program with efforts in the United States to aid Negro youngsters of college age.

Almost from its inception the government organized crèches and kindergartens. These enable mothers to work, thereby serving the state's need for employees and the desire of many women to be part of the labor force. From the child's point of view, these preschool facilities can give the son and daughter of a worker's family some of the social-intellectual stimulation they might not get other-

wise. Only 25 percent of the children nationally and 40 percent in urban areas attend preschool facilities today because, said Hechinger, the mothers do not wish to part with their children at so early an age.

Elementary and secondary schools for all children are essentially academic. The curriculum includes ten years of mathematics, five years of physics and of foreign languages, and four years of chemistry.

Foreign observers are critical of a number of characteristics of Soviet education. The lack of scope for reasonable initiative has recently been criticized by both foreign and Soviet educators. Increasing numbers of students, according to Hechinger, are being siphoned off into "the most fashionable schools," those that give intensive instruction in some one field (foreign language, for example, or mathematics), and many of these children are from what he describes as equivalent to the American middle class. Foreign observers are also impressed by other characteristics. For one thing, educators cannot but take note of the salary and status of their counterparts. The historian James Mulhern writes: "The Soviet state holds teachers in high respect, and the supply of teachers is adequate. . . . As compared with other servants of the state they are well rewarded."[35] But Hechinger has questioned whether the teachers in the grade levels (as compared at least with those in higher education) are very well paid.

American and other foreign observers have also commented on Russian children's attitudes toward school, in particular their intense concentration on study. The government has, of course, emphasized the high value it places on literacy and education. In fact, "An unbiased evaluation shows that between the two World Wars the Communistic educational system in a shorter period of time accomplished more to raise the literacy of an entire nation than had ever before been achieved in all recorded history."[36] The children probably react to the prevailing values and also to the fact that in the Soviet Union, as elsewhere in the advanced nations, higher education is the path to the higher positions and the professions.

The Greeks set a pattern that has served man well insofar as it was a design for quality education, but not well insofar as it was a plan that excluded all but an elite group. In theory the French

challenged such a restricted educational system after the Revolution, as many individual Englishmen had done before and after that point in history, but neither Great Britain nor France nor West Germany has substantially changed the pattern of differential education, although Britain has made much more progress than the other two. The Soviet Revolution, like the French before it, condemned the privileges of the rich, among them the educational privileges. Since 1917 Soviet educators have introduced many measures to counteract the effects of disadvantage in homes of the poor and the poorly educated, but the extent of their success remains to be seen. Their progress and ours—two large nations moving increasingly toward universal secondary and perhaps even higher education—will be a measure of the educability of man.

3

TOWARD FREE EDUCATION IN AMERICA

How different American education might have been if at one of its key points of choice the nation had taken an alternate path. Not long after independence, for example, Dr. Benjamin Rush and Noah Webster argued for a national system of education so that children in all parts of the land, rich or poor, could benefit equally. The wealthy mercantile classes and the slaveowners opposed this plan and any others that would raise taxes to educate children other than their own, or at least other than their own class. Furthermore, the artisans and farmers whose families would have been the chief beneficiaries would not support the establishment of any central institution, having fought first the British and then the Federalists, whose proposals for centralization of governmental power would have benefited the wealthy at a cost to the lower economic groups. Had the country moved toward such a federal plan, the poorer states and school systems would not today be operating with paltry budgets and, as a consequence, offering inferior education. No one can say we were not warned. In a prize-winning essay for which the American Philosophical Society awarded him fifty dollars in 1799, Samuel Knox, teacher, physician, and minister, wrote:

> Great, surely, must be the difference between two communities, in the one of which, good laws are executed only in some particular situations, while in others they are almost totally neglected; and in the other are universally established with equal and impartial authority. Such, surely, must be difference between the effects

> of education when abandoned to the precarious uncertainty of casual, partial or local encouragement; and of that which has been established uniformly and generally by the united wisdom and exertions of a whole nation.[1]

How different our schools would have become if an alliance of southerners and northerners had not destroyed the Reconstruction movement, for it was during this period after the Civil War that the black people themselves set out to democratize education in the South. Had they been able to follow through, the school systems of the South would not have become so clearly inferior to the rest of the country. In fact, had both of these directions been followed—toward a national system and a democratic South—the southern states in particular would have benefited significantly. Most of them have suffered both before and after the Civil War from much lower per capita expenditures for education than those of the northern and western states.

In the middle years of the nineteenth century the country took one direction that was clearly a necessary one, related to the political philosophy that had emerged early in the century. Jeffersonian and Jacksonian democracy was in part at least an expression of the strength and optimism of the common man. The nation was young and virile and it possessed the energy and cockiness characteristic of nations that have liberated themselves in struggle against great odds. Mechanics and artisans believed the future was theirs and they valued education as a necessary means to its realization. The workers had won political equality; now they demanded educational equality—not pauper schools for the children of the impoverished, but free schools for all children.

During the 1820's and 1830's they organized to improve their economic status but equally to secure education for their children. On October 31, 1829, a New York newspaper, the *Working Man's Advocate,* reported on the formation of a new organization whose name itself shows how highly the precursors of today's labor movement regarded education, the Association for the Protection of Industry and for the Promotion of National Education.

The newspaper reported the following:

> *Reasons for the formation of the Association.* Because industry is at present unprotected, oppressed, despised, and indirectly de-

prived of its just reward; and because there is in this republic no system of education befitting a republic; none which secures the equal maintenance, protection, and instruction of youth—of the children of the poor man as of the rich; none which is at once free from sectarian and clerical influences, and from aristocratical distinctions; none which is calculated to induce in the rising generation those habits of industry, those principles of sound morality, those feelings of brotherly love, together with those solid intellectual acquirements, which are necessary to secure to all the fair exercise of those equal political rights set forth in the institutions of the land.[2]

All "honest" men could become members and in doing so they attested that they would defend the rights and promote the interests of the people, and work to carry through the state legislatures a system of equal republican education. These proposals for elementary education, and others like them by the workers of Philadelphia, New York, Boston, and Washington, seem so reasonable, so modest in their demands, and so much in the interest of the community at large, that it is hard to believe that they elicited unfavorable response. But they did. An editorial in the *National Gazette* of Philadelphia, August 19, 1830, attacked a proposal made by "the Mechanics and other Working Men of the City and County of New York" for "the adoption of a general system of instruction at the expense of the State which shall afford the children, however rich or poor, equal means to obtain useful learning."

The editor declared such a plan a gross injustice, "equivalent to the idea of an actual compulsory partition of their substance." The rich would not share their wealth, would not toil for others, would not deprive their own children of the best of educations. Furthermore, the editor said, with a righteousness that has often accompanied the refusal to contribute more to the education of the lower classes, such an arrangement would remove the incentive to industry and would be "a premium for comparative idleness."[3]

Whether the workers' organizations were "the principal force behind the educational achievements . . . or simply the agitators and advertisers for reform," said the historian Rena Vassar,[4] they were instrumental in providing mass backing for leaders like Horace Mann, first secretary of the Massachusetts Board of Education (1837–1848), who succeeded in overcoming the strong resistance of the rich

and powerful in his state. He convinced them that schooling would make the workers more productive and would prepare the working people who now had the vote to use the franchise responsibly. Undoubtedly those in power interpreted Mann's remarks to mean that the schools would direct the thought of the children in support of the kind of stability that the wealthy valued. Mann, who was later a congressman and finally president of Antioch College, won a hard-fought struggle in Massachusetts against property owners who contested his pleas for higher taxes, religious leaders who called his non-denominational schools "godless," and schoolmasters whose efficiency he questioned.

In his victory this great educational statesman helped the country win the war for free public education, a war that by 1900 was won in all the states except those in the South. The demands of the workers that their children be given more than the three R's had been met, for where there had been primary schools (grades one to three) earlier in the century, there were now elementary schools (grades one to seven or eight; later to grade six, when the junior high school idea was introduced). For most American children the victory meant an opportunity for elementary education, for although secondary schools had been established in many communities as a continuation of the elementary school—a number of them even before the Civil War—they were serving only a small fraction of the youth. In 1892 less than 7 percent of the eligible children attended any kind of post-elementary school. In 1893 the report of a well-known committee headed by Charles W. Eliot, president of Harvard University, made it clear that secondary education was not to be universal but only for those who could profit by it and whose parents could support them.[5] This was a time when the champions of free public secondary education were fighting a battle similar to the earlier one for the elementary schools. The arguments of the opposition, as given in a report by the United States Commissioner of Education in 1877, were familiar ones: The state has the right to educate children to understand their duties and carry out their rights as citizens. Primary education is sufficient for this; hence the state has the right to offer that and nothing more. It is unjust to levy a general tax, since the high school is patronized by but few. Further-

more, high-school education will make the poor discontented with their condition and unfit to discharge their duties.[6]

Such were the arguments against high-school education even in 1900, when 11.3 percent of the total population and about 30 to 40 percent of all southerners (depending upon the state) were illiterate.[7] But these arguments did not prevail against the demand of the American people for more education for their children.

A few years after the beginning of this century American education entered a new era. The nation's frontiers were gone, the country was fast becoming urban and industrialized, and unemployment was now a feature of life. In these circumstances laws prohibiting some child labor and requiring school attendance were approved, and free public secondary education was introduced on a large scale.

Within a relatively short time a new breed of adolescent, very different from the children who had formerly been schooled beyond the three R's, populated the high schools. The fathers of these students were mostly workers, many of them recent immigrants born in the Mediterranean regions or in central or eastern Europe, whose foreign-language fluency was of no advantage to the child in his study of Latin or Greek, and especially of English, and whose peasant values and way of life did not provide all the guidelines that a pupil in a strange new city school needed. Many of these children were unable to learn what their contemporaries, American-born and usually from higher social classes, had mastered.

This turn-of-the-century period was hardly the first time that a "new breed" of student found the school door opened for him. Emperors and kings had always made provision for the education of their children and those of the nobility whose intelligence they depended upon. The Renaissance and the Reformation had led to the growth of a powerful mercantile class, and their children, who would also fall heir to wealth, property, and power, had to be trained. The Industrial Revolution had demanded a new type of educated worker and, coinciding as it did with the political revolutions in America and France, it meant that still others of the populace, lower in the socio-economic hierarchy, were to be given the opportunity to learn the three R's and to go beyond that. But at the end of the nineteenth

century, even after the great flowering of American letters during its second half, relatively few people had the benefit of high-school education. In 1900, in a population of 76,000,000, only 95,000 graduated from high school, or 6.4 percent of all those seventeen years old (compared with 61.9 percent in 1965).[8] And today those large segments of the people that are given the least in the way of schooling are known as the "underprivileged" or the "socially deprived."

The "socially deprived" is that portion of the population that was characterized by Franklin D. Roosevelt in the 1930's as being ill-housed, ill-fed, and ill-clothed. To this triad may be added many other forms of deprivation, some of which cut deeply into a person's self-respect, and one very specific one: namely, ill-educated. Further definition is hardly necessary: the socially deprived live "on the other side of the tracks" in the physical and social life of the community. If now a large percentage of them are Negro and Puerto Rican, there are still many white persons among them. Not many years ago they were people from central and eastern Europe and the Mediterranean and the Orient. And before that they were Scandinavian, German, and Irish. There are and were major differences within as well as between these groups, of course. The learning problems of children whose parents fled oppression in western Europe after active involvement in political movements are hardly identical with those of uneducated European peasants or of former American slaves. But the vast majority of the socially deprived occupied the lowest-paid positions in their country of origin and were encouraged to come to America to serve a similar occupational role. With the passing years and the new waves of immigrants (or of in-migrants to northern urban areas), the language has changed, and the skin color and the customs. The country to which they have come has achieved a new status in the world and has new conditions (including better schools, more highly trained teachers) and different educational expectations (high-school education is now the minimum)—but the socially deprived retain essentially the same characteristics: lowliest positions, lowest income, highest unemployment rate, poorest housing, poorest education.[9]

How numerous are the socially deprived now? The estimate depends, of course, on the criteria employed. In the early 1960's the Bureau of Labor Statistics suggested an income of $5,970 as a

minimum in New York City for a family with two children to maintain "a modest but adequate" standard of living. It has been estimated that close to half the families in New York City, and about 70 percent of Negro and Puerto Rican families, earn less than that amount.[10] These two groups are not suffering from the fact of being Negro or Puerto Rican but from being deprived of adequate employment and income, as has been true of all the groups that have occupied this niche in our social structure.

Estimates of poverty in America vary considerably. Michael Harrington suggested in 1963 that there are forty to fifty million people living in poverty. In *The Other America* he quoted a study undertaken for the Senate which came up with a broad range of 16 to 36 percent of the population (or somewhere between thirty and seventy million people).[11] When use is made of the conservative Social Security Administration's poverty index, almost 15 percent are found to fall below it. That source reveals that 27 percent of all in the poverty class are Negroes, although they compose only 10 percent of the population. That fact is no longer a surprising one; what is often lost sight of is another fact, one that highlights an economic rather than a racial problem: 73 percent of the poor are white. Even in the most conservative estimates of poverty in 1966 more than 11 percent of all white families are so classified.[12]

What are the consequences of being poor? The available United States Census data do not provide a direct answer to that question, but they do give some relevant facts associated with being nonwhite. The disadvantages are apparent from the outset. In 1964, for every 1000 live births there were 14.1 white fetal deaths and 28.2 nonwhite fetal deaths. For every 1000 live births the infant mortality during the first year was 21.6 for whites and 41.1 for nonwhites. Finally, for every 100,000 live births the maternal mortality rate was 22.3 for whites and 89.9 for nonwhites.[13]

Accumulated disadvantage manifests itself almost at the moment of conception. Chances of survival are fewer; chances of being orphaned are greater.

As if the differences were not yet intolerable, they have increased rapidly in recent times. In 1930 "pregnant Negro mothers were twice as likely to die in childbirth as pregnant white women." In 1964 Negro mothers were four times as likely to die in childbirth.

"The gap in infant mortality is also widening. In 1950 nonwhite infant mortality was 66 percent higher than the rate of the white, in 1964 the rate for the nonwhite was 90 percent higher."[14]

Most of the data above are for 1964, when the median money income of white families was $6,858 and of nonwhite, $3,839.[15] It was the year when the lowest 20 percent of the population (white and nonwhite) had 3 percent of the aggregate income in the country; the lowest 40 percent had 10 percent of the income; while the top 20 percent received 53 percent of the income; and the top 5 percent received 23 percent.[16]

The pattern is plain. Economic disadvantage gives rise to a host of other disadvantages, including even illness and premature death. The fact that nonwhites experience them to a greater degree than whites is not because of race *per se* but because they have been subject to membership in the lowest social classes.

And the same may be said about learning. Long before the migration of Negroes to the northern urban areas, when the education of the Negro child was not a public problem because he was not being educated, white socially deprived children were having more learning problems than children of the higher classes. Working-class children had lower mean IQ's and they came from families that had had no educational tradition and little formal schooling, where parents were busy trying to provide the necessities for survival, and where family disruption was caused by the new conditions of being unpopular aliens in a strange land. Long ago the socially deprived (whether Irish or Polish or Italian) were accused of being immoral, of making the streets unsafe "for our sisters and daughters," and long ago—as now—the higher incidence of antisocial acts in slum neighborhoods reflected deprivation and frustration—and in some cases prejudiced reporting—rather than a group characteristic, as the history of various ethnic groups shows.[17] And as one psychologist, the late Donald Snygg, has pointed out, when the public high schools first began to be opened to the people for whom almost any education, and especially that beyond the three R's, was a new experience, educators needed help and turned to experts on learning. First came mass public education, then came Edward Thorndike, the psychologist who early in the century was one of a

few who laid the groundwork for the use of psychological knowledge in education.[18]

It should surprise no one that in the America of the first decade of the century, raised to the status of a leading power through the alliance of industry, invention, and science, education too should have been influenced by the scientific winds of the day. Thorndike reported his work on the laws of learning[19] while Cattell, another American pioneer in psychology, was measuring the physical and mental characteristics of college students.[20] Freud lectured here on psychoanalysis, with its stress upon the unconscious motivations of man, and, of special educational pertinence, on the significance of the formative years of his life.[21] The Binet-Simon intelligence test, developed under the leadership of the great French psychologist Alfred Binet to differentiate the backward students of the lower classes from the true defectives,[22] was translated from the French and adapted for American use by another leader in American psychology, Lewis M. Terman.[23]

The First World War saw the birth of the American psychometric movement, the enterprise of measuring all sorts of human abilities, achievements, and characteristics. Before the war one examiner would give a test to one individual, but during this "first modern war" the armed services needed speedy identification of persons with varied talents and aptitudes. This led to the construction of the group intelligence tests (Army Alpha and Beta) by psychologists like Walter Bingham[24] and Arthur Otis, whose names are linked to the development of psychological measurement. Less well known than the others, Frank Parsons of Boston, engineer, economist, educator, and muckraker, became an articulate spokesman for new services called vocational guidance, which along with psychometrics spawned the large guidance, counseling, and testing movement in the country.[25] During all this period John Dewey was voicing the philosophical basis for fundamental change in the purposes of education, the content of the curriculum, and methods of teaching. Sharply critical of an education whose dominant aim was to encourage religious faith and disciplined behavior, and to convey general information, Dewey argued for objectives of individual and social development and vocational usefulness: the school must help a

child understand his world. These objectives can be achieved, Dewey said, only if the school is related to the society, and if the social environment of the school is seen as life itself, from which the child can profit enormously. The program of teaching must be based on an understanding of the child's nature as a bubbling, active, curious being, ready and willing to learn about his world when the methods of instruction and the subject matter are adapted to his needs and interests. With the publication of his influential book, *School and Society,* in 1899, Dewey had become the leading figure and philosophical spokesman for the progressive education movement which broke with lock-step teaching and sought a more solid basis for education in a science of learning. In that book Dewey wrote that our social order had gone through a transformation as a result of industrialization, and that if our education was to have any meaning for life, it must pass through an equally complete transformation.[26] The significant changes that have come about during the years since Dewey pronounced the need are documented in a fascinating account by the historian Lawrence A. Cremin, who borrowed Dewey's concept for the title of his book on progressivism in American education between 1876 and 1957, *The Transformation of the School.*[27] Many of the modifications he reports were strongly influenced by developments in the young science of psychology.

The application of science to education, and to educational psychology in particular, was not fortuitous. The need existed; that is, the people wanted their children to be schooled; their insistence, combined with the technical needs of a great industrial economy, paved the way; the students entered the schools, changed themselves and the schools in the process, and generated new problems. In the previous century students in secondary schools, particularly in the private ones, usually came from families with an educational tradition. The children had absorbed the family's expectations for scholastic achievement and for professional or commercial aspiration. Failures were certainly not unknown then, nor were behavioral problems, but the school and community had learned to accommodate to them. In the late nineteenth and early twentieth century, new students in urban centers—especially the immigrant, or the in-migrant from backward mountain or rural areas—frequently impoverished and living with illiterate parents or those speaking only an

alien tongue, inevitably created problems that the school personnel were unprepared to cope with.

There were various ways to deal with such a situation. One of them was to investigate the way learning takes place, identifying laws of learning behavior that could then be applied to the classroom, guiding the teacher in her work with the class and with individual students. By discovering the process of learning numerical concepts the teacher would be able to facilitate the child's mastery of arithmetic. By discovering the principles underlying memory the teacher could expedite the mastery of language and reading.

Very early in the century Thorndike was already making important contributions to knowledge about learning, providing objective evidence in support of such laws of learning as the one called the "law of effect": when a person gets satisfaction from a learning response (such as subtracting or reading), he is likely to want to repeat and master the learning. Yet fifty years later one of the leading contemporary authorities on learning theory, Ernest Hilgard, author of one of the standard works in the field, wrote, "There are no laws of learning which can be taught with confidence. Even the most obvious facts of improvement with practice, and the regulation of learning under reward and punishment are matters of theoretical dispute."[28] The sterility of learning theory has sometimes been attributed to the fact that it has been largely derived from laboratory studies with rats and pigeons, but laboratory investigations are essential in order to control experiments during the early stages of theory development, and animals are most suitable for such purposes. The important work of both Pavlov and Thorndike stands witness to the possibilities of contributing to our knowledge of *human* behavior through such means. Perhaps Snygg's criticism is more to the point. The tendency, he said, has been to study a learning process rather than the encounter of a human being with his environment.[29] The child sitting at his desk, head bent over his first-grade reader, is engaged in the great task of mastering the basic skill, the one that will open the way to his acquiring the social-historical experience of mankind, in the process of which he develops his intelligence. But he is not alone. Besides the obvious presence of his classmates and the teacher, there are his parents with their values and standards. Already he has acquired a set of attitudes toward

school and learning and developed a sense of the meaning of this activity in his life. Perhaps, as Snygg suggested, the study of learning has been relatively unproductive because it has been insensitive to the total social condition of learning.

Another way to deal with the new situation in the schools was to investigate children's learning ability. Faced with a large number of failing students, along with others doing average, good, and excellent work, some psychologists assumed that the differences were attributable to differences in intellectual ability. They proceeded to determine the "intelligence" of countless children in America, establishing norms or yardsticks which could then be used by school personnel to explain the inadequate scholastic achievement. While the study of the learning process has had an almost insignificant impact upon American education, psychometric theory and the use of tests have held sway. Hardly any adult under sixty-five can have failed to notice that from his own experience with tests. The influence has been far greater than we notice, however, for psychometric theory has provided one of the few pillars upon which all the education in this country has been built.

The two fields of inquiry, learning theory and psychometric theory, held, and still hold, very different promises for education. Their implicit assumptions are fundamentally different. The study of how people learn opens the horizon to vastly improved ways of teaching and also to ways of detecting blocks to learning that occur in the individual or in his relationship to some part of his environment. For those who believe in the malleability of man and in his capacity to adapt to ever increasing demands upon his intelligence, the study of learning can be seen as the scientific instrumentality for hastening change. By contrast, the study of the ways in which individuals differ in learning ability—as it has been carried out by most investigators thus far—sets the limits of probable achievement, classifies students in accordance with the probable limits of their intellectual talents—which are assumed by many psychologists to be largely determined by nature; that is, by inheritance through the genes—and thereby has a major role in predetermining the nature and the quality of the education they receive. For those who believe that man's intelligence, great or little as it may be, is largely foreordained by his genetic potential, and that the function of education

is to release to the utmost all that can be realized from nature's apportionments, then the study of individual differences in scholastic aptitude can be seen as an important scientific enterprise that permits children to be placed among their peers and to be given the quality of school tasks that will challenge but not frustrate them, that will yield the full measure of the potential.

We followed the British pattern. We chose to believe that intelligence is genetically determined, that the potential for high, average, or low ability is fixed by the genes transmitted by parents to embryo. Psychometric tests for the measurement of mental ability became the hallmark of progress in education and of devotion to the hallowed concept of individual differences.

The tests we developed sprang mostly from the pioneer work of Alfred Binet. His intent in the use of the test was different from ours, and his conception of intelligence even more so. It seems strange indeed that in establishing a fixed-intelligence educational system based essentially on social class we drew so heavily on the work of a man who in 1909 wrote:

> . . . some recent philosophers appear to have given their moral support to the deplorable verdict that the intelligence of an individual is a fixed quantity. . . . We must protest and act against this brutal pessimism. . . . A child's mind is like a field for which an expert farmer has advised a change in the method of cultivating, with the result that in place of desert land, we now have a harvest. It is in this particular sense, the one which is significant, that we say that the intelligence of children may be increased. One increases that which constitutes the intelligence of a school child, namely, the capacity to learn, to improve with instruction.[30]

Our direction seems surprising only until we explore the social and historical conditions that led to the choice. Every period in history has witnessed the attempt of the hewers of wood and the drawers of water to get more than crumbs, to win a more equitable share of the fruits of their labor. Through the productivity of labor man has had time to study and, through his studies, to gain greater control over his natural and social environment. Workers and farmers have wanted these benefits for their children and have fought for them.

Typically each forward movement has been followed by a setback,

temporary though it has been. It happened with the Charity Schools in England in the eighteenth century and with primary education in Prussia in the nineteenth century. It is as if people were told, "We have been compelled to give you something, both because of your demands and because of industrial needs, but we withhold from you all but the bare minimum of literacy." This is the equivalent in education of an old political device, of which a classic example is the post–Civil War amendments to our Constitution. Within a few short years actions by the state governments and later by the federal government had shorn them of all but decorative value.

As we look back over the nineteenth century, it seems clear now that the struggle for free public education had been won by mid-century, and the proposition that free public secondary education had to be provided was widely accepted by the end of the century. By that point most of the states had shifted from permissive to compulsory free schools, particularly those in the North and West, although some did not reach that stage for a few years more and Mississippi, the last of the states to do so, did not make education compulsory until 1918. In the period between 1900 and 1920 the schools were making strides to accommodate the growing population, many of the youngsters being the disadvantaged of their day. The junior high school system became established, educational psychology was taught to teachers, vocational guidance was introduced, and vocational training was greatly advanced, especially as a result of federal funds made available through the Smith-Hughes Act of 1917. Because private schools were of much less consequence in America than in Great Britain—though they have had more influence than is generally understood[31]—this nation by the end of the First World War was on the way—a long way, to be sure—toward achieving equal educational opportunity.

But after the war the old elitist doctrine appeared in the form of new theories of human intelligence invoked by psychologists and adopted by educators. Use of the group test of intelligence, first tried in the armed forces, spread rapidly through the schools. By means of the tests, pupils were classified and grouped, and the groupings determined both what was expected of the children and also what was taught to them. The theory of intelligence and the tests it in-

spired contributed, therefore, to the maintenance of a differential type of education.

Did this move go unnoticed? Not entirely. A series of articles on intelligence tests appeared in the *New Republic* in 1922, signed by a man referred to in a psychology book ten years later as "a layman, Lippmann." The internationally known columnist of today, Walter Lippmann, is in fact that same layman. In the early twenties he was infuriated by the assertions of several psychologists, based on mental test results, that the average intelligence of the American people was equivalent to that of the fourteen-year-old, a conclusion based on the fact that samples of fourteen-year-old children did as well on the test as the average soldier.

This was a period when all sorts of groups of people were tested and compared; testing became a fad as well as a scientific tool. Not infrequently the result was a book like that of a Princeton professor, C. C. Brigham, which concluded that intelligence in America was on the decline. Even if immigration were made more selective to eliminate the nationality groups of low intellect, the outlook, according to him, was bleak because of the probable intermixture of the superior Nordic people with the less intelligent Alpines, Mediterraneans, and Negroes. The author expected a serious deterioration—which fortunately has not materialized.[32] In fact what evidence is available points the opposite way. When the scores on the Army Alpha Test of soldiers drafted in the First and Second World Wars were compared, the psychologist Read D. Tuddenham found that those of the soldiers in the later war were higher.[33] As possible reasons for the improvement, he discussed the increase in education, improvement in health, including increase in height and weight, and the greater experience in test-taking of those in the Second World War. Whatever the reasons, the fact is that insofar as the soldiers of 1917–18 and those of 1941–45 were representative of the nation, American intelligence was surely not declining. In the 1930's a dire prediction was also made for Scotland, when psychologists, noting the tendency for children from larger families to have lower IQ's, decided that the average intelligence in Scotland was going to drop.[34] The reason was, of course, that lower-class families were reproducing much faster than the higher-IQ middle- and upper-class

families. Some psychologists have been hard put to explain the dismal failure of this prediction about the general intelligence of the Scots.

It was this kind of outlook that aroused Lippmann and led him to challenge the prevailing beliefs. He rejected the notion that the new tests succeeded in evaluating native human ability. "If, for example, the impression takes root that these tests really measure intelligence, that they constitute a sort of last judgment on the child's capacity, that they reveal 'scientifically' his predestined ability, then it would be a thousand times better if all the intelligence testers and all their questionnaires were sunk without warning in the Sargasso Sea."[35] How can one speak of a certain percentage of the population as intellectually backward or as gifted on the basis of the tests, he asks. There is no scientific evidence for such assertions, he declares, and they are in effect the result of circular reasoning.

He points out that Alfred Binet had been dealing with the practical problem of distinguishing backward from normal children. Binet gave up the elusive task of defining intelligence and sought instead to know what was the normal child. Approving Binet's decision that his standard for a normal child of a particular age would be what an arbitrary percentage of that age could do, Lippmann adds: "Binet therefore decided to consider 'normal' those abilities which were common to between 65 and 75% of the children of a particular age. In deciding on these percentages, he thus decided to consider at least 25% of the children as backward. He might just as easily have fixed a percentage which would have classified 10% of the children as backward, or 50%."[36]

The test result that some percentage is either "backward" or "normal" or "superior" is nothing more than the built-in purpose of a test to classify the same percentage of persons in a particular category. For example, the Army Alpha Test used in the First World War was devised, among other reasons, to select men for commissions as officers. The test items were so selected that only 5 percent or less in any average group would be able to finish the entire series in the allotted time. This was planned because only 5 percent or less were sought after. Lippmann adds: "It is not surprising, therefore, that 5% or less (4½% actually) of the Army made a top score. It

is not surprising that tests devised to pass 5% or less 'A' men should have passed 4½% 'A' men." To conclude, on the basis of the test results, that America has only 4½% top men of intelligence, was, Lippmann thought, to pass beyond the bounds of logic.[37]

In any such system of test construction there must always be the superior, the average, and the retarded, and their proportions in the population must remain the same. This distribution must remain no matter what the effects of unimaginably grand efforts in education might be, and no matter what the future holds in the way of discoveries on the biochemical influence of brain function. And by use of such a distribution, if the average adult, long out of school, performs on these tests at the same level as the average fourteen-year-old, then the claim can be made that the average adult has the mental ability of a fourteen-year-old. The concept, said Lippmann, is "spurious."

His most vehement attack was directed against the fast-growing belief that intelligence tests were evaluating an intangible and unmodifiable human quality. The most prominent testers were claiming, he said, that they were measuring an innate and predetermined capacity "of a human being for all time and that this capacity is fatally fixed by the child's heredity." He was appalled by the tendency to treat people with low intelligence quotients as "congenitally and hopelessly inferior." Retarded children needed something more than classification. They needed special analysis and training to overcome their backwardness.[38]

In one paragraph Lippmann succeeds in crystallizing a problem about intelligence and evaluation that has plagued even psychologists who do not have the blind spots he points out. During the years since the Second World War men like Dr. Benjamin Pasamanick, the child psychiatrist, have investigated the very questions that Lippmann raised in 1922.

> How does it happen that men of science can presume to dogmatize about the mental qualities of the germ plasm when their own observations begin at four years of age? . . . Without offering any data on all that occurs between conception and the age of kindergarten, they announce on the basis of what they have got out of a few thousand questionnaires that they are measuring the

> hereditary mental endowment of human beings. Obviously this is not a conclusion obtained by research. It is a conclusion planted by the will to believe.[39]

Since the time of Lippmann's critique, assertions about human ability can be based on millions rather than thousands of test scores, but this fact does not in the slightest diminish the validity of Lippmann's challenge to those who claim that the tests measure innate ability. Today probably every intelligence test disclaims that the ability it measures is purely native or unaffected by the environment, by parental influence or schooling. Disclaimers notwithstanding, the ideas Lippmann attacked are still influential in practice.

In essence, Lippmann brought charges against what he considered the fundamental assumptions of test theorists and users:

1. What the tests measure is innate, hereditary, and predetermined.
2. Since the intellectual capacity of man is fixed, poor learning ability is irremediable.
3. A static percentage of the population is and remains destined to be superior, normal, and retarded, and the normal or average ability of the American is approximately that of a fourteen-year-old.
4. Education is "essentially impotent because intelligence is hereditary and unchangeable."

The *New Republic* received many letters in response to Lippmann's article. It published two papers, one of them by Lewis M. Terman, who had adapted the work of Binet for use in America, and who later became eminent in American psychology.

Terman's tone throughout his article is reflected in its title: "The Great Conspiracy or The Impulse Imperious of Intelligence Testers, Psychoanalyzed and Exposed by Mr. Lippmann." He devoted three columns to a satirical treatment of Lippmann's naïveté about democracy, as if the journalist had meant that any suggestion that humans differed in ability was as subversive an idea as evolution was to William Jennings Bryan. Yes, Terman said ironically, the psychologists were seeking power and the whole testing movement was motivated by the Nietzschean Impulse Imperious. After Germany established a republic, Terman said jokingly, the psychologists had engaged in an orgy of testing in the schools, and if the German

people didn't wake up, the psychologists would take over the country and then the world![40]

Terman then discussed a number of Lippmann's criticisms, and presented the basis upon which he and other psychologists had classified average adult intelligence as equivalent to that of a fourteen-year-old. His straightforward clarification of the point makes it apparent that Lippmann's and Terman's positions were so different that a reasoned exchange on the particulars of difference was impossible. Terman assumed that since the average adult performed on a test like the average fourteen-year-old, then the average adult intelligence level had been established. Lippmann assumed that there was no way of knowing the average adult's intelligence short of giving him more extensive education and opportunity and evaluating his achievement near the end of his life.

Turning next to Lippmann's claim that the intelligence rating was chiefly predetermined by time limits, Terman chided him for careless reading of the army test reports and failing to note that some soldiers had been given twice the time on the army tests, and that their relative position generally remained the same. Terman was right, but so was Lippmann, who had raised a different argument: the data also showed that double time enabled many soldiers to improve their scores considerably, and thereby to demonstrate greater intellectual powers than under the stricter time limitation. To select 5 percent of the most able people for special service in the army, such a test, said Lippmann, was perfectly appropriate, but to use such a time-restricted test to evaluate the ability of the American people was indefensible.

Terman next turned to the criticism of claims that tests measured pure or native intelligence. He presented as evidence that intelligence was set by the individual's genes the fact that "high and low IQ's are so often found in children of the same family and of the same nursery." Also, he pointed out, identical twins have closer IQ resemblance than fraternal twins. Further, he proposed in support of native differences in intelligence that, notwithstanding what he considered similar nursery environment for Californian Japanese children and Californian Portuguese children, the average Portuguese child "carries through school and into life an IQ of about 80; the average Japanese child soon develops an IQ not far below that

of the average California white child of Nordic descent."[41] He left it to Lippmann to see the import of this comparison.

Terman failed to meet Lippmann's challenge partly because, like other psychologists at the time, he really did not seem to understand Lippmann's main arguments: first, that tests designed to classify a certain predetermined number as bright or dull will surely achieve those results but such a prearranged distribution may have no resemblance whatever to the true distribution of ability; second, psychology cannot claim to measure native or inherited ability without knowing the effects of the first four or five years of life on the development of intelligence.

Recent significant studies show the importance of the early years of life in the development of intelligence. In anticipation of those findings stands the judgment of the British historian Arnold Toynbee, who writes that the contribution of the home to children's education becomes clear when the school doors are opened to a group that had never enjoyed this private presence of the privileged.

> This becomes apparent when children with a poorer cultural heritage are admitted to the minority's schools. They find it difficult to obtain as much benefit as their privileged schoolfellows obtain from the same course of formal education, because they bring less with them. To him that hath shall be given. This is not just, but it is one of the facts of life. It takes more than one generation for a family that has made its way out of a less privileged into a more privileged social class to acquire the full cultural heritage of the class to which it has won admission.[42]

Toynbee does not speak of intelligence or IQ's, but he provides at least a historian's response to Lippmann's question, What happens between conception and the age of four? Although Toynbee does not deal with the first nine months of life and their biological importance, he does point out that the first four years after birth are given to the education of the child in the home. The "curriculum" includes cultural heritage, and the quality of the education here, as in any other situation, depends on the knowledge and skill of the teacher. To the extent that a child's higher mental processes as well as his general knowledge are dependent on such preschool education, the early years can have a telling effect on his intellectual functions.

More than forty years elapsed after Lippmann's stress on the

preschool years before Project Head Start was created. Although this federally supported school program for deprived children four and five years old is a pitifully small response to the need, it is at least a recognition of the significance of the early years of life in laying the groundwork for the mental development of the child. Eight-week summer instruction has already shown the possibility of raising the mental functioning level (the IQ) of Head Start children.

What did it take to get Head Start? Social action. Educational gains like free primary schools, compulsory attendance, laws, tax systems and state support, free high schools, and city and state universities have usually been won through social struggle, and these gains were usually achieved, or the process at least set in motion, during periods of ferment like the Jeffersonian and Jacksonian periods, Reconstruction, the turn of the century, when the Populist and labor groups achieved great influence, and, of course, the 1930's.

With the onset of the Great Depression, educators shifted their attention to the social role of the school. George S. Counts of Teachers College, Columbia, objected to the class bias in the membership of school boards which set policy for the local school systems, and demanded that the schools come to grips with industrial and social realities and avoid the superficialities that were passing for education. Several of his well-known colleagues, including John Dewey and William H. Kilpatrick, contributed to the influential volume *The Educational Frontier*,[43] published in 1933, which urged America to change the school curricula so that they would deal with the facts of modern life, and called for administrative changes so that teachers and students would play a more important part in managing the schools of which they were so much a part.[44]

The New Deal brought forth the Civilian Conservation Corps and its special training for out-of-school youth; the National Youth Administration, which enabled thousands to complete their education; the Works Progress Administration and the Public Works Administration, which together constructed about 18,700 new school buildings. Cremin believes that the abiding impact of the New Deal lay in the greater sensitization of teachers "to the educational predicament of out-of-school youth and to the public's responsibility for contending with it."[45] Of perhaps equal importance was the degree of federal government commitment to the support of local

education through school construction and also through the work programs that financed the education of many of the disadvantaged youth of that decade.

In the ferment of the 1930's the psychological theories that Lippmann had challenged faced their severest tests in the work of many psychologists, a number of them led by George Stoddard, then of the University of Iowa. While educators like Counts, Dewey, and Kilpatrick directed their fire against socially irrelevant curricula and undemocratic school administration, psychologists like Stoddard attacked theories that were close relatives of the Platonic view of educability.

It is an interesting feature of such periods of social ferment that the theories of mental ability are affected by them. It was true during the thirties, as it is today, that the standard concepts about the fixity of ability are challenged and a more open and optimistic view achieves prominence when the people demand more or better schooling.

Why does this occur? Is it not contrary to the spirit of objectivity of science? Theoretically, as the psychologist Hadley Cantril said, science accepts only that which is based "on the objective, rational evaluation of submitted evidence." But in actual practice science behaves "much like other social institutions, complete with hierarchy, dogma, and coercive power. Truth tends to be confused with orthodoxy, science with scientism."[46]

The sociology of knowledge has provided a theory that makes it possible to comprehend the role of society in the developing thought of scientists. One of the great contributions to the literature in this field is Karl Mannheim's *Ideology and Utopia,* originally published in Germany in 1929. Mannheim explains that men "do not confront the objects of the world from the abstract levels of a contemplating mind as such." Their perceptions of nature will be shaped by the ideas and attitudes already learned, and this is as true of their understanding of human intelligence as of anything else. According to Mannheim, a given society does not consist of as many different concepts about an object or problem, nor as many different forms of thought, as there are separate individuals. On the contrary, individuals and their thought may be subdivided into as few as two large categories, which strive either "to change the surrounding

world of nature and society or attempt to maintain it in a given condition."[47] We can place Plato and Galton in the group of thinkers whose ideas tended to assume a static quality in the distribution of intellectual talent. Galton, in fact, saw eugenics as the hope for improvement of the species, and advocated encouraging reproduction by the able and discouraging the backward, in the belief that the germ plasm contained the determinant of intelligence. The group of thinkers who saw the possibility of improving intelligence through social intervention included Locke, Priestley, Godwin, Mills, and Owen. Contemporary American and British psychology has been dominated by those in the first group, with Hall, Thorndike, Kuhlmann, and especially Terman perhaps the most influential American leaders.

In England psychologists like Tredgold, Thomson, and Burt, following the Galton doctrines, declared (in the words of Burt) that intelligence is "inborn, all-round, intellectual ability . . . inherited or at least innate, not due to teaching or training . . . it can be measured with accuracy and ease."[48] It was Thomson and Burt who predicted a dire future for Scotland, with the number of able children declining and the feeble-minded increasing. After the Second World War, when Thomson was confronted with a rise in IQ of eleven-year-olds in Scotland between 1932 and 1942, he attributed the increase to test sophistication on the part of the children. Quite consistently with his theory of intelligence—or perhaps, in Mannheim's words, consistently with his ideology—he made this assumption despite the fact that the data he presented in support of it proved that even those of the 1942 group who had never had an IQ test before showed an increase over the earlier group. The errors and seeming blindness of eminent psychologists are inevitable in assessing even the most objectively assembled data, when their thinking is closed to alternate interpretations. It is not surprising that Britain, only now beginning to break out of the cocoon of a stratified educational system, should have bred a school of psychology so largely dominated by the views of Burt and Thomson.

But in America, along with Thorndike and Terman and Florence Goodenough, there were also those like Stoddard and Beth Wellman, and the conflict between the two camps became heated enough for Terman to write:

> For a more detailed account of the nature-nurture evidence appearing between 1928 and 1940 I refer the reader to Goodenough's two chapters in Part I, which are characterized by critical insight, scientific caution, and just appraisal of others' work. In contrast, the chapter by Stoddard and Wellman (XIV, Part I) impresses me as biased and uncritical.

Terman then proceeded to accuse these two of behavior that can be described as little short of unethical and dishonest for scientists.[49]

Terman's chief target, George Stoddard, declared in 1943, in his *Meaning of Intelligence,* that we had no final answer on educability, but that the final answer would be furnished by science. "When one speaks of hereditary factors in intelligence, he must speak of hereditary *structures,*" that is, of inherited brain structure, not of hereditary behavior. Stoddard emphasized that the genetic process is complex. Human cytoplasm represents an environment for the genes, and the two interact over the years, "producing a vast complexity of organic outcome." The genes are not independent of the cytoplasm, nor the cytoplasm of the experience of the organism, nor the organism of its physical and social surroundings. Human intelligence must be considered in terms of the total organism, not simply of potentiating chemicals known as genes, nor even of hereditary structures of the cerebral cortex and central nervous system.[50]

The debates about theory of intelligence were heated and personal, but the implications of choosing one or the other of the two main arguments were—and are today—of vast social and educational significance. The fixed-intelligence point of view led Brigham to conclude that American intelligence was declining due to racial admixture, that this would probably continue but was not inevitable—it could be avoided if an aroused public prevented it by taking necessary legal steps. "Immigration should not only be restrictive but highly selective." But this would provide only slight relief. "The really important steps are those looking toward the prevention of the continued propagation of defective strains in the present population."[51] The book was recommended by Robert M. Yerkes, a leading psychologist who in the preface referred to the menace of "race deterioration."

In contrast, Stoddard wrote: "We now feel sure that, over the

last six thousand years, literacy need not have been confined to an intellectual aristocracy: the rulers who kept the masses down were strongest in their contempt for their inferiority. . . . The chief advantage of kings is not their lineage; it is the power, often neglected, to establish from birth upwards the right kind of protection and education." Later he says the misuse of genetics "could be termed hilarious, were it not used by the elite to buttress social privilege." Stoddard concludes his book with: "The raw materials of life are good; they are plastic and tremendously varied. The problem of the times is to work steadily toward their preservation and enrichment."[52]

The two different positions have given rise to correspondingly different attitudes about programs of instruction. Those who place special emphasis upon heredity tend to favor rigorous academic instruction for the 20 percent or so who are deemed capable of higher education and to favor programs that prepare students for vocational life and for citizenship (adjustment to that life) for the remainder of the children. As a rule, high expenditures for services intended to compensate for environmental impoverishment will generally be opposed on the grounds that they are educationally invalid. The educationally conservative wing of the fixed-intelligence school will de-emphasize motivation and activity projects in the belief that, with work carefully pitched to the intellectual level of the child, the scholastic demands will not be excessive or frustrating even when challenging. The educationally progressive wing of the fixed-intelligence group will discourage highly structured programs, preferring the kind of unpressured environment wherein the inherent capacities might unfold.

The other group, the "environmentalists" (because of the stress upon nongenetic factors in determining educability), favors massive efforts to offset the preschool disadvantages and consequent impoverishment of millions of children. They recommend preschool education of children and parents, and the provision of large-scale remedial medical, psychological, and sociological services.

Looking back over the history of theories of man's educability, the paths seem more clear and direct than they could possibly have seemed at the time. Whenever the voice of the people was throttled and the subjects of the realm were passive, only an elite were be-

lieved to possess God-given talents for education that enabled them to understand and control the environment, and also to heighten their appreciation of man's cultural heritage. When the common people were sufficiently powerful to demand an improvement in their conditions of life, one or another theory of educability emerged that left open-ended the possibility of mass education. Up to now, the third stage has always been a counterreaction that succeeds in halting if not temporarily reversing the forward trend.

4

THE AMERICAN SCHOOLS CHOOSE

Future historians may well describe our time, more than a hundred years after the Civil War, as the time of the crucial campaign to validate the Constitution and the Bill of Rights in the field of education. Education has always figured prominently in America's development, as part of every generation's aim to make life better for their children. With the quickening pace of the industrial-scientific revolution, the importance of education has increased at seemingly geometric rates in each decade. Its role today in raising the standards of life of citizens in Harlem or Birmingham or Newark is evidenced by the many new job opportunities for educated Negroes, and especially by the newspaper space devoted to actions to improve the schools. The insistent demand for better education is resisted in part because some whites perceive the upward movement of blacks as a threat to their own social and economic position. Other minority groups in America whose economic status and educational opportunities are inferior—such as the migrant, the Indian, the Mexican American, or the vast number of whites of old American lineage, as in Appalachia—get less publicity about their educational needs because they are not exerting enough organized power to change their social status or, with the recent exception of the Mexican Americans, even to be newsworthy. Nevertheless, most Americans are now aware that, especially in a scientific era, inadequate education foredooms these children to failure in and frustration with learning, and to an embittered outlook upon society

because it offers them no opportunity to emerge from the morass of poverty and ignorance. If they develop patterns of behavior disturbing to the school or destructive to the community, their functioning is "normal" under such conditions.

What can school people supported by parents do for these children? They cannot correct the social injustices in the wider community, clear out the rat-infested homes, provide families with adequate food and clothing or get jobs for the parents. They can only do their utmost to give the children fruitful experiences in learning.

Let us see what the schools did at the turn of the century—from about 1900 to 1925—when faced with a somewhat comparable set of conditions. While the need for education was not so compelling then because even most industrialists and businessmen were able to be "self-made," the aspirations of countless working-class families for a better life stirred their interest in education as the best means for attaining it. For their children, too, learning problems and school failure led to consequences not unlike those of today. The school system had to cater to a population that ranged from a social class level just below that of the upper-class old American families and the *nouveaux riches* to that of the unskilled. Differences in preparation for and attitudes toward school were just as vast as the contrast in conditions of life between the upper-middle-class home of the time, with its maid and garden, and the tenement house or the rural shack. The gap between the "uppers" and the "lowers" was further widened by the fact that many of the latter were members of immigrant families whose language was not English and whose way of life was unlike that of the native lower-class American. The lower classes, native and foreign, together supplied, as they still supply, a disproportionately large percentage of failing and retarded students in the public schools.

In retrospect it appears that at that moment in the history of American education two major alternative courses lay ahead. The first was to attribute learning problems and low scholastic performance to native differences in endowment, genetically determined and essentially irremediable. In that case the course to pursue was clear: use our scientific acumen to classify the students intellectually and develop programs of instruction suited to their potential for learning. Such a system of differential education would be humane in

that it would assure each child a greater degree of success, and as a result of success, both a more sympathetic attitude toward school and the likelihood of approbation from teachers and parents. At the same time, no group of children would thereby impede the educational development of any other group by its speed of learning or its classroom behavior. This attitude seemed to show true respect for individual differences in man.

The alternative way of handling disparities in performance was to attribute them to the quality of children's physical and cultural environment—their organic environment from conception, and the cultural and economic environment of their parents and ancestors for many generations. Learning problems would be credited to gross impoverishment in one or more of these environments. The course to follow would be one of providing the encounters with life that enable the child to develop language, to gain mastery over the concepts and the habits of attention, perception, and memory necessary for academic success. Toward that end science would search for the laws of behavior in formal and informal learning situations, so that teacher training, curricula, and the organization of classes could be based on sound knowledge. With the implicit assumption that the limits for learning are unknown and that all children except those handicapped by irremediable disorders of the brain or the central nervous system are capable of academic learning, knowledge of how people learn could be used to remedy children's intellectual inadequacies. The search for causes of learning problems would continue as long as the problems appeared, and remedies would be invented as needed. The emphasis would be on the universality of man's capacity to engage in abstract thought about his physical and social environment. If such a capacity exists, then no child, except perhaps one suffering from brain damage, ought to be classified as ineligible for academic work, and any child exhibiting symptoms of uneducability is a challenge to the wisdom and science of education.

The consequences of choosing between these conceptions of mental ability—the hereditarily "fixed" and the environmentally "open" —go beyond the selection of educational goals and the composition of curricula that are compatible with them. The attitudes of teachers toward their students, an aspect of the learning situation that is now recognized as one of paramount importance, especially in the early

grades, are partially determined by the theories they adopt. How one conceives the nature of a child's learning problem, whether as an inherent defect or as preschool intellectual malnutrition—or as the effect of social inequality or of being the next generation in a line of ne'er-do-wells—cannot fail to affect the relationship of teacher and pupil. A teacher who regards the current functioning of the child as an adequate representation of his ability will expect and be content with the same level of performance. The child learns about himself from other people, and it is especially from teachers that he learns about his intellectual ability. Soon he will set his aspiration at the same level as her expectation of him. In the average overcrowded, understaffed school, the child is almost required to do so. If he does not, he may face the wrath of a teacher who will drive him to disruptive behavior and eventually to dropping out of school altogether.

Most educators are probably not fully aware of their attitudes about the abilities of students, nor do they possess a systematized version of their beliefs. On the contrary, they may profess one theory (for example, one that emphasizes the social determinants of educability) while functioning in terms of another (emphasis on the hereditary factors). But there is a great measure of consistency, for underlying most of the practices in the schools is a doctrine of capacity that is held as widely as if it had been legislated.

No one would claim today that America consciously and definitively chose one path rather than the other or that any group of educators, psychologists, or laymen adopted a resolution that dictated policy in one or the other direction. Prominent psychologists and educators gave representation to both points of view in the books they wrote and the policies they proposed. Yet even a brief review of current educational practices and of their evolution since the beginning of this century reveals that the United States made a choice as decisively as if a central ministry of education had imposed it.

During most of the nineteenth century the forces pressing for free secondary education were building up. The decision as to which of the two alternative paths to follow was made during the years after 1900, and was pretty much set by 1925. We chose to believe that mental ability is largely predetermined by the genes and largely

immutable by the time the child has come to school. The schools' task is therefore to classify, group, and offer instruction to help the children realize their fixed potential.

The genetic theory has had a destructive effect on our school system in its entirety, but most of all on Negroes, Indians, Mexicans, and that large population of poor whites in rural sections. European immigrants fared better than these groups for a number of reasons, first of all because they lived in the cities, whose schools were then clearly superior to those in rural areas. Furthermore, they had migrated to the United States at a period of rapid industrial expansion and were participating directly in it, mostly as workers. Through the trade unions and their ethnic organizations they were able to wield influence over the political machines by offering blocs of votes in return for patronage and other benefits. Their needs, educational and other, had political implications. By contrast, early in the century the Negroes, Indians, Mexicans, and many of the poor whites were disenfranchised and powerless. Today, however, the news media remind us daily that Negroes, at least, are determined to win a share of power, and to spare their children the fate of being excluded from good education on the grounds of supposed genetic inferiority.

The historical route that led to the firm adoption of this theory as the basis of educational policy has not been entirely undeviating. Social circumstances have sometimes made the other major theory a more formidable antagonist, but this competition has occurred intermittently and briefly. The fact that the schools have made the decision is borne out by ways psychologists test students and the ways educators group them.

Pychologists and educators do not usually reveal their beliefs in these matters directly. However, both have spoken out on practical questions wherein their stand on these issues is implicit, and they have described and defended the current school practices that are relevant to the issues.

The way the schools use intelligence tests and group children according to their scores shows that the genetic theory of mental ability is basic to the most important educational decisions and practices. Tests of any kind can be used for good or bad purposes, good if their results are employed to introduce measures to

strengthen the intellect of the child, bad if the scores are used to inform teachers, parents, and the students themselves of alleged ability limits. We can say very much the same about grouping children in accordance with their ability for the purpose of offering different versions of presumably the same subjects to the different ability levels. If such grouping is a temporary measure intended only to accelerate the child's development, to help him overcome a limitation and advance more quickly, then of course it can be a desirable procedure. But when it is used to separate children on a relatively permanent basis, and to give them education presumably suited to established intellectual limitations, then we must consider such action indefensible.

The uses made of these two devices—tests and ability grouping—are symptoms of what is wrong with a school system built upon a fixed-intelligence ideology. The consequences in the form of mental attitudes about the child's ability and the quality of work expected of him, as well as in the quality of his curriculum, are serious indeed.

INTELLIGENCE TESTS

Tests of mental ability have been widely used in the schools ever since the First World War. Data on the sale of tests are not published; however, a cautious estimate made after conversation with test publishers is that in 1966 the major profit-making test publishers sold tests (all tests, that is, not just those on mental ability) valued at twenty million dollars. At an average of fifteen cents a test, more than 133,000,000 tests were sold to schools, colleges, community agencies, and industry in one year. Add to this the business of the minor profit-making publishers and then of the testing program of nonprofit organizations like the Educational Testing Service, and the number gets a substantial boost. The ETS tested 1,143,372 high-school juniors on the Preliminary Scholastic Aptitude Test, 1,413,903 seniors on the Scholastic Aptitude Test, and 662,485 students from grades four through fourteen in the National Guidance Testing Program, all in the 1965–66 academic year.[1]

The 1939 manual of directions for one of the most widely used

group tests of intelligence, the Otis Quick Scoring Mental Ability Test, had this to say about the purposes of mental ability tests:

1. For teaching purposes, to discover which pupils are bright and capable of doing better school work than they are doing and to discover which pupils are dull and may be attempting work beyond their capacity.

2. For administrative purposes, to regrade pupils so that the pupils in any one grade will be more homogeneous in mental ability and therefore able to progress at more nearly the same rate than otherwise.

3. For administrative purposes, to classify pupils into separate groups within grades in order that the brighter or more mature pupils may be given an enriched curriculum and in order that the duller or less mature pupils may be allowed to progress at a slower rate.[2]

Three other purposes are given, each consistent with the general thesis that the test is tapping a stable quality of the individual, one that should determine his educational status and goals.

Manuals for tests developed during the 1940's, and revised manuals for earlier tests, tend to be more circumspect in describing the abilities measured. A number of research studies during the 1930's and 1940's, like those by the educational psychologist George Stoddard and the social psychologist Otto Kleinberg, had raised doubts about a purely genetic explanation of intelligence test performance by pointing up the effects of environmental intervention. But while the authors of test manuals became more cautious and were even prepared to give learning its due, the manuals have not become essentially different in their implicit interpretation of variations in mental capacity. A recently published test manual for the Henmon-Nelson Test of Mental Ability that is a model of excellence in its detail on the development of the test suggests many of the same uses of mental ability tests, although use in combination with other sources of data is often recommended. For classifying groups on the basis of mental ability, "the group intelligence test enables them to do this at the very beginning of the year." While pupil performance usually determines grading and promotions, "in many instances intelligence test data prove to be helpful, particularly in consider-

ing extra promotions or possible retardation." The authors of the test believe that it is "evident that schoolwork should be suited to the intelligence of the pupils" and they do thereby declare themselves in favor of some form of ability grouping.[3]

The two tests whose manuals were quoted above provide a single score, convertible to an IQ. In each case the ability that is appraised is heavily weighted with a verbal factor. Since the Second World War a new and important development in intelligence testing has been the construction of mental ability tests that evaluate more than one or two aspects of intellectual functioning. Some of the new multiple tests evaluate six or more attributes. The manual of one of these, the SRA Primary Mental Abilities, Primary Form, suggests the possibility "that considerable improvement in most abilities for most children can be expected as a result of planned training, especially when such instruction is begun early and utilizes materials specifically designed for this purpose. Work with kindergarten and first-grade classes is potentially most rewarding because in these years the children's minds are growing so rapidly." For a test manual, this is an unusually generous interpretation of human capacities. It is based on the declared belief that so far as the possibility of changing the intelligence of children is concerned, "while the limits of achievement may be established by our heredity, most people never approach the limits of their potential achievement."[4]

This sanguine view offers some hope that man's intellectual resources can achieve a higher level than that fixed by the usual distribution of scores. The author does not explain the meaning of his statement that considerable improvement in most abilities for most children can be expected—that is, whether he believes it is possible for substantial numbers of children to increase their scores from low to average, or even from low or average to high. The implication is that the changes cannot be substantial because the ceiling is determined by heredity.

The manual for a form of the test used in the higher elementary grades suggests that the test constructors were committed to a belief in the stability of intellectual capacity. Students who are low in verbal ability but bright in other ways are to be encouraged through the findings of this test to use their other skills. This shift in emphasis

—that is, to the nonverbal abilities—in the test for older children certainly runs counter to the requirements of academic study and the possibility of higher education.

It seems fair to say that the technicians who construct intelligence tests, or at least those who write the manuals, have the opinion that their instruments are appraising a capacity static enough to be relied on in making important educational decisions—a capacity that is modifiable within limits, but then only through special intensive programs. The learning ability displayed by children in the early grades is regarded as reflecting the limits of their potential educational achievement.

Some psychologists who write textbooks about psychological testing are more prudent than many of the authors of the manuals. Some go to great pains to present data on the handicapping effects of inferior cultural opportunities. Yet one such author concludes a section with the following statement: "The problem now is to determine to what extent our current tests are not 'culture-fair' and to improve upon them."[5] Despite the evidence that justifies doubts about the adequacy of the instruments to make appraisals of the real "potential" of many culturally deprived children, their continued use is not questioned.

Other authors advise caution in interpreting the verbal group intelligence test scores of poor readers and low achievers in arithmetic skills, of those emotionally disturbed at the time of testing, and, finally, of children "whose social and cultural background differs radically from that of the rest of the group."[6]

Teachers in the New York metropolitan area have been advised to look with jaundiced eye at mental test scores of the following groups of children: the emotionally disturbed, the pre-delinquent aggressive, Negro and Puerto Rican, immigrant or first generation, especially from peasant cultures particularly in the Mediterranean area, low socio-economic groups. Frequently the response of the puzzled teacher is, "Who's left?"

The stability of the IQ has occupied the attention of many investigators. Obviously an unstable human condition or an unstable test score does not make for reliable prediction. Tests devised primarily for prediction would have no value. Two psychologists, Donald E. Super and John O. Crites, experts in psychological measure-

ment, after examining the literature on the innateness and constancy of intelligence, concluded: "Whereas both nature and nurture play a part in the development of intelligence, mental ability as indicated by the intelligence quotient is relatively constant from the time a child enters elementary school until late adulthood."[7] The meaning of this statement is clear: Learning ability is fixed by the time the child enters elementary school, and apparently it is not susceptible to change by the offerings of the school. Some less cautious authors describe intelligence as largely innate or as 80 percent innate and immutable. Consider the effects of such interpretations on the behavior of school administrators and teachers. "Teach to his level—Recognize his potential—Place him with his peers—Don't waste time trying to make a silk purse from a sow's ear."

The point of view of two other psychologists, H. H. Remmers and N. Gage, is probably representative of test specialists today. The difference in IQ for the average child on a test and retest even over several years is five points. Such a difference is not educationally or psychologically significant, these authors explain, and "this degree of *average* constancy is highly valuable for predictive and guidance purposes. It means not that environmental changes are irrelevant to IQ but rather that such changes are relatively rare. For most children the environmental factors that affect intelligence do not change markedly from one year to the next. They stay in the same family, neighborhood, and school, and the stimulating or stultifying effects of these factors on their intellectual growth remain roughly constant."[8]

Various circumstances may prevent children from developing and/or revealing learning ability more substantial than that reflected by the recorded scores. This does not mean that the test failed to tap the child's knowledge or that it would evoke a qualitatively different response if repeated on another occasion. On the contrary, the failure of a child to have reached the "prerequisites to first grade" makes him, in the view of those who see great differences in the opportunities available in the United States for such study, *consistently* handicapped both in school learning and in test performance. The gap between the reliability of a test and its validity is very great: a test that seeks to appraise the quality of a child's learning aptitude might be invalid for that purpose, might fail to

evaluate human potential, and yet might do this poor job consistently.

Here emerges a key factor in the question of learning capacity, one that transcends the problem of valid intelligence testing. While the nurturing agents remain constant, prospects for the realization of potential among the deprived are minimal. Following the law of inertia, movement cannot commence without a push. But how many are deprived, and to what extent can they raise themselves or be raised? The "father" of the testing movement, Binet, wrote more than half a century ago: "With practice, ambition and especially method, one can succeed in increasing his attention, memory and judgment, and in literally becoming more intelligent than before."[9] Terman demurred. There was, he said, "no reason to believe that ordinary differences in social environment (apart from heredity), differences such as those obtaining among unselected children attending approximately the same general type of school in a civilized community, upset to any great extent the validity of the scale."[10]

Typically, psychology textbook writers handle the subject of learning capacity in the following sequence: The nature-nurture question has long been debated, they will say, and it remains unresolved and controversial. The evidence as to environmental determinants is especially debatable, those studies reporting the most dramatic changes being open, they indicate, to sharpest criticisms. There can be no doubt that various factors related to social class and to interpersonal relations do affect the IQ and need to be considered. However, since these factors usually remain quite stable during the formative years of life (that is, the community does not dramatically change its attitude toward unpopular groups; parents don't usually dramatically change their approach to life), the IQ—and other measures of functioning learning ability—likewise remain relatively stable. The stability of the IQ over a period of months or years is thus presented as one estimate of its value, and its tendency to correlate positively with school success (which is equally dependent on preschool influences) is given as another estimate of its value. This is an example of the dog chasing its own tail. Many a teacher has been deceived about the children in her class by this kind of reasoning, and many a parent has come to accept failure or

mediocrity as the expected level of performance for a child. Every experienced teacher and parent, however, has a heartening story or two about exceptions. I remember a seventh-grade boy named Ralph, who was lucky enough to have parents who were exceptions.

The junior-high-school counselor urged Ralph to drop some of his academic subjects on the ground that he was not "college material." The boy's dissatisfactions led the parents to see the counselor, who reported to them that Ralph's test results showed him to be "average" in ability. When they questioned the accuracy of the results, he argued that the boy's grades were consistent with the IQ test scores. This seemingly ironclad logic fell apart eighteen months later. After the use of private reading and psychological specialists, Ralph's grades rose from C's to B's and his IQ test scores from approximately 100 to about 120 on comparable tests. Ralph's experience does not mean that every student can be helped in the same way, or so dramatically, but such cases point up the fallacy of supporting the validity of the IQ score by reference to school grades, and vice versa.

Leaders in educational psychology writing about tests may be characterized as weighting the genetic factor much more heavily but giving recognition to the environmental, and urging that the latter be carefully taken into account in test interpretation. One very significant feature of their viewpoint—one that is only implicit, however—concerns their attitude to the cultural factor: since the basic social determinants of educability rarely change, and change little if at all, we cannot expect tests to indicate what might have been if life had been different or what might be if society, perhaps through its schools, could compensate for past omissions in the experiences of the child. Various forces, internal and external, have contributed to make little Johnny's learning and thinking apparatus function as it does when he enters first grade. Current psychological views are predicated on the belief that while modification in the qualitative level of the apparatus is possible, such modifications will usually not occur as a result of regular school activities, hence will not occur at all.

By way of analogy we might take another human activity, a more tangible one than learning, and apply to it the current reasoning about the IQ and learning ability. In discussing walking, for ex-

ample, we would say that nature provided almost all humans with the potential for it, the variegated strides and gaits being dependent in part on hereditary structures, such as length of legs, width of pelvic girdle. The environment, in the form of incentive, encouragement, parental values, and the like, contributes to the rate of learning. Both factors, let us say, contribute to the "walking score" of members of a group of children. Some of these, however, have not learned to walk; at best they falter, drag one or both legs, and their score is very low. Perhaps a number of these "backward walkers" have suffered or still suffer from nutritional deficiency, for which the parallel would be educational deficiency. Any prediction about their capacity for walking, hiking, or running must be predicated on the assumption that their diet will be corrected. If the community does not as a regular practice correct the cause of nutritional deficiency, the child will most likely remain a "backward walker." In such a society a reliable prediction can be made that he will be a backward walker. In the same way, stable predictions can be made that children will be mentally backward if the society fails to provide what is necessary to correct for it.

Faced with alternative theories, the leaders of American schools, under the influence of psychologists like Terman, decided that the ability of first-grade children reflects their native ability and predicts the quality of their subsequent scholastic functioning.

ABILITY GROUPING

The most direct evidence of a school system's stand on ability is the way it educates the mass of its children. If it believes that the postnatal determinants are significant, then it will mobilize its services to overcome learning defects, and it will function as if the vast majority of children, with appropriate help, will be intellectually equipped for successful learning during the period of required attendance. Only the school system which regards the genetic factor as paramount, and the environmental as so insignificant that it has hardly contributed to the child's functioning level at school entry time, would be justified in behaving differently. This latter system would rightly subdivide its population in accordance with the native ability revealed by achievement tests and would proffer a curricu-

lum suitable to the talents of each group. The decision whether it is wise to group children by ability depends upon one's view of the origin of intelligence.

The practice of subdividing students of a particular grade level into ability groups is an old one. It originated in those years around the turn of the century when the schools' composition was in process of change. As early as 1870 at least a half-dozen cities had already introduced the plan. However, not until group mental tests became generally available after the First World War did ability grouping become a standard feature of American education. The widespread use of tests and of grouping coincided with a period of social retrogression in our history, including unpopularity of immigrant groups and the successful attempt to limit their entry. In 1926, according to a United States Bureau of Education report, thirty-six of forty cities with populations of 100,000 or more were classifying elementary-school pupils in some or all grades according to ability. In smaller cities, the corresponding figures were sixty-six of eighty-nine with populations of 30,000 to 100,000, and one hundred forty-five of one hundred sixty-three with populations of 10,000 to 30,000.[11]

A bulletin of the National Education Association presented the status of ability grouping some twenty years later. In 1948, 53 percent of 1598 city school systems used this form of grade organization. The tendency was for the largest school systems to make greatest use of it, the range being from 72 percent in cities of 100,000 and over to 44 percent in cities of 2500 to 5000. A majority of the large systems were grouping the children on the basis of ability, but the percentages had dropped between 1926 and 1948.[12] This period of decline witnessed significant social changes as a result of the demands of the people during the Depression years and the Second World War.

Ten years later the NEA conducted another study on the use of ability grouping. By this time (1958–59) 77.6 percent of all city school systems had full or limited provision for grouping in the elementary grades. In the secondary grades 90.5 percent were using such grouping. In the larger cities the percentages were greater; those in the elementary and secondary schools were about 85 and 98 percent for cities of 100,000 to 500,000, and 89 and 100 percent for cities of half a million and over. The upward trend is marked,

and the tendency in the school systems is toward expanding the use of such grouping.[13]

The post-Sputnik era in the United States has heralded a new wave of ability grouping. In an effort to spur the detection and training of future scientists, special sections for the "talented" are being established. Like sibling rivals at a bare table, the champions of special education for the gifted and those for the retarded jealously guard any scrap that circumstance sends their way, and history has lately been kinder to the top group. This trend continues today, despite the fact that recent studies do not give cause for confidence that it leads to better education. It is interesting that authors of recent textbooks in elementary education display their reservations about such attempts at homogeneous grouping while attempting to present the arguments and research data pro and con in an objective way. One prominent writer said in 1954, "The practice began in public schools in the early 1920's and was heralded by some as the long-sought panacea for meeting individual differences. . . . As the years went by, experience with ability grouping and critical research studies raised many questions and doubts about its values. In spite of the fact that ability grouping still remains as a much debated practice, many school systems continue to use it."[14]

The distinguished authors of a more recent work, the former president of Teachers College, Columbia University, and the director of the Bureau of Educational Research at Ohio State University, reporting on the widespread use of ability grouping in elementary schools, write: "Although many factors in various combinations are used as the grouping basis, intelligence as measured by intelligence tests is usually the dominant factor." The curriculum for each of the ability levels (usually three) is set at different levels of difficulty. In effect, each level has an essentially different curriculum despite numerous common elements. These authors explain that the position one takes on ability grouping stems from "certain basic conceptions of the nature of the individual and of the purposes of education." They proceed to contrast the values that are normally associated with the opposing viewpoints, linking more dynamic and favorable ones with opposition to ability grouping. They say, for example, "If the democratic process is considered one in which real respect for the

personality of every person is basic, with leadership resting on the participation of all and shifting from situation to situation, ability grouping will not be accepted."[15]

Much of the debate about grouping children according to their mental ability has revolved around the question: Is it or isn't it democratic?

More immediately pertinent in a discussion of education than its adherence to the democratic ethic is the question: Does it or doesn't it provide a larger number of children with a better education?

In a book on secondary education edited by the educator H. R. Douglass,[16] the author of the chapter on language arts and literature, G. R. Carlsen, states his opposition to ability grouping in even more explicit terms. The multiple-track system, he says, sets up a kind of hierarchy of the intellectual "that seems objectionable in most schools." He then explains both the attitude of teachers to homogeneity and the consequences of the system. English teachers in general believe that such grouping would solve many of their problems. The plausibility of the plan appeals to many middle-class parents as well as teachers, and it therefore gains wide support from the most vocal and powerful sectors in the community. As a result, the majority of schools practice homogeneous grouping or "intellectual segregation." A few large schools have as many as twelve or fifteen supposedly different levels.

As we examine the evidence, Carlsen believes, we are compelled to conclude that the practice of grouping is usually ineffectual. Although most teachers tend to favor working with homogeneous groups, in general teachers do not want to be assigned to the slow groups. As a result the more experienced faculty members usually teach only the superior classes, and the poor students, including those who are suffering academically from impoverished preschool education and who especially need competent instruction, "are saddled year after year with less qualified teachers."

The program of study for the slower groups may be described as a watered-down version of the usual curriculum, given in smaller doses. Undoubtedly one reason homogeneous grouping appeals to teachers is that theoretically it implies that students in any one class are very much alike and do not require the special and sometimes tedious work of different planning and help for different pupils.

But this, says the author, is a false sense of security, for in actuality the range of differences in classes is only partially reduced. So far as English classes are concerned, Carlsen adds, "When students are grouped in reading they are not homogeneous with respect to their needs in spelling, oral communication or in speech."[17]

Research has shown that a common base for ability grouping is always lacking. Although some children are uniformly bright in all subjects and some are as consistently dull, many are inconsistent, perhaps achieving well in arithmetic, average in reading and badly in writing or spelling. One investigator studied a group of twenty-five pupils who were identical in IQ, mental age, and chronological age. He found average variations of three to five or more years in other traits, one of them being memory, so obviously important in learning. This ability can vary as much as eighty months in a group of children, all of them having an IQ of 107.[18]

Homogeneous grouping does reduce the range of difference, but only to a relatively small degree. And even those who believe that its advantages outweigh all arguments of its opponents must consider whether the gains, even as claimed, are worth the consequences. When homogeneous grouping has been based on IQ, heterogeneity has been reduced by about 20 percent. But note that the same percentage occurs when grouping is based only on chronological age, without regard to intelligence. In either case, whether IQ or chronological age is used, the average difference of, for example, reading ability, is greater *within* a single IQ or chronological group than *between* the several groups.[19]

A similar result was found in a study of pupils subdivided into three groups on the basis of "educational age." This index is heavily weighted in favor of reading-arithmetic scores. The range of ability in each of the groups was reduced by about 20 percent, so that a sixth-grade teacher would have a range of reading ability of six years instead of eight.[20] Hardly a homogeneous group.

Certain facts stand out sharply. Once considered a panacea for "meeting individual differences," ability grouping is now regarded by a number of prominent critics of education as an essential phase in the cure of the school system's defects. These critics, mainly interested in the fullest possible development of the intellectually talented children, call for further enrichment of the curriculum,

and a higher percentage of expenditures, for the ablest students. The strength of their convictions seems unaffected by such conclusions as this, based on a summary of studies on homogeneous ability grouping: "The evidence indicates greatest relative effectiveness for dull children, next greatest for average children and least (frequently harmful) for brightest children."[21]

Two psychologists who stress the difficulty of evaluating ability grouping in general explain that grouping is only the first step.[22] Materials and procedures must be adapted to the group, and this has not often been done. To paraphrase the authors, teaching of these groups calls for intelligent planning and individualized instruction compatible to the needs of the students in the class. They recommend grouping for the highest and lowest 2 or 3 or 5 percent in intelligence, with special provision to accelerate or enrich the training of the very bright. While admitting that there is limited evidence for their recommendations, they do cite a study that gave evidence that "children of high ability who are placed in special groups can master the regular school curriculum more rapidly than they would in regular classes, or engage in a wide range of enrichment activities without falling behind children in regular schools." These authors also write: "Thus, it is still largely a matter of opinion whether the bright child develops better work habits and leadership traits or feelings of snobbishness and superiority from being in a special class group."[23]

Several recent studies have demolished many of the claims for homogeneous ability grouping. Two educators recently reviewed hundreds of studies in which homogeneous and heterogeneous ability groups were compared in terms of subject-matter gain. They concluded that there was no evidence that ability grouping leads to improved mastery of subject matter and that even in cases where a slight balance favors ability grouping (and we should note that these cases are very much in the minority), the difference is "minuscule and has been to the advantage of the low group of students, not the ablest."[24] It should be noted that in these controlled studies both the homogeneous and the heterogeneous groups are taught the same basic content, whereas in actual school practice the content taught to low-ability groups is usually diluted. Consequently, in real life

situations it is likely that the slower students assigned to a homogeneous group get a duller variation of the course that their equals experience in a heterogeneous group.

The most comprehensive evaluation of ability grouping was undertaken in the early 1960's. The study involved a comparison of eighty-six classes in forty-five elementary schools in four of New York City's five boroughs. These classes were organized at the beginning of the fifth grade in one or another ability-group pattern based on IQ and remained intact until the end of the sixth grade. The number of subjects shrank from over 3000 to 2219 because of moving away or absence at the time the tests were given. The schools were described as being in "what might loosely be called 'middle-class' sections of the city."[25] The investigators concluded that, "in predominantly middle-class elementary schools, narrowing the ability range in the classroom on the basis of some measure of general academic aptitude will, by itself, in the absence of carefully planned adaptations of content and methods, produce little positive change in the academic achievement of pupils at any ability level."[26] In brief, they found that grouping is not valid: it does not achieve what it is purported to achieve. Like many other psychologists and educators these investigators still seem to cling to the belief that under the right circumstances (" . . . carefully planned adaptations of content and methods . . .") homogeneous ability grouping might prove itself. The fact is that all kinds of grouping and instruction would benefit from such planning.

Psychologist Glen Heathers recently published a report on the results of a long-term study of a modified plan of grouping originated by George Stoddard, in grades three through six in the elementary schools in two systems in New York State. Children were grouped by grade (that is, heterogeneously) for the English and social studies segments of the curriculum and in physical education, but by ability in mathematics, science, art, and music. A child could be assigned to an advanced mathematics class, a slow science class, and an average class in art, and in each of these classes he would have as teacher a specialist in the respective subject field. Fourteen other school systems in New York, New Jersey, Ohio, Illinois, Florida, and Quebec introduced this plan. The results in the first two systems

that tried the plan, which seem corroborated by less systematic evaluations in the other communities, led Dr. Heathers to conclude that the plan did not accomplish any major improvement in the quality of instruction although students, teachers, and parents endorsed specialist teachers and liked the practice of changing classes for the different subjects. A third finding was that "ability grouping appeared to have some harmful effects on both the academic achievement and the emotional-social adjustment of low-ability students."[27] In personal conversation Dr. Heathers said that other carefully planned studies here and abroad are finding similar negative effects on the slower student at the same time that the abler students show no benefits in achievement or otherwise.

In examining these current ideas about ability grouping, and some of the newest research, the point is only partly to explore its effectiveness and to discuss the wisdom of its use. More importantly, we can infer from its application the position of American education on the central question of human capacities. Notwithstanding the meager evidence in its support, the conflicting results of research over the years, and the veiled or explicit opposition of influential educators—and notwithstanding new evidence that invalidates previous claims—the method of organizing classes in terms of ability and especially in terms of mental ability as appraised by intelligence tests continues unabated. One need not be a member of an "upper-track" class in logic to conclude that the majority of American school systems have decided:

1. That the differences among children subdivided according to ability, especially by the IQ, are such that their intermingling in class handicaps the learning of each of the groups.

2. That the achievement goal for all students except the ablest 20 percent is modest and usually in the nonacademic curriculum, and this because the differences among people are believed to be largely unmodifiable.

3. That such educational objectives as an understanding of the laws that regulate the natural and social environments, a historical orientation, a scientific attitude, and an appreciation of our cultural heritage are not for all or even a majority of American children.

The time has come to say farewell to the nature-nurture contro-

versy. The debate is an important one because it gives voice to two scientific views of man, each associated with a different kind of education. Our discussion has, I hope, clarified some of the reflection and research that have occurred in educational thinking, so that we can go on to the next-higher level of confrontation with the problems of learning—a venture into analyzing the four major determinants of educability.

THE DETERMINANTS OF EDUCABILITY

PART 2

5

BIOLOGICAL

If we are to control and enhance man's learning ability, we need to understand it. If we are to understand it, we must identify and analyze all the factors that contribute to its development. It will no longer suffice to use the terms heredity and environment, which conceal more than they reveal. We replace them with four broad categories, four derminants of educability, each of which includes a number of factors that influence the development of the mind.

These four determinants of educability—biological, social, psychological, educational—stand in no competitive relationship. They are, on the contrary, thoroughly interrelated, and our task is to recognize the manifold ways in which each of them facilitates and expedites, inhibits and frustrates mental development, separately and together. We study them not just to satisfy our curiosity and our need to understand our own behavior (which are perfectly good reasons to study anything), but in the conviction that we are not victims of uncontrollable forces that willy-nilly shape the intelligence of our children as we stand by helplessly; that we can comprehend and to an ever increasing degree can exercise control over our own educability. It is a fact of life that we have had a marvelous capacity to make most people ignorant and some stupid and a few highly intelligent. We ought at least to be able to reverse the order of magnitude.

We humans are all of a piece. One of the fascinations of our behavior is the integrated functioning of the countless component

parts of the organism operating in a complex natural and social environment. Analysis requires close scrutiny of the separate parts—the biological, social, psychological, and educational determinants—of educability, but obviously they never operate in isolation, and their relationships will be evident in the separate chapter devoted to each of them.

"Determinant" as used here refers to certain specified conditions in the individual and the environment, the presence or absence of which accounts for intellectual development. In the discussion that follows, the examples will generally be of situations or cases in which the specified conditions are absent—that is, of defective organs, inadequate diet, a deprecatory self-concept, or an inappropriate school curriculum. This does not mean that the determinants operate only negatively, but rather that under negative conditions the development of educability is retarded. Just as the role of vitamins is clearest in what their absence does to man's health, so here the role of the determinants is emphasized by what the absence of certain biological, social, psychological, and educational conditions does to man's learning ability.

Man is unique. Unlike every other species, he is both part of nature and apart from it. He is inseparable from his natural environment and depends upon it for time and life space and for sustenance, but he has also been able to step back from it, observe, study, and understand it. What is more, he has been able to control much of physical and biological nature.

THE HUMAN BRAIN

Accident or coincidence will not explain his domination. The uniqueness of his brain does account for it, the highly developed cerebral cortex of the brain having given him the power to master nature and not simply to adjust to it as a victim of a limited repertoire of instincts like the lower forms of life. Man has stood up, opposed thumb and fingers, invented tools, made fire, cultivated food, built societies, mastered laws of natural and physical behavior, and by his inventions in communication and transportation conquered time and space. The brain and its necessary connections with the environment were the material basis for his success, the prosaic

stuff involved in the functions of respiration or excretion, but also of language—that remarkable product of the brain in a social environment, the key to man's great advances.

Impairments in any of the equipment for mastering language—to read, to speak, to write—must inevitably affect educability. A valid theory of educability must be able to account for all human learning and learning incapacity. It seems reasonable to believe that we cannot know the limits of man's educability until we know the diversity and degree of organic impairment that impedes learning. Any theory that pretends to know such limits—any theory of fixed genetic predetermination—has neglected significant data about large numbers of persons whose defects relevant to learning are, if not entirely remediable, then preventable in future generations.

One of the peculiar conditions of modern education is that the vast majority of practitioners—teachers, specialists, administrators—have not been given the advantages of knowledge about the functioning of the organs important to learning. When dissatisfaction with the progress of pupils was expressed by educators and parents not long after free public education on the secondary level became widespread in the United States, psychological considerations were largely responsible for modifications in methodology and curriculum. Physiology had little influence. To be sure, from studies like those of Thorndike on the laws of learning one could infer basic mental processes,[1] and the same may be said for the experimentation of most of the learning theorists, like Clark Hull or Edward C. Tolman, who attempt to validate a system of higher mental processes without direct recourse to *organic* behavior.[2]

Such a gap in the education of teachers might have some semblance of justification if mental defectives and retardates (some 3 percent of the population) were the only people whose problems were presumably related to biological factors. As it is, one experienced researcher has proposed the hypothesis that minor deficits in cognition, by which he means even the low performance in one area of achievement of an otherwise competent person as well as minimally deficient general performance, may be due to minor organic lesion rather than only or primarily to the heretofore suspected social and familial etiology.[3] Another veteran worker in the field, Dr. Richard L.

Masland, declared in an introduction to a review of the literature on the biological factors in subnormality:

> I consider it likely, however, that the factor of brain injury can operate throughout the whole range of intelligence, and, in fact, that minor degrees of injury are far more common than are the severe and grossly evident ones. Pathological studies of the brains of mildly retarded persons show minor developmental anomalies in a large proportion of cases, although the significance of these changes has not been established by meticulous correlation with the intellectual traits of normal and retarded persons.[4]

The brain is the great organ of learning, but species man learns with his entire body. Defects in the functioning of any aspect of the total organism may well impair the child's educability. He "learns" with his ears and eyes, his arms and legs, the position and direction of his entire body, with his skin and tongue and hair. If his digestive or respiratory system is malfunctioning, his learning accomplishment is likely to be affected, and if this should be long-lasting, his intellectual development may well be stunted. Not all the organs and bodily processes share an equivalent role in learning, and the brain is clearly preeminent, but the brain's dependence on the rest of the body becomes dramatically evident when we remind ourselves that cutting off the supply of oxygen to the brain even for five or six minutes leads to permanent damage.

The brain is the central, the executive organ of the body. It is the mediating agent of the organism in its interaction with the environment, receiving information from its surroundings, storing and using this information in determining the organism's reactions to and behavior in his physical and social milieu. The brain is dependent upon the sensory organs and the nerve fibers that connect it to the organs to receive information. To see the world about it, the organism must have eyes, connecting nerve fibers, and brain. The parallels are obvious for the auditory, olfactory, and gustatory senses. The final sense, the kinesthetic, is more important to learning than the last two and yet is less well known. The kinesthetic sense informs the organism of the movements of its own body or of its own muscles. Through it the child becomes aware of and experiences movement; through such knowledge he becomes oriented to direction. Nerve endings, or "sensors" as they are called, embedded in the muscles,

tendons, joints, and in the labyrinth of the inner ear, and stimulated by movement, inform the brain via the nerve fibers. Of course, for this sense, as for the others, the brain may return a message to the organs or muscles to continue its action, to alter it, or to cease. All the senses are involved in the process of interaction between an organism and its environment, wherein, through a continual process of feedback, the organism becomes informed of its environment and reacts to it. In the process of reaction, humans have, of course, come to understand and have learned how to control and change the environment; the child learns how to reach the cookie jar; the man, how to reach the moon.

In addition to the brain and the sensory equipment, there are, as we have already noted, other organs—the entire body, in fact—which serve as the necessary basis for all behavior of the organism, not only that involving learning. Generally speaking, disorders localized in these other organs do not have the same effect upon educability as those of the senses or the brain.

Man begins life as a single cell whose needs are all met through its parasitic existence in the womb. This unicellular being is distinctly human, distinctly different from the eggs of other species, because it contains the potentiality of developing into a member of the species. The adult brain is present potentially in this one cell, but what will materialize will depend upon the nature of this egg, the biochemical state of the womb, the general condition of the mother, and all those factors that affect it from the moment of conception through various periods of life to adulthood.

The newborn infant is a helpless creature, and, oddly enough, in that fact lies one of the reasons for human superiority. At birth the unfinished brain is able to function only in limited ways. Its development occurs after birth in the organism's life in a social world, and without such an environment the brain cannot be normal. The child deprived of the stimulation of human communication suffers more than educational deficiencies; that is, he is not only ignorant. He shows cerebral deficiencies; because his brain does not have sufficient opportunity to develop, his loss is irreversible, and he degenerates. It is only with great difficulty that "wolf-children"—young children raised by animals after the death of their parents—can be taught any language skills. Usually it is too late to develop the language

centers of the brain and to acquire that inner language necessary for thought and for control of behavior.

Given adequate human stimulation—and we cannot be sure what optimal stimulation is—the human brain is finished in anatomical development at about the age of seven; that is, the brain possesses a complete nerve network. But although the construction of the brain is completed, the brain is far from complete in a functional sense at that age. The evidence for this shows in electroencephalograms, the graphic records of wavelike changes in electric potential discharged by the brain. EEG's can be helpful supplements in diagnosing mental deficiency, but they do not record differences in mental ability in a normal population. However, they tell us something important about the age at which the brain is still developing, for not until about the age of eighteen is the EEG typically that of an adult. Between birth and the age of eighteen, and especially between birth and seven, the nature of the child's education will determine whether the physiological and functional development of the individual will be enhanced or impeded, whether educational errors committed by a society through its agents—the family, the school, and the local community—will deprive him of some of his intellectual possibilities as a human.

Two factors account for the superiority of the human brain. First is the nature of the brain, particularly the size of the upper centers, including the cerebral cortex, the sections that need not be occupied in handling physical survival processes such as breathing, and are free to engage in "thought." The cortex itself consists of some fourteen billion cells, complexly interconnected. The large number of nerve cells, or neurons, probably acquired in the evolutionary process by the division of these cells, accounts for man's special intellectual prowess, and points to one possible way of coping with defects in children. The neurophysiologist Dr. Paul Chauchard, director of the Neurophysiology Laboratory at the French School of Higher Studies, has said bluntly: "It will therefore undoubtedly be possible one day to augment the brain of a chimpanzee fetus or to give a child more neurons by artificial means."[5]

The second reason for our superior brain is the fact that its completion is a long slow process, dependent upon and subject to the influence of the adult world. While this has meant intellectual

deprivation for countless billions of men during the history of mankind, it has meant for some and holds for all a promise of untold achievement. Four factors play a part in the construction of the human brain; in two of them we are similar to the lower species and in the other two distinctly different. The two factors of our common animal heritage are, first, heredity, or that which is transmitted through the chromosomal structure contained within the egg and which produces a brain of a particular type, and, second, the inner environment of the egg, fetus, infant, and child—the internal interactions and bodily functions that make for harmonious operation of the body and stability for cerebral development.

The third factor, the outer environment, we share only in part with other species. This includes uterine existence and then the outer world, which is the source of the sensory data the brain requires for its development. Human interaction is another, and the most important, aspect of the environment insofar as intelligence is concerned, for it is the means through which children acquire speech and language and the basis for the growth of intellect. The outer environment is most influential during the early period of life because of the special role it plays in the origin of the mind. Since the brain grows most rapidly during the first two years, and continues in its anatomical construction during the first seven, the impact of an abundant or a deprived environment will be greatest in those years. It will still be substantial up to the age of eighteen, when functional construction is presumed to be completed.

The fourth and uniquely human factor is self-intervention. As the active child becomes increasingly conscious of his world, he can intervene on his own behalf in the development of his intellect. This is, of course, a product of the third factor, for the child will engage in such self-helpful activity—exploring, manipulating, learning, storing ideas, exchanging them—if he has the advantage of growing up in a climate in which this is encouraged and practiced by adults. Man has learned to control nature precisely because he has not passively "adjusted" to it but has asserted his mental powers to the task of actively changing it, and in that process he has changed his way of life, of thought, and of being. The child encouraged to do likewise has the greatest opportunity to participate in his own intellectual development.

EDUCATION AS HEIGHTENED CONSCIOUSNESS

Education is the process of heightening the child's consciousness. To say that a child learns is to say that his awareness of the universe has been increased. The world is there before him to be seen, heard, and felt if he is interested and will but look, listen, and feel. The young child explores the world: he looks at objects, he feels them, squeezes, bites and tears them open. His curiosity is endless, interrupted only by fatigue and curtailed only by the imposition of authority. So persistent is this phenomenon that the striving for information and understanding is recognized as among the basic human needs. To know and to understand are essential to the condition of being human and are active until counterforces, really antihuman though long-prevailing forces, censor and inhibit the expression of these needs. Oddly enough, the schools unwittingly have played an important role in achieving that regrettable end. It would be tragic enough if school learning alone were frustrated by the influences that still curiosity, but other learning is no less affected, in childhood and adult life.

There are phenomena all around us, especially those that concern ourselves and our relationships with people, which we can understand and control if we will but allow ourselves to take notice of them. The regard we have for ourselves, the regard for others, the "games" we play—all of this is before us, but we have been taught not to see.

A. R. Luria, a leading Russian psychologist, has proposed the following simple table as a means of analyzing some of the important components of educability.[6]

I	II	III
See	Look	
		Understand
Hear	Listen	

TO SEE AND TO HEAR

Column I refers to the senses. Only vision and hearing are listed, because these are most important in establishing the principles of

learning. Vision and hearing are necessary if the child is to "take in" the world, if he is to store these impressions and facts, organize them, and have them available for recall when the need arises. There are exceptions to this rule in programs especially designed for children handicapped by visual or aural defects that originate in the sensory organs themselves or in the central nervous system or the brain. Even for these children an intake of knowledge is essential through one medium or another, as Helen Keller had to find her way by the sense of touch.

Communication is essential to learning because every word we utter, every thought we have, is social in origin. We acquired them from other people, from our parents and siblings, our teachers and friends. We heard them, and we read them. Then we stored them and called them forth at demand to use them in speech or writing. We learned them in social situations and employed them in the same.

The importance of vision and hearing in learning is clear. The percentage of children who have uncompensated defects is less clear because the various surveys use different age groups, making it awkward to compare the results. Nevertheless, the numbers who are handicapped are exceedingly large no matter what age groups are studied. Ten years ago, seven and a half million children (under age twenty-one) in the United States had handicapping visual conditions. This represented about 12 percent of all in that age group. About one and a quarter to one and a half million had a hearing loss.[7] According to an interview study conducted by the National Center for Health Statistics in 1960–62, more than eight million people had an impairment in one or both ears.[8] More than half a million of them were under seventeen years old. The lower the income group the higher the incidence of impairment.[9] Of more than four million with binaural impairment, at least one third had never been tested by a doctor, a significant fact for those whose impairment might have begun during preschool and early school years.[10]

For the handicapped child to have a chance to learn efficiently, the handicap must be recognized and the necessary corrective measures taken. It is here that we begin to see the interrelation of determinants of educability. One organic or biological determinant is self-evident: the infant must have well-functioning senses. If he

suffers from a defect, he will begin to lag behind in the intake of impressions through the defective sensory organ. The sooner the diagnosis and correction, the fewer the impairments for learning. Pediatricians are advised that, for hearing defects, "early detection, prompt training of residual hearing, and exposure to the spoken word during the early years are essential to the learning process."[11] Medical services are crucial for both sight and hearing corrections. Are these widely available?

In the late 1950's the sociologist Patricia Sexton studied the conditions for education in the schools of a major midwestern city. She found that the elementary schools had no medical report on almost 50 percent of the children in the lowest social class (annual family income, $3000–$5000) who might never have had a health examination. By contrast, only 7 percent of the highest social-class group ($9000 and above) had no report of medical examination. This means that almost half of the children in the lowest group had no chance to have defects identified. When the investigator then looked into treatment, among those who were found to have defects the percentage who received no treatment was about twice as great in the lower social-class group.[12]

Standard defects of sight and hearing are obvious to the physician, and in many instances to parents and teachers, as manifest impairments of the learning process. Less obvious are a variety of other sensory defects, unnoticeable to the parent and teacher and in many instances undetectable by the physician through routine examination, which can also have serious consequences in a child's life. Such symptoms as slowness in language development may be attributed erroneously to backwardness or maturational lag. It is difficult to estimate the number of children with so-called minor sensory handicaps, partly because most do not get the kind of examination necessary to diagnose them. In any case, estimates would be of limited reliability because the more we learn about behavior, the more subtle and hidden problems of educability we discover.

The incidence of these defects is especially high among the same disadvantaged children who are likely to have meager preschool medical attention. The child comes to school unprepared; he is further handicapped by his defect in the process of learning to read;

then come the inevitable sense of defeat and some form of defense, most often resistance. The problem of one child with such a hidden ailment is typical of the unknown but undoubtedly sizable number of children with learning problems. Lewis was eleven, a pupil in the fifth grade in a suburban school in the early 1960's, when he was referred to a psychologist. The symptoms reported by the school officials were: barely passing, poor reader, average intelligence, lethargic and passive. He spent much time daydreaming, and while he was never defiant, he seemed to resist involvement in class activities. His homework was done perfunctorily. The evidence that came from school and from home was such as to suggest a psychological explanation for his behavior, especially since the family doctor reported that Lewis was in excellent health. Psychotherapy was begun.

Lewis had all the characteristics of an underachiever. He was "unmotivated," resistive, uninterested in his schoolwork and unreliable about it. In addition he had no close friends in his neighborhood or in school, and spent much of his time alone, usually watching television. However, these psychological manifestations did not necessarily mean that his problem was psychogenic in origin.

Since his reading was so poor, it seemed appropriate during psychological treatment to try to help him increase his speed and comprehension. These efforts were fruitless. Small gains would show up, but they were ephemeral. There was no carry-over to his school work and the small gains were always lost over a vacation period. The school reading specialist commented on his continuing lassitude. Perhaps he was passively resisting his parents and all authority by refusing to learn to read. Such an interpretation was tempting because those most closely involved felt that he had them "over a barrel."

Another hypothesis was possible: that he was unable to take in the stimuli of the world (in this case words and sentences) efficiently. Even though his vision was acute and he wore no glasses, was it possible that some other defect was impairing his efficiency and draining his energy? If this were so, he would have no way of knowing it. He could only know that his efforts were of no avail, bringing no reward except at best a marginal passing grade, often given as an act of charity by a teacher.

Lewis was referred to an ophthalmologist who specialized in the visual problems of school-age children. He reported that Lewis's accommodation—that is, his ability to adjust and sustain the focus of his eyes for close work—was exceedingly low for his age. Lewis had difficulty in maintaining proper binocular fusion and could not accurately control the aiming of his eyes.

The ophthalmologist began a series of retraining sessions. The psychotherapist continued to work on the effects of the years of frustration and failure—on child and parents. A few months after the retraining had begun, Lewis, reading a paragraph to the therapist, looked up from the book and said with a wide smile on his face: "You know, now when I come to the end of a line, my eyes move to the next line. They don't pop all over the page."

That had been his usual functioning, and he had had no way of knowing that it was abnormal. The defect was not and could not be picked up in routine examination because his sight was otherwise good. There is no way of knowing with certainty the cause of his condition, but his birth had been six weeks premature and the delivery had involved complications—and we do know that children born prematurely or with birth complications are significantly more susceptible to minor as well as major neurological problems. Clearly Lewis was fortunate in that his parents were determined to find the help he needed and able to spend the several thousand dollars it cost for professional services.

Minor brain injury must also be indicted for its part in impairing children's perceptual processes. Once again it is not the gross defect, easily diagnosed, that we are concerned with, but a form of brain damage so difficult to diagnose that thousands of children backward in reading are mistakenly regarded as mentally backward students. *Brain Damage in Children,* edited by Herbert G. Birch, research professor of psychiatry at Albert Einstein Medical College, covers the spectrum of conditions, and Birch himself writes about the problems created by the uneven development of sensory functioning and the absence of intersensory integration.

Children with minor brain injury frequently show signs of awkwardness in their motor activity, a condition that prevents them from establishing an adequate repertoire of motor patterns. These

are the child's earliest learning experiences, and it is from this motor information that later perceptions through the senses acquire meaning. For example, if a child is to learn the differences between "b" and "d," he must be able to "see" the difference, but if he has not developed the concept of direction through his kinesthetic sense, he cannot perceive the difference; that is, if he has not developed an adequate system of right-left relationships, if his nervous system does not inform him of the location of movement within his body, then he lacks the repertoire of knowledge necessary for such discriminations as between "b" and "d" (so important to reading) or between a clockwise and a counterclockwise direction (so important in learning to write).

Even when the child has an adequate body of information based on kinesthetic and tactual experience, his central nervous system and sensory organs must be in good working condition to enable him to make use of it. Newell Kephart, a psychologist, gives as an example the process of matching up incoming perceptual data with past knowledge. When a child cannot reach out and touch an object, he must depend upon his eyes to inform him. His eyes must "feel" the object for him and match this up with the feel of objects he has explored by hand. To do this he must be able to move his eyes voluntarily, be able to know the position of his eyes, and be able to match the movements of eyes with past movements of arms and hands. Any of the following vicissitudes of the organism can impede adequate functioning: motor defect (malfunction of the limbs that limits the repertoire of motor information), visual defect (nystagmus or strabismus or even less recognizable impairments which keep the eye from moving smoothly across a field), or brain injury (which restricts the matching of the two sets of data).[13]

The importance of neurological development is emphasized in a theory proposed by C. H. Delecato that has received considerable publicity: that a deficiency in this development rather than a defect may be a major factor in reading disability. In particular, dominance of laterality has central focus in this theory. Those of us who are right-handed should also be right-dominant in all aspects of laterality, including foot and eye. Since the opposite side of the brain controls these sensory and motor functions, the left hemisphere of

the brain is dominant in right-dominant people. For left-handed individuals, the situation should be similarly consistent, with the right portion of the brain in control. Many children are believed to have incomplete dominance of laterality; that is, some right-handed children have a left-dominant eye. Delecato has reported success in remedial reading when active steps were taken to correct such inadequate neurological development.[14]

Some studies reported in support of Delecato's method were with children whose neurological organization was normal, but the psychologist Gene V. Glass has raised serious doubts about the validity of the claims insofar as they apply to the normal child. His analysis led to the conclusion that the reported research has failed to produce evidence that "Delecato's therapy has any effect whatsover on the reading performance of *normal subjects*. . . ."[15] It is possible that his method is effective with children or adults suffering serious neurological disorganization, but the evidence has not yet been reported.

TO LOOK AND TO LISTEN

To be able to see and hear is essential for learning, and to be able to see and hear clearly without undue use of energy is essential for efficient, successful learning. But it is not enough to have good vision and hearing. It is not enough to be able to hear the teacher read a story and to be able to see the words and pictures in the book. The child must be able and willing to look and listen. It is one thing to have all the necessary apparatus to see the book and to hear the teacher; it is quite another matter to set oneself to the tasks of looking and listening.

The meaning of column II in the table above is that the child must be able to attend to stimuli—to "pay attention"—if he is to learn. In the words of a dictionary of psychological terms, attention is "the active selection of, and emphasis on, one component of a complex experience, and the narrowing of the range of objects to which the organism is responding." The child must be able to maintain a "perceptual set," to hear the teacher and to exclude competing and distracting sounds.

In what ways does the physical condition of the child affect his

ability to look and to listen? We have already seen that even minor defects of hearing and vision interfere with his ability to learn. Such disabilities have cumulative effects, so that the sensory-handicapped child has problems of attention for this reason: The harder it is to hear the teacher or to follow the text, the more is the demand in energy and attention. The child becomes fatigued more quickly. At the same time he must continue to expend greater energy than his classmates in looking and listening. It is a vicious circle: The defect necessitates greater effort at looking or listening; the more effort the child expends, the greater the fatigue; as fatigue increases, the more he must try to look or listen if he is to see or hear; and the more he tries, the greater the difficulty. No wonder he gives up. Not knowing that his learning problems have an organic cause, no wonder he begins to devalue himself. In this fashion a biological determinant (sensory defect) generates a secondary psychological determinant (the concept of himself that develops). The psychological determinant then begins to have its own independent influence on behavior.

The sensory defect has another, related effect upon the child's attention. With each passing week he falls further behind his classmates in knowledge and skills mastered. He now has problems of understanding (column III). Because he cannot comprehend the meaning of what is being studied, the pressure on his capacity to listen and to look becomes excessive. The incentive to learn, to succeed in school, to continue to aspire to higher education, must be far above average if a child is to struggle against such great odds.

It must be made very clear that these problems are not due to *mental* limitations. Intelligence is not the point at issue. Biological defects, specifically those types that impair sensory function, are.

In considering column II of the table, looking and listening, we have seen so far only the effects of sensory impairment. But there are organic impairments that cause attentional defects directly, without sensory involvement. Some children with normal vision and hearing are still unable to listen and hear efficiently. In a later chapter possible psychological causes will be examined. Here we may note two—aphasia and fatigue—that are essentially biological in origin.

Aphasia is an acquired disturbance of language function caused by an organic lesion of the brain. An aphasic person may be unable

to say what he wishes to say because of his poor pronunciation; or he may have difficulty in learning to read, to calculate, or to write; or he may suffer from any combination of these defects. Fatigue, a special feature of this disorder, makes it extremely difficult for the aphasic child to look and listen for more than short periods at a time. He tires with great rapidity because the major cerebral hemisphere is not functioning and the minor hemisphere must do all the attending and comprehending. In a regular classroom, where he is required to be more attentive than his nervous system permits, he is likely to act aggressively. His tendency toward hyperactivity and impulsiveness can create problems for himself and the class. Of course, the consequences of such behavior and the reactions they evoke have a cumulative effect that adds psychological problems to the underlying organic one.

Fred, aged nine, was in many ways a typical aphasic child. From the time he was two his parents had found him difficult to discipline. They described him as "willful and uncooperative." Teachers in kindergarten and first grade described him as extremely aggressive and questioned the parents about their handling of the child, implying that his behavior was due to his relationships with the parents. His performance at the beginning of second grade was at a beginning first-grade level in reading comprehension and in word meaning. Fortunately for Fred, his second-grade teacher had become aware of the fact that organic factors deserved as much consideration as psychological ones in the functioning of a child, and when she found him unresponsive to some of her questions and directions, she suggested to the parents that the child have a neurological examination. The basic problem was diagnosed as aphasia, with some minimal hearing difficulties. When the boy was placed in a school for aphasic and brain-damaged children, with conditions of learning that he could tolerate, his schoolwork and his interpersonal relations at home and in school improved.

There are aphasic children in hundreds of classrooms, and the likelihood is that many are not diagnosed as such. This is costly to the children and to the community, because early diagnosis offers the hope of appropriate instruction and protection from the effects of failure and behavior problems, but the diagnostic process for

aphasia is still difficult and time-consuming, and it calls for the kind of medical and psychological personnel that are inadequately available.

Much more common is the fatigue caused by inadequate nutrition and rest. Food and sleep are so elemental that in a society as affluent as ours they are often overlooked in considering the determinants of educability. Now, however, as we emerge from an era of psyche-oriented views of education and mental health, we have come to recognize that diet is a factor in emotional equilibrium as well as in education. Adequate food and the conditions that make efficient digestion possible are important to the welfare of the organism and specifically to the alertness of the growing child. This means three good meals a day, plus a nourishing snack between meals, all eaten in pleasant circumstances, with at least a brief period of rest or relaxation after the meals.

Nutrition and rest are closely related. The muscles are innervated by glucose, which is formed from starch and sugar and supplies the body with energy and heat. Fatigue comes from the overproduction of acids in the process of breaking down the sugars and starches. In order to replenish the supply of glucose, the muscle cells must dispose of the acid wastes. This action occurs during rest and sleep. Adequate rest is thus essential to overcome fatigue.

Every adult who has struggled to avoid dozing off at a lecture, concert, or sermon knows how difficult it is to fight fatigue. Every teacher who is aware of the inseparability of mind and body will know that many a child who does not "pay attention" cannot do so because he has not eaten the proper food or has not had enough rest.

It hardly needs saying that, although such conditions are often found in middle-class children, they are much more common in children who live in crowded quarters, in conditions of tension and anxiety, in families whose income qualifies them as "the other Americans" who have never known "the affluent society." It is not so well known that children who suffer disabling accidents like those that cause aphasia are also much more likely to come from the lower socio-economic classes. At this point it must be noted that a clear and significant relationship has been found between problems of attention and other behavior disorders and the biological experience of

birth. A higher percentage of children who are born prematurely and those who have other birth complications exhibit behavior that is disruptive to learning—hyperactivity, confusion, and disorganization.

TO UNDERSTAND

Sensation and attention, both required for efficient learning, are impeded by biological disorders. The same is true of understanding. Problems of comprehension are a result of insufficient knowledge and skill, which can be in turn the result of a child's inability to see or to hear or to look or to listen effectively. Once he has fallen behind, new material is "like Greek" to him. It is meaningless. Some problems of comprehension arise directly, for example, in some forms of aphasia. Inability to read is due either to inability to recognize words or inability to comprehend their meaning. Fatigue affects both the child's attention span and his capacity to understand. Mental deficiency which involves damage to the brain obviously reduces the ability to comprehend.

A variety of biological defects are barriers to the mental development of the child. From the moment of conception, the potential child's educability depends to a considerable degree on what society has in store for him—the kind of pregnancy it provides his mother, the kind of birth and postnatal life it provides him. It is an incontrovertible fact that most of the conditions and even most of the biological defects are man-made. They can be prevented, and the effects of many that are not prevented can be alleviated.

Knowledge of nervous-system pathology is still too limited to permit reliable diagnoses in all categories of defect, or even a listing of all possible categories, but tentative classifications are necessary in both diagnosis and research, and will be useful in our attempt to give some order to the large number of possible handicaps. These categories, especially important in the education of those who work with children, may be listed under three major headings: prenatal, those that develop before birth; perinatal, those that occur during the birth process; and postnatal, those that arise after the birth period. In some instances (Rh-blood disease, for example) the

symptoms may arise some hours after birth, but the disease is classified as prenatal because it develops during that period.

PRENATAL PERIOD

Since the turn of the century, childhood has been increasingly recognized as contributory to the development of the person, but educators are still naïve about the role of the preschool years in mental and personality development and in concept formation. They are even more ignorant about the period of fetal life and the birth process itself as influences in scholastic performance. We can make a start in the study of prenatal influences by classifying deficiencies known as genetic or nongenetic.

1. *Deficiencies of Genetic Origin.* The word "genes," derived from the Greek, means determiners, and it is the action of the genes contained within the chromosomes in every cell of the human body that differentiates the cells of the body. The chemical action of the genes produces differences among cells, so that the specialized functions of bone and nerve, for example, are possible. It also produces differences of size, body structure, hair color, and the like. Every cell of the human body except the reproductive cells contains forty-six chromosomes, twenty-three each from mother and father. Each reproductive cell contains only twenty-three chromosomes; thus when the sperm and ovum unite, the newly formed cells, incorporating maternal and paternal inheritance, contain forty-six. (Only as recently as 1956 did medical scientists first demonstrate that man has forty-six and not forty-eight chromosomes, as those of us over the age of thirty were taught.[16])

Among the genes in the forty-six chromosomes are those that determine the size and structure of the brain. In certain tragic instances a single mutant gene may determine abnormal cerebral manifestations such as gross underdevelopment of the head, or microcephaly. Of all the problems of learning these are the least amenable to control. Even taking into account possible legal control of reproduction, with all its social and political dangers, the problem is not easily solvable. If all the disorders that cause mental deficiency were of the single-gene variety, eugenics might provide a solution, but since most types of genetic disorders appear to be re-

cessive, carried by apparently normal persons whose identification remains to be accomplished, the likelihood of control is remote. Denial of children to perhaps large numbers of couples, most of whose children would be normal, would be as unwise as it would be impracticable.

Mental deficiency (which unlike retardation implies central nervous system pathology) is a symptom of various ailments, not a unitary trait. This condition complicates its study, since an attempt to appraise the genetic influence in deficiency calls for the investigation of diseases as diverse as mongolism and epilepsy. A further complicating factor is the interaction of genetic and other conditions, some of them not yet understood. For example, it had been clear for some time prior to 1959 that mongolism had a genetic component. If a fraternal twin is a mongoloid, his twin almost invariably is not. Identical twins, however, who have identical inheritance (identical genes), have a different fate: if one is mongoloid, both are. In 1959 the French investigator J. Lejeune and his colleagues showed that one of the small chromosomes (known as number 21) is present three times rather than twice, for a total of forty-seven rather than forty-six chromosomes, in cases of mongolism. Evidence collected since then shows that the triplication of this chromosome is the cause of the defect. Now, since the incidence of mongolism trebles every five years after the mother's age of thirty at the birth of the child, it seems that the genetic factor—the addition of a third number 21—arises as the mother ages.[17]

Labeling a deficiency as genetic in origin does not always place even these types beyond the power of science to understand and to control. Modifications in the chromosomes and genes have been artificially induced with effects observable in structural and chemical changes in animals. Estimates of the effects of radioactivity in the atmosphere—created by H-bomb testing—in increasing the rate of human mutations, suggest that man has it within his power to alter his genetic functioning, although most mutations are not to the advantage of the species.

Genetic determinants, however, appear to be responsible for only a small fraction of the subnormals, perhaps even of the organic defectives. Dr. Herman Yannet, reporting on a survey of 2500 admissions (the total patient population) at the Southbury Training School

for the Mentally Retarded, in Connecticut, says that only about 5 percent of their cases are due to pathological mutant genes.[18]

Since race figures so prominently in discussions about education and educability today, it is worth looking for a moment at the question of racial differences in genetic defects. Some diseases that cause serious *physical* consequences are associated with particular groups. A case at point is sickle-cell anemia, in which the abnormal functioning of the hemoglobin leads to anemia. The name came from the sickle-like shape of the diseased red-blood cells. This ailment occurs almost exclusively among Negroes. Insofar as diseases that cause *mental* retardation are concerned, there are none that are linked to Negroes or to any particular racial or ethnic group. The British neuropathologist L. Crome pointed out recently that any allegation about racial, religious, or even geographic differences in the incidence of hereditary disease causing mental defect must be seriously questioned.[19]

2. *Deficiencies of Nongenetic or Still Unknown Origin.* One well-known example of a nongenetic prenatal defect is the effect of German or three-day measles (rubella). Pregnant women have rightly feared this disease because of its possible effects on the newborn: cataracts, cardiac anomalies, sometimes mental and physical retardation, and also deafness, which, of course, can retard mental development. In 1964–65, when the United States had its largest rubella epidemic, pediatric experts predicted that as a result thirty thousand defective children would be born, in addition to the many aborted pregnancies and stillbirths.[20]

Surveys of the mentally subnormal, according to Dr. Yannet, have found that approximately 75 percent are minimally, 20 percent moderately, and 5 percent severely retarded. Institutions for the subnormal like the Southbury Training School have a different distribution, with a much lower percentage of the minimal type—because many in this category can make a satisfactory adjustment in the community—and with a higher percentage of the other two, especially the severely deficient. At Southbury, for example, the percentages in 1957 were 40, 30, and 30 respectively.

Using Yannet's estimates of the known and unknown factors in the etiology of the defects in the Southbury patients and applying them to the estimated subnormal population as a whole, we extra-

polate the following: About 2 percent are due to specific pathological mutant genes. About 4 percent are nongenetic and prenatally determined. Approximately 15 percent are prenatal but as yet of unknown cause or origin. Another 4 percent are those injured at birth or in the early postnatal period. This leaves the 75 percent minimally retarded, who are sometimes called the familial or subcultural group because of their tendency to come from families that have a higher than normal incidence of retardation, and who overlap some 80 percent with low social class membership. Experts do not believe their condition is due to pathological genes, and they speculate about the relative contributions of poor biological and social environments, of undetected brain damage, faulty perceptual functioning, and of inheritance from a presumed pool of familial genes associated with lower than average mental functioning.

At this time, then, only about 2 percent of mental defects are unquestionably genetic in origin. Approximately 8 percent are clearly nongenetic. The causes of retardation in the other 90 percent are yet to be determined, but it is probable that the biological and social environments interacting with the organism from the moment of conception will be found of first importance in the backwardness of a major portion of this group.

PERINATAL PERIOD

A book written for pediatricians contains the following:

> Every infant, sick or well, full-term or premature, even under conditions of optimal health, goes through the crisis of birth. To survive, he must make the successful transition from intrauterine dependence to life as an independent organism. . . . Little wonder it has oft been repeated that to be born is to meet the riskiest exigency of life and that no obstetrical attendant—specialist or otherwise—is ever sanguine about the outcome in a given case.[21]

The effects of oxygen loss—asphyxia—during delivery have been studied at a time when the subjects ranged in age from two to eleven. All the subjects were reported to have suffered an extreme degree of asphyxia but to have been normal at the conclusion of delivery. The mean IQ for these children on the Stanford-Binet Test of Intelligence was 88.05, compared with the mean of 100.4 for the

control group consisting of parents and siblings. Despite the appearance of normality after delivery, the asphyxia had affected their mental functioning.[22]

The baby can suffer from oxygen loss before, during, or immediately after delivery, and the brain may suffer permanent damage as a result. Sometimes the placenta separates from the mother before delivery, depriving the child of oxygen. If the umbilical cord becomes wound around the baby's neck in such a way that it is tightened during delivery, it can cause severe damage. After delivery the newborn may have breathing difficulties due to the administration of drugs to the mother during labor or delivery, or to an obstruction (mucus, for example) in the respiratory system, or to a malfunctioning of the lungs.

Long, hard labor can injure the baby's brain, and the obstetrician's use of forceps—necessitated, of course, by birth conditions—can have a similar effect.

POSTNATAL PERIOD

A number of childhood diseases often have serious effects on educability. Three main types are: cerebral vascular diseases (for instance, some cases of infant or childhood hemiplegia), inflammatory and degenerative diseases of the nervous system (encephalitis), and the convulsive disorders. Even the run-of-the mill infectious diseases of childhood damage some children irreparably. Measles, for example, can lead to deafness and also encephalitis and brain damage.

Lead poisoning, which used to be a problem for children of all classes because of the leaded paint on cribs, is a problem now primarily in slum areas, where infants and children eat the peeling paint off the wall. Some children die but most survive, some of them blind and some with cerebral damage.[23] In New York City there were 146 cases of lead poisoning and eighteen deaths reported in 1960, 509 cases and nine deaths in 1964, and 601 and three in 1965.[24]

Children of the slums are much more likely than others to be injured and in the process to suffer head injuries. These can be responsible for aphasia or other neurological problems that impede learning.

One of the two categories of prenatal deficiency is nongenetic in origin, and this, it is believed, is responsible for most cases. None of the perinatal and postnatal problems are primarily genetic. When we consider another fact, we find even further reason to look optimistically at the social opportunities for striking a great blow at mental deficiency: At the other end of the continuum of the clear-cut single-gene disorder there is a type of impairment that "is only a constitutional susceptibility to a stressful agent. . . . The modification of the stressful features of our environment, in the broadest sense of the word, may be an entirely proper and effective means of dealing with many genetic disorders."[25]

Environmental factors apply almost exclusively to the condition of the mother, a status always affected by her physical and social environment. War creates some of the most traumatic experiences, and it is not surprising to find, in one of the few studies made under siege conditions, that a serious increase in reproductive failure (prenatal or perinatal problems leading to defects or stillbirth) occurred during the long siege of Leningrad by the Nazis during the Second World War. These were attributed to near-starvation diet as well as physical and emotional hardships.[26] The war produced dramatic changes in both Great Britain and Germany in the rate of at least one type of maldevelopment at birth, that of anencephaly, the absence of a brain. Despite the hardships of war, food rationing in Great Britain achieved a more equitable distribution than had existed before and consequently improved nutrition there. This accompanied an improved morale in a nation largely united in fighting for its existence. The result, after an initial increase in anencephaly, was a very marked decrease, which continued for several years after the war.[27] (The study ended in 1949.) In Germany, by contrast, the increase in anencephaly during the last two years of the war and for about two after it was even more striking, and was probably associated with the changed circumstances as the productivity of conquered lands, and even its own, became less accessible, and nutrition and morale both declined.[28]

A number of studies in America, Canada, and England suggest that the dietary habits of the mother are an important factor in deficiency, but the nature of the studies compels one to avoid the conclusion that a particular food deficiency is the causative agent,

because only *some* mothers in a deprived group give birth to a defective child. Perhaps we are dealing here with different thresholds of sensitivity to deprivation, in mother and/or fetus. At the very least, however, the dietary factor is contributory. Supplements such as vitamins A, D, and B, calcium, phosphorus, and iron have significantly reduced the rate of stillbirth and perinatal mortality.[29] The intake of protein has been found to be associated with the health of the babies[30] and with birth weight, vitality, and mortality in newborn infants.[31] Vitamin content in the diet of pregnant women seems directly related to their babies' mental development. In a study in the Norfolk, Virginia, area published in 1955, investigators found that under circumstances of inadequate and unbalanced diet, vitamin supplementation given to women during pregnancy and lactation increased the intelligence of their offspring, at least during the first four years of life (when the results were reported). Their findings in a similar study in Kentucky did not corroborate the Virginia outcome, but the investigators attributed the difference to the fact that the Kentucky mothers had a much better diet in respect to vitamin content, and were probably less consistent in taking the vitamin supplement. The investigators concluded that vitamin supplementation to pregnant and lactating mothers with an otherwise inadequate diet does increase the intelligence of their children.[32]

Two other prenatal factors are related to intelligence and other mental development: the age of the mother and the number of pregnancies she has had. One expert on subnormality has said:

> It would appear from these observations that in general the reproductive efficiency of women is impaired with increasing age. In addition, certain specific factors appear to be operative very early in life. . . . In general, most observers report a progressive increase in the incidence of all maldevelopments after the fourth pregnancy and in association with the first.[33]

These findings must be evaluated in relationship to other facts, which then lead one to conclude that mothers need not run as great a risk of producing defective children as a superficial reading of the data would indicate. The youngest mothers of first children tend to come from lower socio-economic classes, where poverty or ignorance are responsible for the pregnant woman's inadequate diet, medical attention, rest, and hygiene. The circumstances of pregnancy for

some of the youngest—such as being unmarried or, if married, being unprepared for an unplanned child—do not always arouse the mother's interest in the survival of the offspring. The older mothers —especially many of those with the largest families—also tend to come from the lower income groups and to suffer from some of the conditions that damage maternal health. When investigators in England studied the relationship between prematurity, height, and the social class of the mother, they found that prematurity was greater in the small mother, regardless of social class, and was also consistently greater in the least favored socio-economic groups.[34]

Similar relationships appear when the influence of another factor is studied. Climate has been found to influence both the rate of conception and the incidence of fetal loss and maldevelopment. Animal experiments with rats in Australia showed that the 7-percent fetal loss when rats were kept at temperatures of 20–28 degrees Centigrade (68–82 degrees Fahrenheit) rose to a 58-percent loss when the temperature was raised to 35 degrees Centigrade (95 Fahrenheit).[35] More relevant is a series of studies in the Midwest concerning the effects of climate on human reproduction.[36] The investigators were interested in noting the effect of summer heat on reproductive practices and on pregnancy. One question was whether summer heat during the early months of pregnancy, especially the crucial third month, led to complications of pregnancy and also to the birth of mental defectives. Pregnancy complications can cause damage to the extent of mental deficiency, but they can also lead to minor damage that has a smaller but still significant effect on educability. "A significant peak in the births of mental defectives in the first three months of the year, corresponding to a summer occurrence of the third month of pregnancy," was found. Hotter summers were found to produce more mental defectives, whereas cooler summers caused no increase over the other months of the year. A significantly higher rate of the complications of pregnancy that are associated with brain damage occurred in the mothers who delivered in January, February, and March.

These findings too become especially meaningful when seen in the light of social class differences. The lower socio-economic groups produce a far higher proportion of maldeveloped and brain-damaged children due to environmental conditions that affect them more than

others. An example is the effect of summer heat which aggravates the fatigue of the hard-working lower-class mother. The effect of the heat shows even in the number of conceptions, which tend to decline during the summer months. The upper economic group is, of course, better able to control the discomforting and deleterious effects of hot weather by air-conditioning, the use of servants, extended vacations, and a more appropriate diet. The same study reports that this group does not show a decline in conceptions during the summer.

One of the important birth conditions occurring in about eight of every hundred deliveries is prematurity. The literature on the psychological correlates of premature birth (that is, a birth weight of less than five pounds) shows that prematurely born children have slower developmental rates, are prone to a wide variety of personality aberrations, and have impaired reading and writing achievement.[37]

Medical investigators and some psychologists here and in Britain have been studying these phenomena of early life for many years, but especially since the early fifties. Their work is important not only for those who experience prematurity or complications of pregnancy or of birth, numerous as they are. Its significance for all education is enormous.

Two of the leading investigators, Benjamin Pasamanick and Hilda Knobloch, a husband and wife who are both physicians, have coined the term "reproductive casualty."[38] It refers to the results of harmful events during pregnancy that cause damage to the fetus and those during birth that cause damage to the newborn infant. Four propositions have guided their series of studies:

> (1) Since prematurity and complications of pregnancy are associated with fetal and neonatal death, usually on the basis of injury to the brain, there must remain a fraction so injured who do not die. (2) Depending upon the degree and location of the damage, the survivors may develop a series of disorders. These extend from cerebral palsy, epilepsy, and mental deficiency through all types of behavioral and learning disabilities which are a result of lesser degrees of damage sufficient to disorganize behavioral development and lower thresholds to stress. . . . (3) Further, these abnormalities of pregnancy are associated with certain life experiences, usually socio-economically determined, and consequently (4) they themselves and their resulting neuropsychiatric disorders are found in greater aggregation in the lower strata of our society.[39]

In their studies the investigators first obtained "a large population of children diagnosed as having the particular condition under scrutiny." Thus they obtained separate samples of children for each of the following: cerebral palsy, epilepsy, mental deficiency, behavior disorders, reading disabilities, tics, speech disorder, strabismus, hearing defects, being accident-prone, infantile autism, and juvenile delinquency.

A control group was necessary for comparison with each sample group. With one exception, the control in all the studies "was the next surviving infant in the birth certificate register of the same race, sex, and socioeconomic status as the case, who was born in the same hospital to a mother of the same age. In the behavior disorder study, the control was the next child alphabetically of the same sex in the same school class as the case. This controlled for teacher bias in reporting and automatically controlled for race since the study was done [in Baltimore] prior to integration."[40]

The studies sought answers to this question: If you compare children who have a disorder with children who are in other respects very similar to them, will more of the children with the disorder have a history of either premature birth or birth complications? Here are the answers they got.

Eight of the twelve conditions were found to be significantly associated with both prematurity and complications of pregnancy: cerebral palsy, epilepsy, mental deficiency, behavior disorders, reading disabilities, strabismus, hearing defects, and infantile autism. Tics were found to be associated with complications of pregnancy but not prematurity. Accident-proneness was related to premature birth but not to complications. The complications that were associated with these disorders were "the prolonged and probably anoxia-producing complications of pregnancy such as the toxemias and maternal bleeding."[41]

Each of these ten conditions is manifestly important in child development and education. What is more, insofar as they are the result of circumstances that create prematurity and prenatal maternal abnormalities, they are subject to considerable control. That is to say flatly, many of them can be prevented.

Who are the prematures? About 8 percent of the children in the country are born prematurely. The distribution is very uneven

among the social classes. In one slum area in Brooklyn, about 13 percent of all children are prematures, and of the Negroes almost 20 percent are in that category.[42]

In Baltimore, where Drs. Pasamanick and Knobloch made a great many of their studies, 5 percent in the highest economic tenth of whites were premature, compared to almost 8 percent in the lowest economic tenth of whites. Nonwhites had more than 11 percent. For complications of birth and pregnancy, there was a 5-percent incidence in the highest economic fifth of whites, almost 15 percent in the lowest fifth of whites, and over 50 percent for nonwhites.[43]

The most common reasons for pregnancy complications and premature birth are poor nutrition, inadequate medical attention, overwork and fatigue, and illness. No wonder the consequent defects occur so much more often among the children of the poor.

The increasing possibility of control and prevention of early-life injury is highlighted by two dramatic medical advances and another on the horizon. Each of these discoveries can reach its full potential when good medical service is readily available for pregnancy, birth, and childhood. Together these three will save the lives of thousands of children and will protect many thousands from serious learning disorders.

A disease with the technical name of erythroblastosis fetalis, more commonly known as the Rh-blood disease, kills about 10,000 babies in the United States every year (and an estimated 200,000 in the world). The Rh-factor is a chemical substance on the surface of the red blood cells of about 85 percent of the population of the United States and probably of the world. Individuals who lack this substance are known as Rh-negative. The disease can occur only when an Rh-negative woman is impregnated by an Rh-positive man, which happens in about one out of every eight marriages. The first child is rarely affected, but if some of the infant's Rh-positive cells enter the mother's system during delivery, she manufactures antibodies as an adaptive measure against the foreign cells. These antibodies take their toll in subsequent pregnancies, when they pass through the umbilical cord to the fetus, whose blood cells they then attack and destroy.[44] The result is either stillbirth or mental and physical retardation. A 1952 discovery that the amniotic fluid of an Rh-immunized patient contains products of hemoglobin opened up the

way to diagnose whether the fetus *in utero* is Rh-positive. In 1961 Dr. A. W. Lilly of New Zealand reported on the development of a technique for analysis of the fluid, so that the obstetrician can now evaluate the situation during pregnancy and decide whether to interrupt the pregnancy, with the possibility of damage or death due to prematurity, or to allow it to run its course, with the risk of fetal death. Since the decision must be made early in the pregnancy, medical attention at that time is essential.[45]

Those infants who develop early signs of mental and physical retardation (apparent, if at all, within about forty-eight hours after birth) can be treated by exchange transfusions whereby their entire blood supply is replaced, but only about one in four of the afflicted infants can be saved by this means. Now at last, doctors have created a vaccine that is nearly 100 percent effective; it can be injected into the Rh-negative mother within seventy-two hours after delivery. The antibodies in the vaccine will destroy the Rh-positive cells in her body before her own defense system begins manufacturing the antibodies which would be hazardous to her subsequent pregnancies.[46]

Another disease, measles, which has attacked nearly all children and left many of them mentally and physically retarded, is also at last subject to man's control. The vaccines available make it a preventable disease, with the possibility of eradicating it by 1970.[47]

Third, medical researchers are close to a final breakthrough in conquering German measles. Scientists isolated the rubella virus in 1962 and reported on preliminary studies of immunization in 1965.[48]

We remain ignorant about the causes of some forms of backwardness. Yet there is no reason to despair. On the contrary, the advances in brain research in recent years allow for considerable optimism. We have already noted Chauchard's prediction that we shall be able to increase the quantity of brain cells, a fact of importance to both the damaged and the normal child. Another possibility lies in the use of sensory prosthetic devices "to provide useful input information to individuals who have suffered damage to crucial brain areas." Such devices, which have already been tested and have had some success, were invented as a result of the formulation of two laws about the behavior of the brain. According to the law of mass action, the deficit in function of the brain after damage "is proportional to the

mass of tissue destroyed, relatively independent of its specific location, provided that the primary sensory receiving areas of the brain are spared." The second is the law of equipotentiality: many areas of the brain are functionally interchangeable and can therefore perform a function formerly carried by a damaged area. A functional relationship is established between regions of the brain which are active simultaneously. As brain researcher E. R. John reports, investigators have been successful in establishing connections—learned responses in the brain to direct electrical stimulation of particular brain regions. The sensory prosthetic device, substituting for damaged tissue in crucial areas, can provide the stimulation for other areas.[49]

Many investigators are asking what basic factors affect the total learning process. Either inadequate or excessive stimulation of the brain disturbs its effective functioning in learning. Variation of metabolic process can alter the excitability of nervous tissue. What are the effects of such excitability on learning? Success in answering this question as it applies to one entity of mental defectiveness is an example of what the future may hold for many more. Phenylketonuria is a rare disease occurring in about one in every 25,000 persons in the general population, for a total of about an estimated 8000 cases in the United States. It is believed, however, that about one in every 173 persons carries a recessive gene.[50] When both the mother and father are carriers of the recessive gene, their offspring will have phenylketonuria, which causes mental and physical deficiency as a result of the malfunctioning of metabolism: the body does not produce the necessary enzymes to handle the phenylaline in the blood. When this substance is removed from their diet early in life, such children, whose mental deficit is behaviorally indistinguishable from those who are defective for other reasons, show dramatic improvement. Recently British psychiatrists L. T. Hilliard and Brian H. Kirman wrote: "Every undiagnosed case represents a tragedy and a lost opportunity."[51]

The genetically caused abnormality in these children was not in the anatomical structure of the brain, but in an enzyme system, and it may well be so for others who are markedly deviant in intellectual functioning. Perhaps for them too, as Dr. John has said, the differences "may arise from variations in the activity of particular enzyme sys-

tems responsible for the regulation of chemical reactions which play a role in nervous excitability."[52]

Studies have sought to find chemical means of facilitating memory through alterations in excitability. Some drugs have been found to improve the rate of learning, and others to interfere with it. Precisely what accounts for the differences in learning ability? We have no answer. But investigators studying groups of rats, some selectively bred as bright in maze-learning and some as dull, found that, given an optimal dose of excitatory substance, both improved, but the dull improved to such an extent that the differences between the two groups were eliminated.[53]

False optimism and self-delusion have no place in science nor in the applications of science to education and child-rearing. Nor does a static view of human intelligence deserve such a place, when it is possible to conquer some mental deficiencies and to raise the level of functioning of normal persons through eliminating biological hazards to educability.

The outlook for human intelligence is highly promising. Many of the causes of damage to the egg, the fetus, and the infant are subject to control now without further investigation. It requires the conviction that the conservation of human intelligence and welfare is an imperative need, that it deserves the availability of our resources to provide adequate housing, nutrition, medical and hospital care, and postnatal attention for child and mother.

6

PSYCHOLOGICAL

In 1909 the great Binet warned psychologists and educators: Do not believe that a child's intelligence is fixed. We did not heed the warning, and we have suffered immeasurably.

Some ten years later a young Swiss psychologist, Jean Piaget, went to work in Binet's laboratory in Paris. His experiences there awakened his interest in the intellectual development of children. Called to Geneva to be director of studies at the Institut J. J. Rousseau, he began a series of studies on child development unequaled in the history of psychology. Over a period of forty-five years his work, as he reported it in more than twenty-five books and some hundred and fifty articles, has yielded results of enormous significance to education and psychology. Yet the 1950 edition of the leading American textbook on the history of experimental psychology devotes half a sentence to Piaget;[1] the 1948 edition of one of the most widely used textbooks in general psychology does not mention him at all in its nearly eight hundred pages;[2] the 1956 edition of one of the leading texts on theories of learning doesn't mention him;[3] neither one of two leading texts on educational psychology (1956 and 1958) includes his name in the index;[4] he has no place in a leading work on the psychology of adjustment (1956).[5]

How did it happen that American psychology and education largely neglected the man who more than any other has shown how the human mind grows, the stages it passes through, the structures it must develop? It was not a willful conspiratorial act of disregard,

nor can it be attributed to the complexity of the theory or the language of original publication. Freud's theory is also complex, and it too was first published in German. And American literature on learning theory is highly complex.

American education's preoccupation with the fixed-ability theory inevitably shut out Piaget. When the major task is to measure and classify the intelligence of children so that they may be placed in classes appropriate to their ability, studies of how the mind develops are not necessarily enthralling. A person who believes that inherent potential "unfolds," that there is something in each individual that with proper sunshine and water will blossom into a totally predictable kind of flower, need not concern himself with a psychologist who sees the adult, the school, the community as having a major role in what the child becomes. In the foreword of his book entitled *The Moral Judgment of the Child,* Piaget wrote: "It is my sincere hope that it may supply a scaffolding which those living with children and observing their spontaneous reactions can use in erecting the actual edifice. In a sense, child morality throws light on adult morality. If we want to form men and women, nothing will fit us so well for the task as to study the laws that govern their formation."[6]

The laws that govern the formation of the mind are of interest primarily to those who believe that the mind is not preformed in the womb. Those who, without denigrating the contribution of the genes, believe that they as adults do influence the development of the child and can form and facilitate his mental and moral growth welcome Piaget's work. Some Americans always have, but it is only within the past few years that he has even begun to receive the attention he deserves. It is in these same few years that the insistent call of the American people, and particularly of Negro Americans, for a share of equality in education has had its impact on educators. To measure and classify children according to their IQ—which often means according to their social class—will no longer do because it will no longer be accepted. Change is being demanded with ever increasing intensity, and when the demand is strong enough, it is heeded at least to the extent of new legislation authorizing a Head Start program, or of some innovations like busing children to overcome racial segregation. The heeding involves educators and psychologists, and it involves their theories and their practices.

To whom can these professionals turn for dependable theory about learning behavior of the child? Certainly not to the school of learning theorists whose long and arduous work has led to the conclusion quoted earlier, that "there are no laws of learning which can be taught with confidence."[7] Such theory obviously has nothing practical to offer a teacher, a parent, or anyone who wants to help a child learn. The psychologists have been occupied in studying a learning process as if it were a separate entity quite detached from people. Instead, they should study the encounter of a human being with his environment.[8]

Educators can turn instead to Piaget and his associates, and to other psychologists who have been studying the child in his encounter with his universe—and fortunately they have begun to do so. Two British educators wrote recently about Piaget: "The ideas themselves are revolutionary in that they seek to explain the child's intellectual life in terms of his own action and its internalisation rather than as the emergence and training of an inherited ability. As Nathan Isaacs says, 'we owe to him a strikingly fresh picture of the child himself as the main architect of this [intellectual] growth.' "[9]

The child is the main architect only in the sense that he alone can use in the development of his mind the experience that his world provides him. The adults in his life are the architects of his experience. As a species, we inherit a mode of intellectual functioning. Man's intellect has enabled him to achieve a high level of adaptation, but it is not only his intellect that has helped him. Biological processes such as digestion have obviously been involved too. The intake of food and the incorporation of nutrition-providing elements into the organism are comparable to those involved in the intellectual development and adaptation of the organism, because the two vital functions for human life are both dependent upon a balanced relationship with the environment. This requires the successful completion of two processes upon which survival and adaptation depend. The first is *assimilation:* the individual must be able to take this foreign substance into his system, to chew and swallow and absorb it until it has lost its identity and is, in effect, an integral part of his organism. It has become incorporated.

It is not only the food substance itself that must be amenable to change. The organism must adapt itself to the object. To be

digested it must be chewed, then the digestive operations within the system must *accommodate* to the special properties of the food. The complete act of acquiring nourishment consists of two aspects of adaptation: assimilation, whereby objects must be made to adapt to the structure of the organism; and accommodation, whereby the organism must adapt to the special demands of the object. To assimilate a shrimp or a clam one need only chew; a steak is a different matter—it must be cut into pieces to adapt it to the structure of the organism. To accommodate to a bowl of hot cereal is quite different from accommodating to three hot pastrami sandwiches.

Assimilation and accommodation are inseparable. When they are in balance, the organism is in a state of adaptation. It takes in the necessary nutritive substances and assimilates them by accommodating itself to them. All this is external and subject to observation—the assimilative and accommodative acts of selecting, chewing, digesting. What is not evident is the underlying organization. Organisms are not robots. Adaptive behavior is directed and organized. Usually this organization—a repository of experiences—guides the organism in determining what it can accommodate, hence what it can assimilate. A healthy adult rejects food to which he cannot accommodate.

Intellectual functioning follows the same pattern. Intellectual adaptation consists of assimilation and accommodation. In its encounters with objects in the world, the organism assimilates not the object itself but that structuring of it which it can accommodate at a particular time. What it can accommodate depends upon what has already been assimilated. The infant's first experience with a dog cannot mean the same as subsequent experiences. Assimilation really means making the unfamiliar familiar, the new more like the old. To do this, past experience must possess something that strikes a relationship between it and the new encounter. The more encounters the child has with the animal, the more he is able to accommodate what is new about it, and the more he is able to assimilate. His mental structures of dog are revised and improved; they come closer to the reality of "dog."

We "take in" the world. That is the stuff of our intelligence. The more we assimilate, the more we can accommodate. The more we can accommodate, the more we are able to assimilate. What we can learn depends upon what we have already learned. New learning

can be built only upon former learning. To a child who is seeing a dog for the first time its meaning cannot be the same as to a child who has seen it ten times. The latter has assimilated a structure of dog and has revised this with subsequent assimilations. And two children seeing a cow for the first time will interpret the experience differently if one is seeing his first four-legged mammal while the other has seen dogs and horses.

Through assimilation and accommodation, those two inseparable aspects of adaptation, and through the underlying organization, humans develop cognitive structures. These structures constitute our knowledge and enable us to control our lives and our environment. "Structures come into being in the course of intellectual functioning; it is through functioning, and only through functioning, that cognitive structures get formed."[10]

Through functioning and only through functioning does the child learn. Functioning is social. It is the interaction of child with adult. Through such interaction the child learns to associate words with objects. Through those interactions he learns to assimilate behavioral changes. Hearing his mother, the young child repeats the words. He repeats them in her presence. Later, when he is alone, he repeats them aloud to himself. Still later he thinks them to himself. *Speech* of the adult, assimilated by the child, has been transformed into the *thought* of the child, and the thought of the child has become the guide to his behavior. The child does become the architect of his growth, but the kind of growth will depend on the material the adult world provides for him. The speed with which children and adolescents can assimilate new experience, and the amount they can accommodate, varies on what is in part, at least, a biological basis, but the ability to assimilate and accommodate is universal. It requires guided social experience.

Piaget studied the evolution of language and thought from infancy through adolescence. He identified the progressive stages in the development of logic. He studied the process of mastering the concepts essential to thought and learning: space, time, number, movement, and others. But of all his important work what is most relevant to the question of educability is his theory that the structures of the mind are learned; that what the individual learns depends in large part upon his experience; that new learning is possible

only insofar as the prerequisites are available, only insofar as old structures are there upon which new structures can be built. We might think of learning as a pyramid, with each new structure representing a block. To build the second level of blocks the first must already be there. The third can be built only on the second, and the fourth on the third. Finally, the pinnacle can be set on only when the fourth is complete. More advanced learning may be conceived of as structures built upon the pinnacles of already constructed pyramids. What the child accommodates depends upon what he has already learned. Calculus cannot follow straight upon addition. Reading cannot follow straight upon the acquisition of a limited vocabulary.

Experience is vital to learning, and the small child cannot provide his own. As he gets older, he can intervene on his own behalf in the development of his mind; in fact, unless he does, his mind cannot possibly even approach the higher levels. For the older child or adolescent there is no substitute for self-intervention in learning, in which he determines some of his own experiences on the basis of his own interests and values, but the groundwork is laid in infancy and childhood, when the individual has almost no control over his encounters with the environment. It is adults who have it in their power to proffer or withhold the experiences that construct the actual intelligence of the child. It is the adult world that determines the intellectual fate of the newborn infant by the conditions for learning that it provides. We have already seen that the society has a large measure of responsibility for the *organic* determinants of educability. The same is true for the *psychological* determinants.

Following Piaget's system, what are the psychological determinants of educability? What psychological conditions are necessary for the child to use efficiently the experiences for learning that are made available? How must he feel about himself and how relate to others if he is to learn in school? What circumstances are necessary for a child who can see and hear to assure that he will look and listen and comprehend? The questions really ask for the conditions that help shape the fully realized person.

Mental development is not a thing apart from the rest of development. First the *biological* state of the organism must be good. Next, the growth of the mind requires *cognitive* experience. This demands

good *social* relationships. This in turn demands that the organism think well enough of itself, have a sufficiently good *self-concept,* to enter into such relationships. Self-intervention, a *sine qua non* of successful intellectual development, requires that in growing up the individual find some inherent interest and value in the tasks that teachers and parents assign.

We might adapt for our use here a well-known theory of needs, formulated by the psychologist A. H. Maslow.[11] For beings whose "humanness" is to be realized, the following needs must be satisfied. Our special focus will be on their relevance to educability. It is to be noted that they are given in the order of primacy, the satisfaction (partial, at least) of one being essential for the next to be experienced as need.

1. The Physiological Needs. Certainly food and liquid and shelter from extremes of temperature are necessary for survival. Unless these needs are met, the organism cannot concern itself with other needs, even that of safety.

Needless to say, infants and children are unable to satisfy physiological needs independently. In a most basic sense, nobody is. Even Thoreau came into town from Walden Pond to supplement his supply of berries. The movement toward independence from the vagaries of nature led early man to introduce primitive forms of agriculture, a step that hastened socialization and language development. We satisfy our physiological needs through social relationships, from the basic one of an infant at its mother's breast to the complex ones of automated industry's sprawling food-processing plants.

Clinical observation of humans and research with both humans and animals show that deprivation of these needs early in life has a permanent effect on behavior. Such deprivation, whether in a backward nation or in the heart of an affluent one, affects the educability of the child. Once nature was to blame for unfulfillment of these needs; now, except for rare situations, it is man and only man, by which is meant his social organization.

2. The Safety Needs. With adequate food and shelter the organism's will to survive manifests itself in defense against threats. Whatever meaning death may have to the child, he abhors it. Few adults welcome it, even those who have dissociated it from punishment

(in response to their feelings of guilt) or those who have associated it with the mystique of an after life.

Insecurity surrounds the lives of all children today. The high rate of crime, especially crimes of violence, assaults the tranquility of the child and arouses fear in proportion to the effect of such reports on parents and teachers. Almost all minority-group children in the United States are confronted with violence on the streets, in the school playground, and in TV news reports of lynchings and riots. The reactions of such groups, especially at the moment those of Negroes, are given wide publicity, which arouses insecurity in members of the majority, including their children. Children cannot be shielded from awareness of social conflicts; on the contrary, the best defense they can have is an understanding of the problems and involvement in the resolutions.

Hanging over the lives of all children is The Bomb. Several studies have shown that children even of elementary-school age are very much aware of this danger, and the probability is that their lives—like those of all adults—are affected by nuclear cold war.[12] To younger children especially, the insecurity lies in the threat of separation from parents. Anna Freud observed that nursery school children in London during the Second World War found the war of little significance as long as only their comforts and food were affected or their lives threatened. But war "becomes enormously significant the moment it breaks up family life."[13]

In a study of the reactions of children to the dangers of war made in 1961 and 1962, junior and senior high-school students in urban, suburban, and rural areas in the Northeast wrote papers on these questions: Do I think there will be a war? Do I care? What will happen if there is? What do I think of fallout shelters? Through the results—through all the essays and the data they yielded—runs the theme, clearly and consistently, that children know and fear the dangers of nuclear disaster; that the more they know it, the more they fear it and wish for peaceful solutions. And those who have no such hope live in dread of the future.[14]

This and other similar studies offer no valid measure of the degree to which mental anguish has been converted into pathology. In most instances the responses do not indicate the extent to which the students are preoccupied with these concerns; they do not indi-

cate the intensity of the students' feelings at times other than that spent responding to the questions, or their defensive maneuvers. The question of the effects of cold war on mental health is even more difficult to research than the somatic pathology caused by radioactive fallout. Only epidemiological studies some years hence will be able to give us more definitive, but even then perhaps not conclusive, answers to questions about the effects of either test fallout or the fears induced by cold war. Yet in the absence of conclusive empirical data we hardly need suspend judgment and avoid professional encounters with the problem. Wars hot or cold, like depressions, unemployment, and poverty, breed social problems that are incontrovertibly related to individual behavior. They influence morality and hence interpersonal relations; they shake security and thus shape perceptions of the social scheme and expectations for the future. Time and again the students in the study described their universe as highly uncertain, its people greedy and irrational, its future questionable. Their great hope lay in the fact that no nation could win and that rational people would not choose suicide, or that at least conflict would be postponed until they had had a chance "to live," by which they meant to work, experience adult love, have children.

For the disturbed child, like some of the students who wrote that they cried themselves to sleep terrified by thoughts of war, the extra burden of fear may be more than he can bear. For the normal child, the uncertainty of the future is not in the forefront of his thoughts, but it has its eroding effects in more indirect form. High-school girls are frightened by the danger of having deformed babies, and boys and girls are cynical about preparing for a future which they say they are being cheated out of.

Some students, like those who said they did not permit themselves to think about the world, are defending themselves against stress by the mechanisms of suppression, avoidance, and denial. These mechanisms can be effective, but only at a price, and the more efficient a child becomes, the greater the price he pays. To keep the danger of nuclear war out of his mind, he must avoid thinking of world conflict and of everything else that might remind him of war. Current events in school, news reports on television and radio and in the daily papers, all unsettle him. To defend himself he avoids reading and listening to the news, and to play it safe, gradu-

ally extends this to other listening and reading matter. Of course he must carefully censor his thoughts, lest they bring the dangerous threats to mind. To defend himself from the disturbing effects of the times, he sacrifices some of his powers to read, to listen with comprehension, and to think.

There are, in general, two paths open to children, the same two that are available to adults in the face of a threat to survival. The first, recognition that the threat of a destructive nuclear war exists, involves a burden of fear which can be lightened by involvement in discussions and actions aimed at reducing the danger. The second is denial of the existence of danger by using every possible means to avoid reminders of threats to peace. The cost of the second way of life is a partial blindness to the world, and the habit of discouraging knowledge, thought, and understanding about one's own problems.

Accident and disease are other realistic threats to safety at all ages. They can have serious consequences in education, career, love relationships, and, of course, mental functioning as well.

The healthy response to the dangers of life is recognition of their existence accompanied by appropriate measures to guard against them. Clearly it is unhealthy to be preoccupied with danger to the point where life cannot be enjoyed. It is equally unhealthy to deny the existence of danger and thus be unequipped to deal with the inescapable realities of health and safety.

3. The Love Needs. One need only ask himself the role of secure love, of affection and friendship in his own life to begin to appreciate its importance to the child. In the view of Ralph Linton, a distinguished anthropologist, "In the Götterdämmerung which over-wise science and over-foolish statesmanship are preparing for us, the last man will spend his last hours searching for his wife and child."[15]

Love gives a child stability. It provides a sound base for learning. Yet fundamentally its effects cannot be differentiated from other adult activity that contributes to the child's learning. A loving parent (or parent substitute) smiles and coos and talks, giving the baby language along with trust, structures to assimilate along with warmth.

A classic little study with an unusual follow-up points up the inseparability of these two adult functions, love and stimulation.

In the late 1930's two psychologists selected for study twenty-five orphan girls between the ages of seven and thirty months. The institution they were in provided exceedingly little "mothering" or stimulation.

According to mental tests given to the twenty-five children, they were all functioning at a mentally retarded level. Twelve of the children remained in the orphanage. The other thirteen, who had somewhat lower IQ's, were placed in an institution for mental defectives. Each of these children was put in a separate ward with older, high-grade mentally defective girls. The babies evoked a very positive response in these girls, who gave them much attention, affection, and stimulation. Two years later both groups of orphans were retested. The children who had been placed with the older girls showed an average increase of twenty-seven points on the IQ test. In contrast, the children who had remained in the orphanage had shown an average decrease of twenty-six points.[16]

At the time this study was reported, it was subjected to severe criticism on the grounds that tests appropriate to that age level are not dependable. It is a fact that infant tests are not so reliable as those given to children who have reached reading age, and that predictive tests are more accurate when they deal with shorter time spans. For these reasons a test given at age six is a better predictor of school success at age twelve than a test given at age one. This is not surprising; the weatherman is more reliable on short-term forecasts. But there is a deeper reason for the increased reliability of school-age tests. By the age of six the biological, social, psychological, and educational determinants have had time to make a great imprint on the child.

Wedded to the status quo theory of immutable intelligence, critics saw the thirteen orphans' dramatic changes as proof that the tests were questionable. They might have noted that the experimenters had rearranged the children's lives so that the determinants could have positive effects.

Twenty-one years later one of the psychologists involved in the original investigation followed up the twenty-five subjects. Of the twelve children who remained in the orphanage, six, as adults, were wards of some institution. The average schooling completed by this group was about third grade. Of the children who were placed with

the older girls in the institution for mental defectives, all thirteen were self-supporting. The average schooling completed was approximately the twelfth grade.[17] These striking findings are consistent with the present viewpoint that love, security, and mental stimulation available early in life are important to intellectual development.

The need for love is so apparent and so much reported in professional and popular publications that it needs little documentation. Abundant evidence shows that children deprived of the love and stimulation of a mother or a mother substitute frequently become physically and emotionally ill.[18]

Teachers know that disturbances at home have a distracting effect upon children. Even when the child is not suffering the precursors of neurosis he can be disabled for learning on a particular day when breakfast was marred by a family argument or by the displacement of a parent's anger or frustration upon the child. It need hardly be added that a chronic condition of discord sets the stage for massive effects upon all of the child's general behavior, naturally including the academic. The fantasies of children in this unfortunate situation, as they sit in class staring into space, are filled with attempts at achieving harmony and reuniting parents, or perhaps serving as substitute for one of them.

Vicissitudes in relationships with parents, especially with the mother, account for the distractibility of other children whose subsequent failure or underachievement leads them into a state of resistance. The child does not feel loved, senses that a sibling is preferred, finds "confirmation" in mother's devotion to a younger sibling, perhaps one still being breast-fed. The child misinterprets a parent's marital unhappiness or preoccupations with other distressing events in life as rejection. Sometimes, of course, the child is not misinterpreting, but reacting to a hostile, rejecting parent, possibly one who envies the child's dependency and freedom from responsibility.

Life is full of examples of the ways in which threats to love and outright rejection of a child subvert his learning effectiveness. Some cases are poignant human dramas, the stuff of which *King Lear* and *Tom Jones* are made. Here we may concentrate on the underlying currents that effectively thwart love and its expressions.

For fulfillment, humans must love and be loved. For a long time,

but now in our times at an accelerating rate, major dehumanizing currents have been at work to frustrate this need. Dehumanization has been conceived of "as a particular type of psychic defense mechanism," and "its increasing prevalence" has been attributed to its being "a social consequence of the nuclear age. . . . Dehumanization as a defense against painful or overwhelming emotions entails a decrease in a person's sense of his own individuality and in his perception of the humanness of other people." The term alienation, which refers to the tendency to become estranged from other people and from one's own emotions, is similar in meaning to dehumanization. The process of alienation drains those most human of qualities, tenderness and love and concern for the welfare of other humans.

In a distinguished paper, from which this definition of dehumanization was drawn, the three authors, psychiatrists Viola W. Bernard and Perry Ottenberg, and psychologist Fritz Redl, analyzed the consequences of dehumanization. In summary they are:

1. Increased emotional distance from other human beings.
2. Diminished sense of personal responsibility for the consequences of one's actions.
3. Increasing involvement with procedural problems to the detriment of human needs.
4. Inability to oppose dominant group attitudes or pressures.
5. Feelings of personal helplessness and estrangement.

People have responded to the sheer brutality of our time with a kind of self-inflicted anesthetic. For lynchings, terror, the break-up of families, the slow erosion of manhood, the genocide of six million Jews, Hiroshima and Nagasaki, starving Asian Indians, 300,000 Indonesians massacred, the statistics from Vietnam—numbness is a sane response if there is no way of comprehending the meaning or enlisting in the act of opposing such monstrosities. But the cost of numbness, of denial and repression—of dehumanization—is to see other people as lacking in humane qualities and to experience this lack in oneself.[19]

One cannot reproduce in the laboratory the kinds of all-pervasive but intangible effects on humanization of brutal discrimination and of cold and hot wars. Often enough laboratory studies have shown that artificially induced conflicts will take the vitality, the selfness, the "animal-ness" from the animal subject. The serious

counterpart in man is alienation, the incapacity to feel and to love. This affective numbness denies many children the full birthright of parental love and robs some of them of the equanimity important to effective learning.

4. The Need for Esteem. We need to like ourselves. We learn to like ourselves when we are loved and liked by others. We should not need to be liked by everyone, a condition that leads us to expend endless energy in anticipating and satisfying the wishes and preferences of others. It may offer occupational fulfillment for Geisha girls, whose job is to please clients; for most other people it is the road to denial of self. When we like ourselves, we strive for fulfillment as self-respecting persons in relationships of equality.

Powerful social forces are at work to undermine esteem. Naturally, their effect is strongest in minority and deprived groups, where individual self-esteem is damaged through a "group image." Black children growing up with parents who have been intimidated and who teach their young to avoid antagonizing the white citizenry do not have much of a chance to develop self-esteem. For years, for centuries, such parents had no other way to counter the inhumane treatment by the "master race." With changing conditions, as people insist on their human rights, minority self-attitudes are also changing.

Every human has experienced humiliation. It requires only to recall our feelings at that moment to share to some extent the experience of growing up as a member of an unpopular group. In many parts of the United States the Negro child hears on the radio news in the morning that a robbery was committed not by John Smith, a man, but John Smith, a colored man. He hears that a Negro leader's home has been blasted by dynamite. On the way to school a group of whites driving past yell "nigger," and the white policemen look menacingly, not at the carful of provocateurs, but at him and his friends, whose fists are clenched in frustrated response. In school, if it is "integrated," he goes to the lower, vocationally directed, "ability-grouped" classes while the higher, college-directed classes that he walks by are composed largely of white youth. And so it goes, driving home the demoralizing fact that he is a member of an inherently inferior group and that for life itself he must cringe and bow low, or compensate by his success in sports or music, fields that were open to him early.

It has never meant that for all Negroes, not even in the worst days of slavery, as the history of the Negro people reveals. But for many Negroes, as for other groups forcibly placed in chains or in ghettos, it has meant that.

What are the educational consequences of damaged self-esteem? It has the insidious effect of shaking the child's self-confidence, weakening his ability to concentrate, and convincing him that he should not succeed because members of his group are not intended to, or expected to, or welcome to succeed. Usually his "group" is racial, religious, ethnic, or social-class.[20]

Psychologists and sociologists have given their attention over the years to the educational fate of lower-social-class children.[21] Reviewing studies on the social background of teaching in a recent handbook on research on teaching, W. W. Charters, Jr., a professor at Washington University, wrote that the evidence is so substantial that we may regard the following relationship as a law: The social class position of parents stands in the same general rank order as the scholastic success and extent of participation of their children in the school system. He added that in any institution where there is some diversity in social class, right up to and including university, the social class position "predicts grades, achievement and intelligence test scores, retentions at grade level, course failures, truancy, suspensions from school, high-school dropouts, plans for college attendance, and total amount of formal schooling."[22] Academic honors, awards, elective offices, and extent of extracurricular and social participation in the school can all be predicted.

Psychologists M. Sherif and H. Cantril indicated as early as the 1940's that in studying the psychological dynamics at work within the individual members of such a group, one fundamental fact emerges: Members of unpopular groups tend to see themselves as members of the majority group see them.[23] The concept we develop of ourselves is sketched from the one we see reflected in the eyes of others, the important others being those in positions of authority. If your community regards you as unworthy of respect, position, status, education, it is almost impossible not to incorporate some of the devalued view of yourself, even if at the same time it conflicts with a more favorable one. This erosive process takes its toll even before the child enters school,[24] and its insidious destruction of character is

not easily countered by encouragement from even the most dedicated teacher. The hardy child whose self-esteem has been strongly bolstered by his parents is still faced with the fact of life that formal education is not for him the royal road to comfort and status that it is for others in his community. Adults who are ignorant of the interplay between socio-economic realities and psychological dynamics interpret the behavior of children of various groups as evidence of group inferiority, of a group character. Yet once we are truly aware of the world as perceived through the eyes of a child in a group to whom some or much of life is closed, we see that the child's behavior is precisely what is to be expected.

Sometimes his "group" is his family. In this category of causes, the child avoids learning because scholastic success carries with it the danger of alienation. Members of my family do not succeed in this activity and I must not. An example of this was recently reported by a school counselor. A high-school sophomore in the business curriculum, with a grade average of 75, told the counselor that she planned to quit when she was sixteen. "I want to work," she said. The counselor asked if she thought a job would satisfy her. "I don't know. My older brother quit when he was sixteen, and my parents told me to quit." Asked if they thought she would be better off if she quit school, she responded: "Well, my father thinks kids shouldn't waste their time in school. I have two younger sisters in elementary school and they already aren't doing too well, and they'll quit when they get to be sixteen." The counselor asked if she was happy about quitting. The girl hesitated for a moment, then said, "I'm going to quit and get a job." She is saying what countless high-school and college students in America have felt, many of whom dropped out: "I cannot remain comfortable in my family if I become a successful student or a graduate." In this case the girl's father may be reflecting ignorance or cynicism about education, or perhaps his interpretation of the family's need for more "working hands." To go contrary to the norms of behavior in any family often evokes punitive measures.

In another version of this kind of self-denial, the motives go to a deeper layer of the personality. Sometimes a bad student is responding to the hostile competitiveness of a parent who cannot tolerate a child's success—especially if the child is the same sex—even while

the parent is ostensibly punishing the child for inadequate performance. To the child the subtle disapproval of his success is a lesson in being wary of it. A bright boy of fifteen, failing all his subjects in his sophomore year, recounted his experiences in eighth grade when, at the beginning of the term, he got high grades on a few papers and tests. "A few of the boys in my class were kind of 'rocky.' When the teacher called out my grade they came up after school and made wisecracks, and one of them threatened me. They didn't want me to do well. The same thing happened in my other classes." Only some time later did he realize that he had gotten the same feeling from his father, who, unable to use his talents, was envious and competitive with all males including his son. Of course, the behavior of these two fathers has no mysterious origins. To attribute it to "instincts" or to an "unconscious" is only to confound us. The attitudes and values that motivated these parents were acquired in their real-life experiences and are prominent features in society.

A child's self-esteem may be impaired just because he is very different from his parents and siblings in certain basic characteristics of behavior. Several psychiatrists in New York City have been studying an upper-middle-class set of children and a lower-class group from the time they were only a few days or weeks old. Many of the first sample of about a hundred are nearly ten years old. The investigators found a great deal of consistency of behavior, so that the child whose activity level was high at three months (kicked and splashed in the tub and moved much during sleep) was still very active at ages two, five, and eight. Correspondingly, an equally normal but low-activity infant continued so through childhood. Similar consistency was found in such other characteristics as the tendency to approach or withdraw from new situations (despite adequate adjustment to them subsequently even in the case of the initial withdrawers), and the tendency to be rhythmic (regular) or arhythmic in repetitive functions like sleep, eating, rest, and bowel and bladder functions. This continuing study has implications for child-rearing. Conflict can arise when there are markedly different types in the same family, as for example when a high-activity mother regards her low-activity child as slow, lazy, or dull when in fact he is simply responding to what may be a different biochemistry, or when a mother thinks her high-activity child is wild and needs to be "broken." Problems also arise

when parents misinterpret differences in behavioral characteristics among their children.[25]

It would be a serious mistake to believe that only members of unpopular groups suffer a loss of self-esteem. The point may be made again that considerably more people in the poverty class are white than Negro and that they have been made to feel many of the self-demoralizing effects of their class position. Furthermore, a society that breeds group hatred cannot contain it any more than tuberculosis, bred in poverty, could be contained in the slums. People whose lives are dominated by a hostile competitiveness and who have a need to crush others cannot leave this motivating force in the office or on their doorstep. They bring it home. They learned it in a society that says one must love but teaches hate; that says one must cooperate but rewards hostile competitiveness. They learned it, and they pass it on to their children.

5. The Need for Information and Understanding. We humans need to know. Allegorically, when Adam plucked the apple from the tree, he changed nothing in the world but his own consciousness. And in that process he changed much in the sense that he—or that species that evolved with a developed cerebral cortex—could now be more than an object in the operation of natural laws. He could step back, examining the universe; he could begin to comprehend its laws, and in comprehending them, he could control them.

The infant examines and tries to understand. The instructive and often charming reports of Piaget's observations of his own children as infants bring this truism fully to life. The first realization that the infant displays curiosity comes as a surprise to the parent of a first child. So young—five years before school. Further thought makes clear that the infant is manifesting adaptive behavior. To know and to understand is to survive. The problem in educating children is not that of instilling or arousing curiosity but of instructing in such a way as not to stifle it.

Curiosity is stifled in many ways, most frequently by teaching both implicitly and explicitly that (1) one should not know; (2) one should not engage in particular activities; (3) one must not try.

The inquiring mind of the child leads him to ask many questions, some of them about tabooed subjects. He is given intensive training in *not knowing* and not inquiring. If he is taught that knowing is

evil, carrying with it the threat of severe punishment or death, he may institute severe controls over his thoughts. It is not simply that he must not look into that book with those pictures, or must not ask this question, but soon must be cautious about asking, thinking, and learning. Books can be dangerous.

During periods in which liberties are abridged and freedom of speech infringed by overt or subtle forms of intimidation, children are taught to avoid controversial issues. In the mid-fifties the well-known sociologist David Riesman proposed the abandonment of social studies in the public schools. He thought this action necessary "since they could not, without more protection for the teachers, be taught with any vigor or candor."[26] The public schools were not alone during this period, for in a study published in 1958 two other sociologists reported that social scientists in our colleges and universities felt constraints in the classroom that led them to give students "an altered version of what, in their best judgment, was the truth" or to detach themselves from personal responsibility for the views they discussed, or to take elaborate precautions to avoid getting into difficulty over controversial issues.[27] Ideas can be dangerous.

Two unfortunate consequences of such a social situation are especially relevant to a discussion of learning. If ideas are dangerous, and controversial issues to be avoided, education is arid as a desert, and involvement in learning becomes only a process of jumping the academic hurdles for incentives that have little relationship to learning. For the child who has already been taught that curiosity is dangerous and to be discouraged, suppression of controversy in the classroom further reinforces this disabling attitude.

As to the second sure way to stifle curiosity, the admonition not to engage in a particular activity most frequently says, aloud or not, "because it is contrary to the sex role in your society or subcultural group." Only girls and sissies like to read and mind the teacher and get all the schoolwork done. Real boys play ball and fight and don't let the women in school make them do all the sissy stuff. A few years later, and even into adulthood, there is a variation of this theme: Real he-men don't go for art, music and literature. They are interested in mechanics, sports, and, if bright, in engineering and science. If a boy or young man is to adhere to the norm and identify with the models of masculinity, he will tend to resist "feminized" activities.

As members of the largest underprivileged group in America, females too have restrictions, and many of them. It is no accident that the percentage of women attending the major professional schools in America is no greater than it was in 1910, when the suffragist movement had helped to break the barriers; nor is it an accident that the restrictions continue to exist as long as they serve to limit competition and protect against male unemployment. Regardless of the reasons, unequal opportunity and an unequal share of rewards and promotional possibilities discourage girls from participating in various intellectual and professional activities. An interesting account of this is given by Betty Friedan, who believes that even in sexual and marital life, a woman's success depends upon her inhibiting her intellectual development.[28]

For both sexes and all classes there is a further inhibition: One must not engage in intellectual activities because "eggheads" are suspect. The mad scientist has been with us for a long time, and it took the first Sputnik to give science some status toward scholarship, but young people still do not feel they can be unrestrainedly intellectual with impunity. A recent study in New York revealed that academically brilliant adolescents prefer to conform to the popular traits of well-rounded average amiability. As a result, some students with high potential for scholarly excellence play down their talents in order to become acceptable in high-school society.[29]

There are four basic variations of the "one must not try" theme, each representing a different type of defensive measure against the real or imagined consequences of trying. In the first, to avoid the danger of failure, the child actually invites failure, but in such a way as to protect himself from a devaluation that he fears, expects, and cannot tolerate. When he becomes fully aware of his action, he can verbalize it as: "If I don't try, I and others won't know my limitations." Resistance is a defensive reaction to lack of confidence, enabling one to attribute failure to insufficient motivation rather than limited intelligence. So long as one avoids a test of his competence, he can continue to have grandiose fantasies about himself, or can at least protect himself from a low evaluation of his potential by teachers or parents. Resistance thus becomes an avoidance of commitment, comparable to that of the shy person who remains silent during conversation in fear of appearing ignorant or naïve and feel-

ing humiliated by the reactions of others. A home in which scholastic success is so highly accented that the child considers it inseparable from love and self-worth is likely to produce resistant children.

Second, to avoid the dangers of revealing himself the individual must not try. Were he to exercise his talents, his successes might reveal his antisocial motives, for which he would suffer some horrible punishment. Such ideas clearly verge on the pathological. Students in this group have suffered an emotional deprivation that has made them hostile and filled their fantasies with violent acts of vengeance. Successful learning does call for assertiveness, a healthy human quality of using one's energy and talents unsparingly. The student who hates and fears this emotion sometimes confuses assertiveness with hostile aggression and suppresses it. High grades are a form of crushing other people, and for his own survival he must defend himself against his hostility. He must inhibit efforts to be successful. He must not try.

Third, to avoid the dangers of growing up he must not try to learn. Well-intentioned parents who are overanxious about their children train them in dependence and in fear of intense involvement with life. His skills in coping with life's problems underdeveloped and his confidence undermined, the child fears and avoids activity. But the community and the school insist upon a certain minimum of involvement, and the socially frail child inevitably encounters difficulties which only reinforce his concepts about a frightening world. Adult experiences which the healthy child will anticipate with pleasure and even await impatiently, such as high school and college, work, sexual love, marriage, and children, each represent to him insufferable social expectations fraught with danger. The average child or adolescent may well have some anxiety about the new adventures of life before him, just because the new and unknown are fear-provoking, but not so much anxiety as to dampen enthusiasm and curiosity. For the anxious child, the scales are tipped in the other direction, and whatever attraction growing up has for him is more than offset by the dread it arouses in him.

Fourth, to avoid the danger of losing his identity as an individual he must not try. Children who are subjected to autocratic control will find covert means of resisting a stranglehold on their sense of integrity as a person. They will seek to exert their own power, some-

times by displacing their anger upon a safer target than the parent—another child, or a teacher—sometimes by "forgetting" to perform a chore at home, and not infrequently by resisting learning. The latter is used especially when the schoolwork becomes a theater of warfare for the family. To the child it is a well-selected battlefield because "you can't help it if you can't remember what you learned when you take a test" or if you "can't keep your mind on your studies." The child is usually unaware of his motives and certainly is not acting out of spite. School and learning have taken on very negative meanings: they represent his existence as an extension of his parents, a human puppet who has that quality that leads slaves to rebel against their status and leads the most submissive to resent their position and to resist it even when they neurotically continue to place themselves in a submissive and dependent role. Many a college student who has gone to college or professional school as an act of obedience to the expressed or implicit wish of a parent, has resisted learning and then for reasons "beyond my control" been compelled to leave the chosen college or curriculum. Even a dutiful child can fail!

Resistance to learning is the method of defense used by many sons of ambitious mothers. Unknowingly and without malice, such women respond to their exploited position by exploiting their sons. Passive resistance provides the son a safe outlet for hostility, a means of punishing her by thwarting her ambitions. The boy preserves his autonomy in his struggle with an engulfing mother. Since such a parent often seems to the child to set perfectionist standards, he understandably resists involvement in activities which can only lead to failure and humiliation. The ambitions of such a mother often stem from highly competitive tendencies which, with too few socially acceptable outlets, give rise to the conflicting needs to be the best through her son and simultaneously to be the best by preventing him from outdoing her. The outcome of the conflicting forces, of being pushed and having no way out, is lethargy, a "beaten" feeling.[30]

6. The Need for Self-Actualization. In a sense, this need is met when all those which precede it have been met. When one has food and shelter, safety, love and esteem from those whose esteem one

values, has knowledge and understanding of the laws of man and nature and uses them in behalf of mankind in an interdependent relationship with others of his species—such a person has the feeling of having realized himself. He is not an alienated man. Work is satisfying, even exhilarating, and does not demand periods of induced relaxation to reduce built-up tension. Work, friendship, love, sex are all part of his life.

Such a man's world is not seen through rose-colored glasses. There is conflict and struggle, and he sees them, seeks to understand and to participate wisely. Because he is not alienated, he will avoid the posture of neutrality, knowing there cannot be neutrality in a world in which silence amounts to acceptance of things as they are. So-called neutral behavior in the face of conflict is an avoidance of the risks of commitment.

Human personality, like human intelligence, is not fixed. It is subject to modification. People can change themselves by changing their behavior. What does this entail? Carl Rogers, a well-known psychotherapist, gave this view of "the good life": It is not a destination but a direction, not a state of being but a process. An individual can realize it when he feels free and unafraid to see clearly and to act in terms of his perception of the world. One of the characteristics of such a person is an increasing openness to experience. He is not reluctant to examine and reexamine any phenomenon, whether it be about himself (what he does to other people) or about his country (how it relates to other nations). He refuses to rely on the observations and interpretations of others. Even if he is unsophisticated in science, even if he is untutored, he is, nonetheless, a person who has a scientific orientation; that is, a rational approach to life.

Increasing trust in himself and his reactions is another characteristic. This enables him to express his views at a public meeting, to talk up at a social gathering, to feel confident about his feelings for others, to establish close personal relationships as he wishes, to take leadership in support of what he believes.

Such a person increasingly experiences fulfillment: he lives fully each moment. He needs no escape from boredom because life is full of excitement; he needs no escape from freedom because he glories in his freedom; he needs no escape from people because they do not

arouse anxiety or tension; he needs no escape from work because work is not the constantly nagging way to prove himself; self-fulfilled, he has no need to prove himself.[31]

This, of course, is a sketch of human fulfillment that few of us ever achieve, and in our imperfect condition even fewer achieve it consistently. But even those who fall far short of such a state are not necessarily suffering from "personality problems." More likely, our problem is simply lack of knowledge, knowledge about the world (including self) which we have been taught to shut out, or denied the opportunity to learn. In Piaget's terms, man can assimilate from his environment only that which he can accommodate. His ability to accommodate depends upon his previous assimilations. If he has not been given a foundation or if he has been taught not to pry and explore and to ask questions, if he has been taught to fear the unknown, he will not be open to new experience.

A study of the way mothers supervise their young children is very much to the point here. Bright children were tested periodically between the ages of three and ten. For those who showed the largest IQ increases from the ages of four and a half to six, a study was made of their upbringing. The findings suggested that those with accelerating learning ability had been free to be curious and to explore; they were unafraid to investigate and to assimilate more. They were increasingly open to experience.[32]

In a book called *The Souls of Black Folk,* published some forty years after the Emancipation Proclamation, the historian W. E. B. Du Bois tells of Negroes' centuries-old yearning for freedom. Then came the Civil War and its bright hopes, which were dashed by the events that followed. The vision of political power faded as a result of terror and disillusion. It was replaced by a new vision, education.

> Up the new path the advance guard toiled, slowly, heavily, doggedly; only those who have watched and guided the faltering feet, the misty minds, the dull understandings, of the dark pupils of these schools know how faithfully, how piteously, this people strove to learn. It was weary work. The cold statistician wrote down the inches of progress here and there, noted also where here and there a foot had slipped or someone had fallen. To the tired climbers, the horizon was ever dark, the mists were often cold, the Canaan was always dim and far away. If, however, the vistas disclosed as yet no goal, no resting-place, little but flattery and criti-

> cism, the journey at least gave leisure for reflection and self-examination; it changed the child of Emancipation to the youth with dawning self-consciousness, self-realization, self-respect. In those somber forests of his striving his own soul rose before him, and he saw himself, darkly as through a veil; and yet he saw in himself some faint revelation of his power, of his mission. He began to have a dim feeling that, to attain his place in the world, he must be himself, and not another.[33]

Self-fulfilled people experience a revelation of their own power, and they know they must be themselves. They can be neither slaves nor puppets, neither as a group nor as individuals.

To be open to new experience and to be free to act in accordance with new understanding one must have a modicum of satisfaction of the physiological and safety needs, of the love and esteem needs, and especially of the need for information and understanding. Physiological and security need satisfactions safeguard the individual's capacities to see and to hear. Security, love, esteem, and information and understanding need satisfactions enable the child to look and to listen and to understand. If these needs are frustrated, the school experience becomes meaningless, an endless bore, a form of incarceration from which the student, following the adaptive patterns of man, seeks escape. Depending on the age and background of the child, this takes many forms: dropout, overt defiance of school authorities, apathetic submission, or passive resistance. The last is one of the most widespread modes of response.

Resistance to learning appears at every educational level. In the kindergarten or nursery school, as teacher and children pick up the blocks and place them on a shelf, one child spitefully kicks or throws a block, or stubbornly refuses to cooperate. In the primary grades some children stare out the window or are preoccupied in other ways as the teacher reads a story, or as other children practice their writing. In the upper grades or in high school, perhaps at the teacher's desk after class, students say, "I'm sorry, but I just couldn't get the assignment done—I left the book in school and I couldn't do it." Or "I put down the wrong assignment date in my book." Or "My mother made me do some job around the house and I couldn't get to it."

In college the excuses are only more sophisticated. If one were

to slip unnoticed into a typical classroom in which a teacher or professor was lecturing, the evidences of resistance would simply take a different form. Many students would be taking notes assiduously, but were they to be questioned, a few would reveal that they had been recording mechanically, their minds partly engaged in fantasy. Others in a similar state of mind would be doodling in their notebooks. A few might be surreptitiously writing to a friend or even reading a book. It would be a mistake to think that the fault was entirely the lecturer's, for even the classes of the most gifted teachers include students of this sort.

Resistance to learning is a social product. As with ignorance and stupidity, the degree to which it exists is a measure of a society's inability and unwillingness to satisfy the human needs that make for ever fuller functioning, for wisdom and clarity.

Individuals conscious of the psychological determinants of educability can use their own resources and those of society to intervene in their own lives and those of their children to attain these most human qualities of man, qualities that differentiate him most from all other species.

7

SOCIAL

It has been by custom and law determined
for the eye, what it is supposed to see and not to see,
for the ear, what it is supposed to hear and not to hear,
for the tongue, what it is supposed to say and not to say,
for the hand, what it is supposed to do and not to do,
for the foot, whither it is supposed to proceed and not to proceed,
for the heart, what it is supposed to want and not to want.

Seeing a newborn baby in its mother's arms, adults wonder what goes on in its mind. They speculate on the infant's reactions to the mother, to other children, and to themselves.

Knowledge about the baby's mind is far from complete, but it seems clear that the infant does not experience the people before him as different individuals, not even as different from himself. In fact he does not experience himself as a separate being and is not conscious of himself. Whatever sensations and awareness he has are not experienced as something separate and apart from mother and the rest of the environment. The process of maturing, growing, and developing as a person involves differentiating himself, seeing himself increasingly as a separate, independent organism.

This characteristic of the evolution of the individual follows the pattern of the evolution of the species. Species *homo sapiens* is thought to be nearly nine hundred thousand years old. During all but the past five thousand years he was probably not conscious of an inner life. The fact that his wishes, feelings, and ideas emanated

from him and his experience with other people and that they were the source of his actions was not known to him.[1]

The man Homer portrays, the man of the *Iliad* and the *Odyssey,* "has not yet awakened to the fact that he possesses in his own soul the source of his powers, but neither does he attach the forces to his person by means of magical practices [as had his ancestors]; he receives them as a natural and fitting donation from the gods."[2] Even after the Homeric period the early Greek lyric poets saw love "not as an emotion which breaks forth from within, but the intervention of a deity."[3] Sappho wrote:

> Once more Eros, looser of limbs, drives me about, a bitter-sweet creature which puts me at a loss.[4]

Neither she nor the other poets of the time were using metaphors. Their lines depicted the way they understood the forces that controlled their lives. Between the time of Homer (about 1000 B.C.) and that of Aristotle (384–322 B.C.) man achieved a consciousness of himself that enabled him to differentiate himself from external forces enough to lay the groundwork for science, for political thought, and for an individual ethic. He had acquired a greater sense of the unity of thought and action, for he now attributed these to himself and not to magic or to the gods. Knowing now that thoughts resided within himself, he could come to understand the influences that shaped those thoughts.

The new consciousness opened man's eyes to the realizations so well expressed by Antiphon, the Sophist, the author of the lines at the beginning of this chapter. Challenge it as he might, man could not alter the basic law of social behavior that what we see and hear and what we understand are socially conditioned and socially determined. There is nothing inherently good or evil in the existence of this law. The operation of it is a different matter. *What,* "by custom and law" the eye may see, the ear hear, the tongue say, and the heart feel—*what,* is the determining factor as to good or evil, constructive or destructive, healthy or unhealthy, for man or against him.

This basic law has operated at all times and places, but differently. Various governments in our own time and earlier have been openly despotic and restrictive in the dissemination of knowl-

edge. While the chronicle of history gives the impression that censorship of ideas has been the major form of thought control, the fact is that it has been only the most blatant and conscious manifestation of the law. Much more subtle and unconscious is the phenomenon whereby the functioning of our perceptual processes is affected. It is not a question then as to whether we have the ability to see and hear, but rather that the ability we have is conditioned to inhibition. In Antiphon's words, our culture determines, for the eye, what it is supposed to see and not see, by cultivating a reduction in visual perception.

Today, according to the European psychologist and historian Barbu, 85 percent of our "intake" of the world is visual. Barbu writes that man's perceptual world was very different in times past. His analysis of the written language of the time shows that the sixteenth-century Frenchman suffered from what has been called "visual backwardness," that his olfactory, tactile, and auditory functions were relatively more developed than his sight. In part this is explained by the fact that hearing had to play a much more prominent role because of the scarcity of books, mass illiteracy, and the oral transmission of literature through song and story, in addition to the simple scarcity of artificial light. But there is another and more important explanation, one much closer to our interests. Sixteenth-century France was still in many respects medieval, with its people described as high-strung in temperament and with violence as the tenor of life. The period was dominated by magic; everybody believed in and dealt with ghosts. The line between real and imaginary, natural and supernatural was thin. In a world of ignorance, in which man was relatively helpless, he found security in the prevailing beliefs and superstitions. The "affective senses" of touch, smell, and hearing support to a higher degree than vision the magical character of the world. Visual perceptions could only cast doubt and weaken the basic beliefs, and they had to be repressed. In a prescientific age, spirits, angels, and demons were explanatory agencies as well as symbols of order in an otherwise incomprehensible and capricious universe.

The role of sight changed as the old order changed, as religious faith declined, as life became more secular, as science and reason began to pervade more of life. For now that man began to seek his

security in mastering his environment, by learning its secrets, he depended primarily upon his visual sense. As the old beliefs weakened, new sources of security were found in the intrinsic order of nature and the rational processes of the mind, as well as in the norms of a new society.[5]

Changes in consciousness induced by social factors may occur in much shorter periods of time, and they can show themselves in many forms, including the biological. One example is the perforated peptic ulcer. This is of course an organic condition, but it generally occurs in people who have conflicting feelings toward the same person, dependency and hostility, which they try to suppress. On the one hand they are dependent on, for example, a wife or a husband, but reject their dependency needs and compensate for them by great strivings. On the other hand they cover up the hostility they feel toward that person. In the second half of the nineteenth century this ailment consistently affected more females than males in the Western world. In New York for the period 1880–1900 the ratio was seven females to six males. In thirty years the ratio shifted markedly; for 1932–39 it was twelve males to one female. During the intervening years the changes in sex role had been dramatic. Women had achieved a considerable degree of emancipation, and whatever the negative consequences for them, the movement had left them with less of a tendency "to eat away at their insides." To the extent that the Depression and other social changes of the 1930's were contributing factors, they obviously affected the two sexes differently.[6]

Differences in time are matched by those in space. Social anthropologists have given ample evidence of differences in concepts, language, and thought. In the United States, when asked the date of birth, one automatically gives the month, the day of the month, and the year. A Balinese gives the day of the week and probably doesn't know the month. He will not give and will not even know the year. To the man of the Western world the changing years denote social movement and progress. Past, present, and future are experienced as sequential but different. To the man of Bali (at least when Gregory Bateson and Margaret Mead studied him in the early 1940's) the present is only a repetition of the past, and the future of the present. If Piaget's theory of the development of concepts is correct,

the Balinese and the Western child will acquire temporal structures at about the same stage of life, but their content will be different.

The experience of being adolescent was once thought to be associated with universally consistent responses. The biological changes of puberty presumably evoked intense reactions as their natural consequence. Yet Margaret Mead's well-known study of adolescence in Samoa in the late 1920's revealed that the adolescent's problems of adjustment to the demands of his or her burgeoning sexual needs, so characteristic of the Western world, were not found there. Differences in attitude toward sexual behavior, differences in role and in family organization elicit markedly different concepts and behavior.[7]

Along the same line of intercultural comparisons, but on a topic more directly related to learning, is the way in which upbringing affects the child's development of the ability to abstract, to recognize that dogs, cats, horses, and cows, different as they are, have like qualities that classify them as animals. This ability is essential for the flowering of intelligence, and it is lacking in the few known cases of children raised by animals and in the organically mentally defective children. Some societies require the use of abstraction more than others and cultivate it in the young.

The word for "child" in the language of the Pacific island of Truk means "does not comprehend." Children are given very little instruction and a great deal of freedom until they are old enough to begin work. Compared with the children of Western countries, those in Truk have relatively little adult supervision. By the time the American child has begun to move from a stage of dependence upon a code of behavior taught by his parents and others to a level of independence and self-evaluation of behavior, the Trukese child, having had practically no guidance from his parents or other adults, arrives at a stage of dependence upon concrete instruction, a level of functioning that he never leaves. He never has the American child's opportunity to experiment with choices, especially the American child fortunate enough to have parents with whom it is safe to err. Instead, the Trukese child learns from concrete experience to utilize always the least controversial response, the one most likely to be socially acceptable. This rigid way of life is nonprovocative. It is also nonproductive when one is confronted with a new type of

problem that requires the weighing of alternatives or inductive thinking and freedom from anxiety about mistakes, whether these problems arise on an intelligence test or in daily schoolwork. Without these abilities, so essential for success in school and in industrial societies, Trukese children who are perfectly adequate for life in their own culture would probably function inadequately in highly disproportionate numbers, compared to native Americans, were they to come en masse to the United States. They would no doubt contribute in like proportion to the mentally retarded rolls. This would occur not because of any inherent inferiority but because the demands upon them, especially during the crucial early years, did not elicit or develop their abstracting capacities.[8]

Even temporal or spatial distance is not necessary for very marked differences in conceptualization to exist. To paraphrase Antiphon, it has been by custom and law determined, separately for each social class, what it may see, hear, say, and feel. The social determinants of educability operate differentially even in the same community and neighborhood.

The Trukese approach to child-rearing studied after the Second World War bears some resemblance to that in the lower socioeconomic groups in the United States. An interview study in Chicago in the mid-1940's in which the subjects were two hundred mothers—a hundred middle- and a hundred lower-class, half of each Negro and white—showed that lower-class children had a great deal more physical freedom from the time they were able to care for their basic needs, and that the middle-class children had more restrictions and responsibilities. The latter were prepared for the methods of school-learning through the supervision they received in solving their problems, whereas lower-class children had to rely on trial and error. They had no opportunity to build up the body of knowledge which serves as a basis upon which the three R's are firmly established and the standards of middle-class teachers satisfied.[9]

When this cognitive deficit is combined with lesser motivation for academic achievement, we have a truly massive handicap. To cite only one of many motivational studies, one investigator has used a verbal projective achievement test on 427 New England boys, aged eight to fourteen. Using a system devised by David McClelland to measure the strength of the achievement motive, the examiner gives

the boys a brief verbal picture (for example, a boy sits at a desk over an open book, his chin on one hand, looking out toward the viewer) and they are to tell what is happening. Some will describe him as thinking deeply about the subject he is studying; to others, he is daydreaming about leaving home. The subjects were ranked for motivation in terms of ethnic group, religion, and social class. The last, social class, was found to be the strongest determinant of motivation. When religious and ethnic groups were ranked, Negroes were lowest, but when only middle-class groups were ranked, the Negroes were not significantly different in score from the white Protestant youth.[10]

Our discussion about parent-child relationships and their effect on abstracting ability should not be construed to mean that these relationships are the only crucial factor in mental development. The expectations the parent has for the child constitute a culturally generated condition, and what the culture generates depends on many factors, all of them interrelated. The pioneer anthropologist Malinowski showed that the behavior patterns of a community are not at all independent of each other, as they may appear, but are all part of an interlocking system. Starting his analysis at any point in the society, as for example the economy, the anthropologist will find it leading him to the practices at every other point in the society. The activities basic to life, the food-getting systems of hunting, fishing, and agriculture, are in an interdependent relationship with all other aspects of the culture, with its system of family and kinship, with its language, with its religion, and no less so with its expression in various art forms. Each of these in turn is in a similar interlocking relationship with all the other phases of community life. The behavior patterns of a people truly form an interdependent unity.[11]

This organic approach to cultural phenomena should also be applied to educability. Any other approach fails to reveal the multiplicity of factors and their interdependence. Attempts to understand human intelligence for the purpose of controlling, modifying, enhancing it, are likely to fail if they are not truly comprehensive.

The danger to truth in being less than comprehensive is illustrated by the more than half-century-old history of the Kallikak family. That famous study, published in 1912, reported on two

lineages stemming from a soldier of the American Revolutionary Army. Martin Kallikak had an illegitimate son by a feebleminded girl. Later he married a daughter of a "good family." Descendants from the illegitimate son numbered 480, many of them feebleminded, some of them illegitimate, some prostitutes and alcoholics, and a few criminals. Only 46 were known to be normal. From the marriage, 496 descendants were traced, of whom 491 were classified as normal, many of whom were successful in business and in the professions.[12]

For a period of more than ten years after publication no one challenged the author's conclusion that the differences between these two lineages were attributable to the different maternal hereditary input. With paternity held constant, the only contrast seen between these two family lines was in the genes of the two mothers. It took a later time and more sober thought, bound less to "divine right" of class and good family, to recognize that, besides her genes, each mother gave her child a life very different from the other. It would be more accurate to say that a whole set of interrelated conditions acted in very different ways, beginning with the circumstances of their own birth and childhood, upon the respectably married mother and the mother of a bastard. And whatever the difference between the two offspring at the moment of conception, social influences began to act upon them immediately. The marital status of the mother affected her economic well-being and her psychological state; these in turn influenced her biological condition and simultaneously that of the growing fetus. At the moment of birth one infant was welcomed by two parents; the other perhaps less warmly welcomed and by only one. Thereafter the opportunities for love, stimulation, and supervision were probably very different. Any such comparative study needs to take into account the probability that physiological, security, love, esteem, and information and understanding needs will not be met equally. On the contrary, we can expect that the difference in need satisfaction will be as great as the differences reflected in the two familial lines.

Besides genes, parents give their children the only kind of upbringing they know. They speak the language the only way they have learned. They serve as the only adult models they can be. They engage in conversation with whatever form and content they have

available. They can accommodate only those new experiences that their own past assimilations permit. They can provide only those opportunities open to their use.

This is all of a piece. It seems like a tautology: parents are what they are and cannot be otherwise. They cannot change so long as the conditions that make them what they are remain unaltered. But these conditions are not unalterable, and the conditions that are subject to change—those that affect large numbers of people—are social in nature.

Just as good food, rest, and medical attention for the mother are important to the health and mental condition of the child, these are in turn dependent on the mother's income and the social class of the family. There is evidence from the work of behavioral scientists to suggest that the child's health is at least partially determined long before his conception. Two of them, A. Wolf and C. M. Drillien, have made a study that demonstrates a correlation between the economic status of the family (mother and father) and the incidence of prematurity. There is also a correlation between the incidence of prematurity and the economic class of the mother's father. The investigators discovered that the correlation here was even closer than the correlation between prematurity and the economic class of the father—an interesting observation, but difficult to interpret. Possibly the nutritional status of the mother during childhood and adolescence has had an influence on her subsequent pregnancy. Possibly the habits of her childhood environment with respect to diet and other matters of hygiene carry over into her married life and influence her actual nutritional status throughout the pregnancy.[13]

Profound changes that will begin to tap the actual educability of the species may have to start with the mother's childhood. At any rate, we know there is no one easy way to bring about significant changes in the educational level of people, and no possible way should be neglected. "Head Starts" are not and can never be more than one of many types of beginnings, but this fact must not be used as an argument against immediate and massive improvements in the schools. Decent food, housing, neighborhood parks, steady employment, human dignity, adequate medical, hospital, and psychological services are all part of the social fabric that determines the educ-

ability of every individual. The schools are only part of it. The schools must be changed, but that is not enough. The people, as the grand designer, must change the elements in the fabric if the educability—the humanity—of the young is to be developed. In the process of modifying the system, the adults—parents and teachers among them—change their own thinking and their own behavior.

The interdependence of all the aspects of living as they bear upon mental development and education is probably nowhere better illustrated than in the performance of American Negroes in comparison with American Caucasians. Until 1946 comparative studies of the intellectual functioning of black and white children contradicted the view of most modern scientists that there are no innately inferior races. The notion of difference came into prominence after the First World War, when the significantly higher average scores of white soldiers on the Army Alpha and Beta tests were publicized. The fact that northern Negroes and whites both scored higher than their southern counterparts received less public attention. Northern Negroes were merely assumed to be the superior members of their race, as further proved by their migration to better conditions. Various investigators later studied the differences between the two regional groups and found that the newly arrived children in the North were not a sample of superior members of the race insofar as IQ's were concerned. Compared with the Negro children born or long resident there, they were inferior, but given time and the advantage of northern schools, and probably the greater incentives for education for a Negro in the North, their IQ scores rose and approximated those of the long-term northerners.[14] But still some difference between the races in IQ scores remained.

We have seen some of the basic reasons for this: Negroes have a much higher incidence of premature birth and other pregnancy and birth complications. Deprived children start life at a disadvantage, social handicaps having already been converted to organic defects even at birth. From then on the gap usually widens with each passing day, sometimes because of the greater incidence of injury, and generally because of inadequate opportunities for intellectual stimulation and for the variety of experience that is prerequisite to

concept formation and scholastic success. But in spite of these differences, under the proper circumstances equivalence of ability between black and white racial groups can be recognized. Life in New Haven, Connecticut, during the Second World War provided some of those circumstances and permitted Dr. Pasamanick to compare developmental quotients of children of the two races who then had approximate equivalence in social and medical conditions. Having found in his previous studies of racial differences in intellect that when data on the physical status of the children were given, the two racial groups were significantly different in this way too, he reasoned that children who were intellectually slower but also physically smaller might well be manifesting organic disadvantage. He looked for a set of conditions that might circumvent both of these disadvantages, the organic and the intellectual, and found an approximation of them in New Haven, where employment was high and many workers, including Negroes, enjoyed a higher standard of living than they had known before. For the purposes of a hypothesis that the physical health, nutritional standards, and obstetrical care of the pregnant woman are significant ingredients in the mental functioning of the child, as well as in his general health, the minimal conditions were satisfied, though it was impossible, of course, to eliminate all the effects of "being a Negro" on parents or children. Using the Gesell Developmental Examination, Pasamanick found the adaptive behavioral development of Negro infants proceeding at the same rate as that of the whites, contrary to all previous comparative studies. Similarly, the two groups progressed from birth onward at the same rate in both weight and height. These children were followed into their eighth year, and at the age of seven the Negro children had mean scores equivalent to the white children on the Stanford-Binet and the Arthur Performance tests.

The results were unambiguous: With socio-economic and health factors controlled, Negro and white infants and young children were not different in their mental development.[15] Shortly afterward, two other investigators, working in another part of the Northeast, found no significant race differences in IQ's of five-year-old Negro and white children matched on socio-economic factors.[16] These researchers used the Goodenough Draw-A-Man Test, in which

the child is simply instructed to draw a person and the IQ is inferred from the quality of the drawing compared with those of other children of the same age.

At this point in contemporary research one can only speculate about what group differences, if any, exist at the moment of conception. Judging by the studies just mentioned, however, there is every reason to believe that there is no difference at that time, but that at the moment life starts, harsh social disadvantage begins to take its toll.

If this is true, we should expect the differences to be smaller earlier in life, and so they are. In a study of the literature on psychophysical, psychomotor, and intellectual functions published between 1943 and 1958, white persons were found to show a general superiority, with smaller differences among young children.[17] One investigator who, after a study of the literature, concluded that racial differences in intelligence are native, nevertheless pointed out that the differences are smaller at a younger age.[18]

But they grow all too quickly, as a typical study shows. More than 800 white children and almost 450 Negro children, tested when they were in grades six, eight, and ten, revealed reading and arithmetic achievement differences between the Negro and white groups that increased progressively from the sixth to the tenth grade.[19]

The extent to which the gap widens undoubtedly depends upon the quality of the school system and the milieu in which the child is reared. This can be inferred at least from Otto Klineberg's well-known studies reported thirty years ago. Correlating average scores on group mental tests with length of residence in New York, he was the first to hypothesize an increase in IQ of southern Negro migrants to New York. Using the Stanford-Binet, he also found a very striking tendency toward a relationship between length of residence and IQ.[20] About fifteen years later, Klineberg's hypothesis was substantiated by independent evidence in Philadelphia, where retests of the same subjects were used—a sounder method than Klineberg's, though more difficult to arrange. An analysis of the scores on the Primary Mental Abilities Test indicated increases, for all categories except memory, consistent with length of residence.[21]

The research literature on comparison of racial functioning is vast, and the reported results are seemingly contradictory in that

some show early differences and others do not. Yet it is clear that in several of the best-controlled studies differences in mental functioning were not found in infancy and early childhood. With passing years and increased disadvantage, the differences that emerged suggested the very viable hypothesis that racial differences in the capacity to master the concepts of an advanced society are socially produced.

The research we have discussed here does not mean that the question of educability is of prime concern only to Negroes, or only to Negroes and white ethnic minorities, or only to the lower socioeconomic classes. The question would be well worth a thorough analysis even if its benefits were to be restricted to one group, but a basic principle would be missed. That the lower classes have been the more deprived educationally as every other way, and lower-class nonwhites most of all, does not alter the fact that a false theory of educability does injury to members of every group. Not infrequently school people give up on a white middle-class child in a suburban school, in the belief that the youngster's ability, presumably fixed at too low a level for academic success, is not susceptible to alteration. Whatever disarms education harms all children exposed to it. Whatever leaves teachers impotent impedes the mental development of all the children they teach.

The concept of "intellectual potential" is an artifact. It was born of necessity in a nation that espouses egalitarianism but fails to provide the conditions necessary for it. In the United States as a whole the mean current expenditure per pupil was $455 in the 1963–64 academic year. In Kentucky and West Virginia the average was $300, and in the depressed rural areas of those states (part of Appalachia) the expenditure fell well below that figure. Surely it is not coincidence that children's school achievement showed similar discrepancies. The national norm or average score on the High School Senior Achievement Tests is 100. In eastern Kentucky 69 percent of the school districts had *average* scores below 80—not 100, but 80. Not one county averaged as high as 100, and only one had an average over 90. On the College Qualifying Test, designed to measure both cultural background and scholastic achievement, the average score of Virginia and Tennessee students in 1960 was 80 percent. But in Kentucky outside the plateau, the averages were 55

to 65 percent, and in a number of eastern counties the average was a pitiable 17.5.[22]

Poorly supported schools and poor pupil performance are likely to go together. In the case of poor counties one need not go far for an explanation: There is just not enough money to raise the per capita expenditure materially, at least not without considerably more aid from the state or federal government. In the case of urban areas where children have been short-changed over the years, the answer is not so simple. This is not to suggest, however, that it is mysterious. The greater expenditures have quite consistently gone to the schools that serve the middle classes. Those who exert community power have succeeded in obtaining for their children the better teachers, buildings, and facilities. Combined with the other good things that contribute to learning and educational achievement, these advantages have produced discrepancies in achievement of a magnitude similar to those between Appalachia and other more blessed areas of the country.

How are these achievement differentials to be explained to the public? One obvious way is the frank exposure of the difference in expenditure and quality. That, however, is really spilling the beans. All parents have a tendency to be outraged when they hear that their children are being short-changed. To those who are enjoying the benefits of the present inequitable distribution it is far better to avoid that kind of disclosure. A rationale unrelated to economics and cloaked in the vocabulary of science can avoid recrimination. Furthermore, it can be very convincing, for are people not unmistakably different in intelligence? That being so, the variance between the Appalachias and Harlems on the one hand and the more privileged areas on the other can be imputed to a difference in potential.

Once you inject a social organism with even a single myth, no part of the system can escape its effect. The concept of potential cannot be applied only to children in the depressed rural areas and the slums. It must reach into the privileged schools as well. One distortion calls for another, and that for another, and soon the entire social organism is infused.

The self-serving interests of the more affluent that created differential education in the first place also set constraints upon what

teachers may teach and students discuss. Information that reveals inequalities is to be scrupulously avoided, and the only issues to be discussed are those unlikely to arouse the suspicions of that large portion of the population that is not affluent, or the racial and class pride of the disadvantaged. In a democracy, however, major concerns of the people like income, jobs, equal opportunity, war, and police behavior are bound to be brought into the classroom in one form or another, and the established way for the system and the teacher to handle them with impunity is to give them partial, superficial treatment and prepackaged answers. By carefully skirting any controversy the teacher succeeds in destroying student interest even in dealing with relevant topics.

This is the state of affairs that led David Riesman to argue for the abandonment of social studies in the secondary schools.[23] The anthropologist Jules Henry, commenting on education generally, uses stronger language: "Learning social studies is, to no small extent, whether in the elementary school or the university, learning to be stupid." The intellectually creative child may even fail at the task because he cannot understand the stupidities that are presented as fact. Because much that he is asked to learn seems absurd and because he is unable to think of the absurd as the truth, he finds himself a failure and considers himself stupid.[24]

Antiphon said, "by custom and by law." When a society compromises with its own basic values, it must creat a custom and a law that will appease the victims while it assuages the guilt of men of good will among those who benefit. A successful rationale hides all semblance of class interest, so that those most intimately engaged in developing a palpable theory protest honestly that their motives are purely scientific and professional. In reality, if it were possible to be completely scientific and professional, we would be forced to see that the "truth" about human ability has been contaminated by social-class self-interest. Then the consequences might be circumscribed, the distortions limited. But our ideals, as well as guilt and fear, prevent us from an open and rational form of unequal treatment, with the result that a whole structure of distortions has been built. They influence psychologist and teacher as well as parent and child, and objectivity and truth are hard-pressed to hold a place in the classroom.

As a part of society teachers and principals have helped to create the problem, but they are also among its victims. They are the ones who must try to help or at least control students who are impatient with absurdity, dulled by issues that are not relevant or discussions that exclude real controversy. Teachers disseminate and interpret knowledge; they do not generate it. They teach what the curriculum writers set forth and what the textbook authors have prepared. The publishers want books that will sell, which means books that ultimately meet the approval of the members of boards of education. Our text writers are not necessarily poor scholars, nor our curriculum specialists badly informed. Except during periods of special repression, they do not knowingly omit very much as too highly controversial and unwelcome to potential publishers and pressure groups. Their own disciplines have learned to accommodate themselves to the prevailing implicit values.

There are many just complaints about the limited way history is taught, including the history of minorities, and many parents know that "civics" courses are laughably far from reality, but we seldom recognize the inadequacies of the science courses. At first glance it would seem that the natural and physical sciences and mathematics are not susceptible to unconscious attitudes that influence the direction and productivity of thought. But ideological thinking—that is, in the terms of the sociology of knowledge, thinking determined by class or caste need—knows no bounds, and the natural and physical sciences have been the scene of a theoretical controversy not unlike that in education. The familiar figure of Plato appears as the first champion of the idealist side of the conflict, the side that in effect stands for order, aristocracy, and established religion. In its view, as the British physicist and science historian J. D. Bernal wrote, "the objective of science . . . is to explain why things are as they are and how impossible, as well as impious, it is to hope to change them in essentials." The other position, the practical or materialist one, which dominated science after the Industrial Revolution, is "a philosophy of objects and their movements. . . . It emphasizes the inexhaustible stability of the ever-moving material world and man's power to change it by learning its rules."[25]

Einstein's general theory of relativity was a decisive step in challenging Newton's principles of mechanics and opened great

possibilities for new knowledge of the universe. At the same time, according to Bernal, one effect was that some popularizers of science seized upon the Einstein theory to support the view that "everything is relative" and reality really "depends upon what you mean." Reality so defined then was what was in the mind of man rather than in an objective material world. This was a refuge from harsh realities of life. According to Bernal, whose ideas on the subject were first organized for presentation in the Charles Beard Lectures at Ruskin College, Oxford, in 1948, "The physical theories of the twentieth century are no freer than those of earlier centuries from influences derived from idealistic trends from outside science."[26] Conflicts about scientific and philosophical views do not always take the form of intellectual controversy nor always rely upon evidence and logic as the chief means for resolving differences. At some periods new ideas confront the raw and ugly force of threatened power or prejudiced public opinion. The careers of Galileo, Copernicus, Bruno, and Darwin, and the Scopes trial are dramatic instances in which established authority felt threatened by new knowledge. The dampening effects of repression can stifle creative thought in every field, in inorganic chemistry as in biology, in theoretical mathematics as in physics. What happens then is that the flow of new knowledge can become deflected from the mainstream into inconsequential eddies.

The recent history in the United States of the biosocial science of psychology is an example. During the 1930's and the war years of the 1940's many behavioral scientists were studying problems of war and peace, of prejudice and resolution of conflict between people, of overcoming the learning deficiencies and handicaps of the deprived. Either through sheer coincidence or, more likely, in response to postwar recognition of mental health needs combined with response to the different pressures of the postwar years, by the early 1950's psychology was considerably preoccupied with the inner problems of the individual man. The dominant theory of personality directed attention to problems of instinctual gratification and intrapsychic imbalance. This was, of course, one or another adaptation of the theories of Freud, who some twenty-five years earlier had expressed pessimism about world peace because of the inherent aggressiveness of man.

It was safe to introspect. It was safe to find the root, at least the major root, of man's problems of adaptation within his psyche, just as it was safe to find the cause of man's learning problems within his intellectual potential. "Contemplation of the navel," as psychoanalysis was facetiously or lovingly caricatured, became a conversation piece but also the most enticing topic at meetings of psychologists. These developments in psychology had a substantial effect on the schools. Now not only the IQ but the psyche of the individual was held responsible for his deficiencies. This was dual protection against the possible charge of social determination of learning problems. At the same time the theories of Carl Rogers that there should be less directiveness in counseling and guidance, for all their merit in overcoming authoritarian approaches to student guidance, provided—unwittingly, of course—another means of avoiding commitment or involvement during a period when neutrality and strict conformity meant security.

Happily, this state of affairs has been changing. With the advent of "The Triple Revolution"—civil rights, nuclear science, automation—numerous psychologists are engaged, as a few never ceased to be, in using their science to tackle the basic problems of contemporary man. They are not less interested in the conflicts that erode the spirit and shackle the minds of individual men, but they are finding new evidence that the psyche is not a thing apart, that it is a material brain, part of a unitary organism, that assimilates new experiences in its relationships in a social world.

One other tendency in contemporary psychology applies very much to its sister behavioral science, sociology. Although science has acquired an aura of mystique, all science is nothing more than formalized and controlled human thought. It is the kind of thought for which, as Piaget has found, humans are equipped by the time they are preadolescents or young teen-agers. The logic of mathematics is sometimes important in conceptualizing problems and frequently in designing and testing hypotheses. To that extent mathematics serves an essential function for behavioral scientists. It can also be used as a refuge, as a sophisticated escape from those real but controversial issues that stare both psychologists and sociologists in the face. In our time some social scientists—the late C.

Wright Mills is a good example—have lost a measure of respectability and to a few people become pariahs for daring to meet these issues forthrightly.

One attribute that some claim as essential to science, and a virtue at that, is neutrality. "The true scientist is neutral," so the slogan goes. If this is so, the scientist must never take a stand on an issue. He just goes on collecting data; let Rome burn if it will. This is a case of confusion between objectivity, an indispensable quality, and neutrality, a luxury that only those who give preeminence to unenlightened self-interest can afford. Darwin declared that no scientist can be neutral. He has chosen a hypothesis to test because he has reason to believe that it is correct. He is not likely to spend a year or two or more of his life evaluating a point of view in which he has no faith. Inescapably he favors it and wants to see it upheld, which is all the more reason why he must be strictly objective in his research.

The scholar who insists on withholding a position for action until "all the facts are known" is making postponement inevitable and infinite, for "*all* the facts" will never be known. Certainly it will be years—centuries, perhaps—before the descendants of those who are now deprived have been freed of the biological, psychological, social, and educational handicaps to learning and of their consequences. By that time the scholar will long be dead, today's problems solved or replaced by others, and courage, decisions, and action no longer necessary for their solution.

A society that contains inequity while espousing equality pays for this in many ways, and one of them is in the unconscious injury to the integrity of knowledge. The damage is minimized during periods of history like the present, when the clamor for improved education pries open the closet door that hides the skeleton, and it is maximized during periods of repression, when scholars, scientists, and teachers consciously suppress unpopular ideas and controversial issues. It can never fully teach its children the truth because it is busy avoiding the basic conflict between its expressed and implicit values.

What happens when the subject matter of the various disciplines reaches the student? By now it has gone through the sieve of author, publisher, and the public as vested in the board of education. Their standards are borne in mind in the teaching as well as in the writing

and revision. They reach the hands of the student in a condition that the historian Oscar Handlin described as "dogmatic and dull, an obstacle rather than an aid to learning."[27] Some subjects are taught as the study of facts without organizing principles. Biology is remembered as "lists of muscles and bones," whereas it is vibrant with problems of living and has much to say about group relations and even, in the study of genetics and the epidemiology of disease, about our major social issues. Literature is studied out of context of the times, as if Shakespeare, Byron and Wordsworth, Ibsen, Tolstoy, and Gorky were deeply meaningful and vital to an adolescent without reference to the social conditions that shaped their thoughts. Shakespeare "in modern dress" should not be a substitute but an adjunct, for the universal meaning of a great work can best be evoked in terms of the stresses and struggles contemporary to the artist.

This is not, to be sure, the advocacy of "sugar-coating" or titillation to delight and hold the fancy of uninterested adolescents. On the contrary, it is the recognition that learning in depth requires a holistic approach. A literary work without its social-historical background is partial knowledge, and a fragmented approach to knowledge makes for obscurantism and leaves students bewildered. The well-motivated student will swallow the undigestible stuff because he knows that if he can manage it for a limited number of years, there is caviar ahead for him. In fact, his parents see that he gets some of it on the side, along with the other stuff. Because there are social and intellectual rewards for him not only in the future but contemporaneously, he can manage to learn the rules and play the game. For other children, with no experience in the family of having won the sought-for prize, there are few rewards in the present to make the sacrifice of study worthwhile.

What is "by custom and law" prescribed for learning in school is not worth the candle to some students. Many lower-class children and not a few creative middle- and upper-class children bide their time. The poor performance of the latter is written off as underachievement, that of the former as evidence of poor potential. The teacher who is in his position because he learned to play the game—that is, to discipline himself to learn subjects that had little inherent interest or meaning in order to reach his present status—is not in

the best position to be aware of the sterility of his field. He cannot possibly hold either the content or the form of his course accountable for his students' behavior. The circle has been joined. The testimony is here to reinforce the original theory. Original sin—innate deficiency—is the cause.

8

EDUCATIONAL

"I quit school when I were sixteen," the sign on the wall of the New York subway car reads. Spot advertisements on radio and television advise the young in their audience, and their parents, that the quality of their job and the size of their income depend upon their completion of high school.

Automation, a great product of the human mind, hangs like a specter over our economy, threatening to unbalance even more the uneasy relationship between labor supply and demand. Induction of large numbers of men into the armed forces serves as a temporary abatement. Prolonged education can be a permanent measure to postpone for four years or more the entry of millions into the labor market. This is not the first time that economic need has combined with a long-held wish of the people to achieve major educational gains. Laws against child labor and for extended compulsory education to age fourteen were passed only after more than half a century of demand, and after child labor had become unprofitable for major industries.

Child labor was unprofitable by 1900; today unskilled labor is in the same position. The lowest socio-economic classes, which supplied the pool of those workers, have no place to go but upward or out. "Out" means to become unemployed, or unemployable as a result of the corruption and demoralization of years of unemployment and marginal support by the local welfare organization. "Upward" means acquiring the kind of education that enables young people to com-

pete for semiskilled, skilled, clerical, personal service, managerial, or professional jobs. While the semiskilled occupations require no more than literacy for successful performance, that category is most vulnerable to the otherwise welcome onslaughts of automatic production. Whether a high-school education is necessary for the job or not, the possession of a diploma is a distinct advantage in the competition for it.

Upward movement is the understandable aspiration of parents for their children, and of parents in the urban slums as much as of those in suburbia. They want their children to enjoy more of the good things in life. These are often labeled "middle-class values," as if education, travel, comfortable cars, and pleasant or luxurious homes were attractive only to those who have achieved the level of middle-classness. Both classes are desirous of upward movement, or, for the middle class at least, of having their offspring maintain the same status and material advantages they have. Whereas for the lower social classes the striving is for a high-school diploma and the dream is for college education, for the upper classes it is a degree from a college of distinction and then, for those who do not enter a father's business, for a higher degree and a profession. When parents are dissatisfied with a school, their criticism is motivated by a child's failure or by the slow pace of instruction. Rare is the parent who is dissatisfied because the school is a diploma mill successfully turning out students who have not changed much since they entered except in age.

The standards of the parents may be little different from those of the teachers and educators whose greatest satisfaction is an increase in the number and percent of their students admitted to college. Although college admission is an inadequate measure of the quality of education, and although spending the four years of high school working only toward college application rather than sharpening one's intelligence and learning is a pitiful waste of years, the fact remains that satisfaction in increased college-going does show a growing appreciation for higher education for more people. New nations around the world who condemn much about the American way of life and its foreign affairs set their sights to match our achievement in the steadily accelerating rate of college attendance.

During the 1950's the public schools came under severe attack.

Some of the critics were simply opposed to the very idea of good education for the general public, but others were genuinely troubled by what they believed to be a lack of quality. They contended with the question: Can you have quality along with equality, or are the two incompatible? What action is necessary, they asked, if there is to be a "restoration of learning," to borrow the title of the book of one of the soundest critics, Arthur Bestor, a university professor.[1]

Whatever the differences among them, the critics agreed that learning must be the central, the chief, if not the *only* purpose of the schools. The words of Admiral H. G. Rickover, "father" of the nuclear-powered submarine, illustrate this attitude: "The school's concern is with the intellect alone." Athletics and other extracurricular activities were to be subsidiary if they must be allowed at all, and the needs of young people in the realm of interpersonal relations were to be served, at least in the schools, only through the medium of such established and tested courses as literature and history.[2] The critics did not denigrate the importance of personal adjustment but were quick to add that society provides other agencies besides the school to foster social education.

These attacks upon education came during a period when most school systems were accommodating themselves to anti-intellectualism and severe restriction upon academic freedom. The tendency toward self-searching, toward encouraging the child to look inward and to find the sources of his problems within himself rather than in his society, was a way of avoiding controversy. Certainly not all the critics were aware of this, but Robert Hutchins was. "At least during a cold war," he wrote, "the doctrine of adaptability leads remorselessly to indoctrination."[3] Irving Adler, a teacher and author, agreed that we should pay attention to the child's emotional and social adjustment but criticized other formulas of progressive education. Commenting about the life-adjustment program in city schools, especially in the nonacademic program, designed to help children deal with problems of family and other interpersonal relations, he said that "the real-life problems of adolescents tend to crowd out of the schools the study of science, mathematics, and foreign languages."[4]

Proposals for the restoration of learning were various. The extremists, motivated by hostility against public education and school taxes, wanted to produce automatons as economically as possible, not

people educated to think independently or critically. As Adler described them, "They believe it is wrong to teach people *how* to think; they want the schools to teach children *what* to think, instead."[5]

On the other hand James B. Conant, former president of Harvard University, became a leading spokesman for the American high school, a status earned by his leadership in reappraising the functions and goals of the school. In *The Revolutionary Transformation of the American High School* he advocated academic study for able students only. He made his position clear in a statement during a discussion of vocational training and the education of those who have "great difficulty" with their studies: "I should start by questioning the dogma one often hears that all the youth, irrespective of academic ability and interest, should complete grade twelve."[6] His view was based on the belief that the young people who have little academic ability and who really want a job in a manual skill would be bored and frustrated in school. Perhaps it would be at least equally accurate to say that the school bores and frustrates such children.

Admiral Rickover was more optimistic than Conant about the intellectual appeal of the schools. He wanted to raise standards of all education and stressed the need for higher pay to attract better teachers, preferring to expend money on faculty rather than new buildings. He cited the inadequate budgets of recent years which had failed to keep up with increased enrollment. In his *Education and Freedom,* published soon after the Soviet Union's Sputnik made history, he described American education as inferior to European, although we exceed the per capita expenditures, he reported, of all European countries except the Soviet Union. He recommended a faster, more intensive pace in all schools, and wished to see the United States model its education on the European pattern. He emphasized the high quality of Soviet education and urged that the United States try to overtake that country. It is a curious fact that Rickover advocated ability grouping, separate education for select students, and failed to point out that a marked feature of the schools of the Soviet Union, whose educational achievements he admired, was a single curriculum for all students and the absence of grouping.

Professor Bestor came directly to grips with the problems that

come from the diverse backgrounds represented in the schools. The most dangerous misinterpretation of the scholastic performance of this heterogeneous school population, so different from the selected group of the private school and of the nineteenth-century high school, he said, "consists in confusing lack of intellectual and cultural background with absence of innate mental ability." The "masses of men" are educable, he wrote in *The Restoration of Learning*. What is necessary is the kind of systematic learning experience that offsets intellectual impoverishment. This he proposed to accomplish by means of an educational system whose structure would be based on selective ability grouping, so that, for example, bright children would go from kindergarten to second grade, and backward ones would repeat kindergarten. Some children needed more time to offset the disadvantaging experiences of their preschool life, but that did not mean they could not benefit from a rich academic program.[7]

Another critic, James D. Koerner, former professor in the humanities and later executive director of the Council on Basic Education, declared that the book he edited, *The Case for Basic Education*, would distress professional educators because the authors could not accept the "dreary estimate based on the vaguest of evidence, that only fifteen or twenty percent of American students can master a foreign language or a high-school course in physics or advanced mathematics." No attempt had ever been made, he asserted, "to give a serious education to all students or even to, say, sixty or seventy percent of an average student body—and thus to find out how many can indeed profit from a solid curriculum. Public school men, far from having the answer to this most fundamental of educational problems, appear not even to have asked the question."[8]

Here, in Koerner's statement, the issue was clearly drawn. The vast superstructure of education, its superintendencies and teacher education, its curricula and pedagogical methodology, its faculty attitudes and student relationships, is built upon the prevalent conception of mankind. If, as Koerner asserted, public school men had not even questioned the general view that only a relatively small minority of children are capable of benefiting from a rich experience of academic education, they were only reflecting the ideology of

the times about the severely limited capacities of the great mass of humanity.

No critic has been more consistent and, in a sense, more "traditionalistic" than Robert Hutchins, former president of the University of Chicago. The term traditionalist seems incongruous for one who condemned the practice of training people to adjust to the status quo and who said, "Our mission here on earth is to change our environment, not to adjust ourselves to it." Yet his educational views are close to traditional American principles of equalitarianism and high valuation of education. The old myth that every child has a chance to be President is implicit in his recommended curriculum, which would offer every child the great heritage of the past and the ability to use his resources as a thinking, reasonable being to unlock new knowledge. It is ironic that the man who, as president of a distinguished university, fostered a curriculum akin to that of upper-class British universities is the champion of the same academic education for all youth, and that many of his opponents, who favor differential education in accordance with ability, are the leading spokesmen for public education in this country.

According to Hutchins, the current ideal of American education is the successful man whose primary requisite is not a well-trained mind but, more likely, the ability to get along with people, "which is often oddly interpreted to mean the ability to get ahead of them. Since we have little else to measure, we tend to measure time spent. These results do not follow from the great American doctrine of education for all, but from the hasty and ill-considered application of that doctrine." In a penetrating analysis, he said that "the underlying paradox in American education is the belief in the capacity of people. This we reject, but we don't dare say it. So we continue to proclaim education for all, but surreptitiously substitute accommodation for education. There is no evidence that ordinary people cannot understand great philosophers, historians, scientists and artists, or if they try to understand them without distinguished success they will be any the worse for the effort."[9]

So it seems that we are victims of our own subterfuges. Declaring ourselves for excellence, we are stymied from the start by a theory of human ability that asserts the intellectual mediocrity of most

people. We are less than a decade removed from the general belief that no more than 15 or 20 percent of the college-age population can benefit from higher education, and there are still many in high places who have not forsaken that prejudice. The logical sequel to their cynical view is a curriculum that substitutes "accommodation for education," superficial knowledge devoid of inherent interest and functionalism. Lacking substance and meaning, for many in the college-bound curriculum as well as those in the others, such schooling encourages the memory of fragmented, undigestible material.

Those who cannot muster enough external motivation to discipline themselves for that kind of unproductive labor often become burdensome to the class. The teacher must be a good entertainer, using all his wits to titillate his class, competing with the television programs and movies that hold the attention of children, adolescents, and adults. Because most teachers are not and should not need to be entertainers, they often fail to maintain class interest. To them the bored and unruly behavior is what one expects of students who "don't have it." That knowledge is inherently exciting, that the search for new knowledge is adventure to match that in popular entertainment and sport, escapes many teachers and principals because their own education had no such joys. That knowledge is power in ways far more significant than as a route to occupation and income has not usually been programmed into their own education. Teachers and professors who have not known the excitement and adventure of learning cannot stir the minds of their students. Teaching then is wooden, and learning mechanical, and the incentives for the child must be external to the act of learning. On the other hand, a good teacher—and there are many in the public schools—transmits the challenge and satisfaction of exploring new realms of knowledge.

With all our good will and effort to have a truly democratic school system, we have succeeded in evolving programs that are completely contrary to our intent. Great Britain has one kind of class-based school system, France another, and the United States still another. While ours provides more opportunity for a higher percentage of children, it is, nonetheless, very much of a stratified system.

Teachers, like other workers, get some of their satisfaction from "a job well done." But success in the school system's terms means that the students have learned what the syllabus for the course has called for. They have passed with good grades and are college bound, or, in non-college-bound curricula, they have been orderly and remained in school until graduation. If the relationship between teacher and students has been friendly and the classroom atmosphere has had at least the semblance of stimulation and interaction, this is a very welcome fringe benefit. Wanting both kinds of success, the teacher responds most positively to the students who enable him to achieve them, and those students benefit from his satisfaction. For them he becomes the interesting instructor that he could not be under different circumstances, and as good a teacher as his own mental development and education permit. Through them he has the chance to experience fulfillment in his work.

Most of such students were born to the expectation that they would go to college. They have been conditioned by love, approval, and material rewards to strive for the goal which with age they themselves saw was associated with the same returns. They are mastering "the academic game." To paraphrase the well-known lines:

Ours not to wonder why;
Ours but to learn and sigh.

Inevitably in the course of reading and such independent thinking as is encouraged, some children find for themselves the excitement of discovery. Often they provoke classroom controversy or arouse the teacher's sense of inadequacy. In other cases they may be found, one or two of them, in a class of conscientious students, those good soldiers who will do as they have been trained—learn anything assigned, without zest but with good spirit. It is as if everyone had agreed there was a job to be done from which all would profit—complete the course successfully with a grade that will be an asset to a college application—and agreed to make it as pleasant an experience as possible.

In the interdependency created between those students and the

teacher, the students benefit from the efforts and attitudes of a satisfied professional worker. Their response reinforces his, and his theirs. A camaraderie of like interests and values is established between the professional who has had higher education and those who have every expectation of acquiring it. Under circumstances like these, in which a holistic, unfragmented approach to education is not taken and the great minds and issues of the real world are not the major focus of study, the two forces, college-educated teachers and their college-bound students, establish the best possible modus vivendi. Their relationship is strongly approved and rewarded by parents and school authorities, while teachers and students who behave in a contrary fashion suffer disapproval: the student who rebels against restrictive school practices or against teacher or textbook interpretations given as "the truth" which he regards as dogma; the teacher who nurtures independent thought and critical inquiry about controversial matters such as "black power," religious bigotry, family planning, biochemistry and the creation of life, social action, or open housing. Teachers who open the doors to lively or even lifelike debate are quickly reminded of their professional role, sometimes called a "neutral role," by which is meant a dormant role. The teachers learn, and they teach their students, that the rewards are given to those who learn well *what* to think from those who have decided, consciously or not, what may be safely thought about.

A very recent study of high-school teachers in Oregon has revealed that they are more politically conservative than other population groups, and that the longer they teach the more conservative they become.[10] In another recent study the investigators observed the way in which human likeness and difference (race and religion, for example) are handled in the schools, and found that they were seldom treated by direct confrontation of the issues. Instead the methods used were either total avoidance ("a wall of silence") or discussion of such problems in far-off lands but not in this country or in the community, or restriction of discussion to the safe facts in the textbook.[11] Trained in this way themselves and further conditioned by experience in the school, teachers are understandably most comfortable with students who play the game, do assignments unquestioningly or at least ask only the safe "literary" questions.

Other students cannot elicit the same positive response from the

teacher. They cannot mobilize enough external incentive to work at meaningless material. Not for them, as it is for their middle-class peers, is it the clearly perceived open road to status and security. Vocational and commercial programs at least have a substance of "reality" about them and, even more, a clearer relation to future occupation. If they can program one of these curricula into their own future, those students usually classified as "not college material" can manage to tolerate the watered-down general education courses in such fields as English and social studies. If they cannot, they leave school as soon as they can.

Another important reason for their difficulty and withdrawal from general education is to be found in the problems they encounter in learning. Two propositions may help to account for these learning difficulties.

1. Most students, unable by themselves to create a productive relationship with a teacher, never achieve that happy state because their teachers, not comprehending the nature of the problem, are unable to help them. American educators, following American psychologists, have measured the so-called intelligence of the child rather than his deficiencies—and what help he needs—in mastering each stage of mental development.

2. The fragmented curriculum, with its emphasis on fast, safe, acceptable fact and its de-emphasis of controversy and discovery, not only stifles inquiry, imagination, and interest and deprives students of inherent incentives in learning; it also ignores the mental developmental needs of children.

The mental development of the child is central to education. It should serve as the basis for determining the sequence of studies, the content of the curriculum, and the methods of instruction. It is the yardstick against which the appropriateness of judgments about education must be evaluated. Piaget provides a detailed analysis of four periods in the growth of intelligence that constitute the nearest thing to a yardstick we have so far in the less than precise field of human behavior.

Piaget, as we have read, explained learning as a process of assimilation, with the individual assimilating only what he can accommodate at any particular time in life. Piaget's observations led to the identification of four periods in the origin of what we regard as

mature or adult intelligence. Taken as a whole, intelligence tests really measure the level at which children or adults are performing in the use of several types of mental abilities such as the verbal or mathematical or perceptual. Each of these is one-dimensional; that is, each is like a ladder ranging from the simplest items at the preschool age to the most complex on tests designed for candidates for graduate study, from the simplest problems in mathematics to the most complex. The difference in that span of age and mental ability is in the complexity or difficulty of the items. It is fair to say that psychologists and educators regard the tests designed for children as being easier than those for adults, or, stated differently, as being at an earlier point in a single continuum ranging from the easiest to the most difficult. Piaget's work has shown this up as primitive. In former eras—pre-Freudian and pre-Pavlovian—the popular and professional conception of the child was that of a "little man or woman." Having forgotten the experience of being a child and having repressed much that would have revealed qualitatively different modes of thought and behavioral acts, adults attributed to the child the capacity for rational behavior that they believed they themselves possessed. With the introduction of Freudian theory, however, the unmasking of adult consciousness disclosed deep veins of egocentric thought that had persisted from early childhood. How clear it then became that the mode and content of childhood thought were qualitatively different from those of maturity.

Freud and Pavlov, each in his separate way, contributed to the beginnings of an archeological perspective on human psychological development. Piaget carried this on in the cognitive domain, saving us from the "little man" view of the intelligence testers. In his view the continuity between infant and man is incorrectly portrayed as problem solving at ever greater degrees of complexity, when in fact there are four distinctly different periods in the developmental life of the human species, and the problems that are solvable in each are qualitatively different. Continuity is there, of course, in the sense that each period is prerequisite to the next one, and that vestiges of the first three remain throughout life. But the intellectual gap between each and the other three requires that four, not one, different yardsticks be used if we are to know an individual's problems and success in assimilating and ordering his environment.

If we were to picture the study of man's intellect as an archeological study of the earth, we would say that Piaget discovered between the cave and the topsoil four differentiable strata. As we carry our analogy further, carbon-14 tests (used to determine the age of long-buried artifacts) reveal the chronology and age periods. The artifacts show that each successive period borrowed from but built distinctly different structures upon the former, so that a clear, though not abrupt, transition is apparent. From the infantile or primitive period of human thought, when there is no awareness of the constancy of objects in the environment, to the advanced period of scientific thought, the evolution of the individual corresponds to the evolution of the species. Ontogeny follows phylogeny.

As we examine the four periods of intellectual development in detail, it is worth keeping the following questions in mind:

1. What conditions are necessary during the preschool life of the child to assure him of mastery of the operations associated with the preschool period?

2. What provisions must be made for identifying inadequacies in development and remedying them?

3. Are the content and the processes of education in school geared to the laws of mental development through the three periods that overlap with schooling?

The Sensory-Motor Period (birth to about eighteen months). The newborn infant is a cute blob of protoplasm, displaying uncoordinated gross bodily movements and reflexes like sucking and swallowing. During the approximately eighteen months of life that constitute this period, the infant makes very marked, if not very dramatic, progress and lays the groundwork for the advances of the future. By the end of it, but not before, the organism has developed an elementary form of imagery, the first and very primitive inner use of some representation of the environment recorded in the brain.

During this period the infant advances from the first stage of inchoate use of his reflexes to a later stage of circular reactions. By chance he has some new experience, such as grasping the edge of his crib sheet with his fingers. He tries to recapture the experience, and when he succeeds, he repeats and repeats this until he has this ability in his repertoire. He is learning to control the environment, but mostly the environment that his own organism represents, for now

he is more intent on the act of grasping than on what is grasped. He shows this progress in the development of his visual, hearing, vocalization, and sucking activities as well as grasping.

Soon the infant's attention is directed to objects external to his body. He begins to recognize them in his surroundings, and he learns to hold and shake and drop and pick up and examine. He recognizes familiar objects at a distance, for example, a doll across the room. As another development in his growing control, he becomes able to make interesting sights or sounds persist. Enjoying the drumming sound his father made on a tin box, one of Piaget's children at age seven months uses the reactions he has available to make the phenomenon recur. He turns toward the box and shakes his arms while looking at it. When an attentive parent is available, the infant can get enough response to reinforce his own actions as methods of communication.

Before the end of the first year of life the infant is able to remove an obstacle that blocks his way to a desired object. He pushes aside a cushion to get at a toy. He learns to use instruments to attain his goal, like taking a parent's hand and pressing it against a moving toy he could not get going. He anticipates events, as, for instance, crying at the sight of his mother putting on her coat.

During the final six or so months of this first period, as the sensory and motor apparatus develop and become integrated, the infant shows further advances in his goal-directed behavior. Now he is not content with reproducing only those experiences that have occurred by chance; he welcomes novelty and is not satisfied simply with the reproduction of a new event or object. He can accommodate novelty and is fascinated by it. He seeks variations in the new experience, as if to discover fluctuations and novelty as the result of a repetition. Of this development Piaget said: "The 'experiment in order to see,' consequently, from the very beginning, has the tendency to extend to the conquest of the external environment."[12]

The crowning achievement of the sensory-motor period is the development of a form of representation. Thus even before language the child has mental images with which he can engage in limited internal manipulation of reality prior to an action. Piaget cites an example of this in the behavior of another of his own children:

> In the same kind of inventions, that is to say, in the realm of kinematic representations, the following fact should be cited. At 1; 10 (27) [i.e., age one year, ten months, twenty-seven days] Lucienne tries to kneel before a stool but, by leaning against it, pushes it further away. She then raises herself up, takes it and places it against a sofa. When it is firmly set there she leans against it and kneels without difficulty.[13]

Lucienne did not have to rely on a random experience of stool-leaning-against-sofa nor on training in the use of the two, nor did she have to engage in trial-and-error activity. From past assimilations she now had an internal representation of an object like the stool against a solid object like the sofa. She could now apply her "knowledge."

The Preoperational Period (about eighteen months to about the age of six). The child begins to build his conception of the world. Because he starts life without any cognitive organization, and this period with little in the way of an organization of his simple representations, he cannot easily make the world coherent.

His world is highly concrete. His representations of the world are mental pictures of specific objects and events. Whereas the adult uses symbols to represent past experience, and this with great rapidity, the young child has available only images of specific experience. It is as if he projects a film slide on the screen of his mind, or a series of these, a slow process compared with the manipulation of advanced and symbolic representations.

One of the most prominent characteristics of preoperational thought is what Piaget calls "egocentrism." The child is a social being, and he can learn and develop only because there are those upon whom he can be dependent. Not until the end of this period, however, can he begin to take the role of another person and see things as others see them, as the following test shows. The child of four or five is placed before a large model of a town. When the examiner has him stand at point A and asks for a description of the view from there, he will give an accurate one. Standing at, let us say, point B on the opposite side and observing a different view, he will report his observations accurately. Now, while he is standing at B, ask him what a friend standing at A would see, and he will report

the view he has at B. He cannot yet put himself in the shoes of another. His representations are egocentric.

Another characteristic is "centration." The child centers on a striking feature of an object or an event and neglects others, just as he does in his drawings of people, in which the major characteristic may be a head or a hand. This gives him only partial or fragmented understanding and leads to distortions in reasoning. Shown two thin beakers with identical quantities of liquid, he recognizes the identity. When the contents of one are poured into a short, broad beaker before his eyes, he now declares that there is more in the taller beaker. He assimilates the more obvious feature of the higher column of water in the tall, thin beaker. He is not yet able to decenter and take into account width as well as height of the column of water.

Preoperational thought is "irreversible." The child cannot yet change his direction of thought and start anew. The water from the wide beaker is poured back into the tall thin one from which it came. The child sees identity of content again. Were he not now sensory-bound and irreversible in his thinking, he would begin again and perhaps invoke a concept of constancy in the water. But he cannot, and when the water is poured from the tall thin one to the short wide beaker, once again he reports a difference in quantity.

The young child makes great developmental strides during this period. He has language; he is vastly more of a social being; he is searching, exploring, and constructing his conception of reality. Such a view of the world as he is able to devise is an insufficient one for social control of the environment. It is as shifting as his perceptions. The line between what he sees in his dreams and in his waking hours is very narrow. The concepts, or "preconcepts" as Piaget calls them at this period, do not yet have an abstract generalizing quality about them, and they shift with the egocentrically perceived experiences of the child. This is hardly the kind of thinking that can delineate an adequate and functional conception of the world. It is the developmental mission of the next period to provide the stable operational structures essential to that task.

The Concrete Operational Period (approximately ages seven to eleven). During the first, sensory-motor period the infant's ability to learn is limited to direct and immediate experience. Only in transi-

tion to the next period does he begin to be able to manipulate the environment "in his mind"—by representations of past experience. During the second, the preoperational period, this ability develops so that the young child can, with increasing accuracy (in the mental reflection of reality), use representations of past events in solving current problems. Not being part of a stable classified system, his representations are subject to the vicissitudes of shifting perceptions. He has a concept of more and less and recognizes the difference so long as only one class of magnitude is involved. He can see which of two columns of water is taller *or* which of two columns of water is broader, and in those instances he knows which one in each of the two sets contains more water, but he cannot apply the two concepts at one time. He has a single-dimensional representation. Because he lacks a stable system of more and less, he also lacks the concept that the quantity of water is conserved no matter what the size of the vessel. To him, the greater quantity in the taller one is lost when it is poured into a broad beaker and is now a shorter column.

During the period of concrete operations the child, now in the middle years of childhood, acquires an enduring conceptual system. This new stability in his mental operations does not mean rigidity. What he gets from his social experience (including formal education) is the wherewithal to give order to the multiplicity of concrete phenomena that confront him. He loses the egocentricity that has characterized his thought, as the healthy corrective of interaction and communication with others rids him of many distortions about the world of objects and people and about himself. The world becomes more comprehensible and manageable.

The greatest mass of work by Piaget and his associates was applied to this period. For our purposes we will try only to characterize the meaning of cognitive systems in concrete operations and to present some of the specific developments of these years which precede adolescence.

We have witnessed a change in the degree to which cognitive actions are internal. At first, as when the infant brings thumb to mouth, the action is largely external. By the preoperational period some of it is "in the head," and by the time the child is in the middle of the concrete-operations period, much of it is internal.

The mind is not a chaotic storage bin. It is systematic. The cogni-

tive representations of the external world become organized into tightly knit systems. Piaget applies the term "cognitive operations" —any representational act which is an integral part of an organized network of related acts—to these mental structures.[14] It is in the period of concrete operations that these operations are really established and, before the end of it, consolidated. Examples are the logical operations of arithmetic such as adding or subtracting or those involving quantity, time, and space, or operations concerning classes of values. The stable systems can be established because the child's thought processes have become more logical. Operations can now be reversed. If $5 + 2 = 7$, then also $7 - 5 = 2$. If the tall column of water is poured from the narrow to the broad beaker, the child can symbolically reverse the process and recognize the invariant quantity of water.

He acquires other mental characteristics which, on the face of it, may appear to be trivial or at best infrequently used qualities of thought. They are, in fact, indispensable for mature and logical reasoning. For example, the child learns that any two or more classes may be combined into a more comprehensive one that embraces them all; that is, all men and all women = all adults. During this period children also develop the conception of conservation of numbers and quantities and approach an adult-level conception of space and time. They can serialize items in terms of size or shape. Along with the systematizing of the concrete world, there is a parallel development of operations related to the more directly social. Just as the child learns that there are norms in the behavior of natural phenomena—as, for example, the conservation of water—so too he discovers there are norms in the relationships of people. There are rules of behavior and moral norms in transactions with parents, siblings, friends, teachers, classmates, and strangers. Just as hierarchies of concepts arise, the comprehension of one being essential for the understanding of the second, so too there are hierarchies of goals. The child learns that to achieve goal two he must first reach goal one.

At the threshold to adolescence the individual has a firm conception of the world. He is ready to move on to the most advanced development in human thought.

The Period of Formal Operations. The previous period, that of concrete operations, witnessed many gains, but important limitations

in the quality and flexibility of thought remained. The very name given to the period indicates the major limitation. Whereas his ready availability of representations gives him the freedom from immediacy lacking in the sensory-motor period, and the availability of reversibility and other cognitive processes gives him flexibility unavailable to the preoperational child, he is nonetheless largely bound to the concrete. He can manipulate objects mentally because he has mental representations of the consequences of, say, moving pieces on a chess board. What he cannot yet do with ease and what he rarely does is to deal with the potential, with the consequences of events for which there is no concrete representation, with that which is not there, not concrete, at all.

Piaget and his colleagues differentiate between the actual and the potential. The child in the age period of about seven to eleven is largely preoccupied with the task of ordering a world of clearly perceived phenomena. In his problem solutions he begins and ends with the actual. Faced with conflict, he considers the potential; that is, the potential effects of specific actions. To paraphrase the psychologist J. H. Flavell, who has studied with Piaget, the possible becomes a special case of the real.[15] The child starts with the real and, manipulating it on the basis of experience, searches for a solution. The possibilities available to him—and they are limited because he is tied to the concrete—are regarded as real rather than possible. He cannot indulge in flights of hypothesis building because he is fixed to the real and is limited in his solutions to those largely inherent in what he perceives.

By contrast, the adolescent, capable of engaging in formal operations, is not bound to the actual in this fashion. Problems lead to the postulation of all the possibles, and these hypotheses are then tested in the real before him. "The real becomes a special case of the possible."[16]

An analogy can be drawn by turning to a different category of behavior. A large qualitative gap exists between the person who can perform a task only in a prescribed manner and the one who is sufficiently confident, secure, and free to experiment with fresh ways of action. The adolescent is free in the sense that he can engage in hypothetical and deductive thinking. He ventures into the domain of the possible by posing the spectrum of hypotheses, then through

deductive reasoning he can test each of them by examination of the facts before him, discarding those which are not supported by the data and retaining those which are.

One operation in the adolescent's thinking is a technique he mastered during the previous period. He learned how to manipulate mentally the concrete objects and events of his experience. He put them into a state of organization, using classes, serials, and the like. Automobiles are convertible and hard-top, Fords and Cadillacs, sports cars and limousines, different in horsepower, length, and so on. Now, during the final period in the development of intelligence, he takes the processed concrete data and engages in propositional thinking; that is, he transforms the data into propositional statements which he uses in the operations of formal thought. He can take the data on automobiles and cast them into propositions about the length, weight, and tire gauges of the cars, the horsepower of the motors, and so on; then, through the process of logic, he copes with problems about speed in traveling between two points. These formal operations are impossible without the prior concrete operations, but the concrete operations alone are not enough for solving problems that demand the logical manipulation of propositions.

It is evident that during this fourth period, when humans develop the greatest command of reality up to this point in life, they can learn to exhaust the possible hypotheses about a question or problem. This means that they consider all the potential combinations of propositions. These combinations are then the hypotheses which are subjected to investigation through examination of the data which will or will not confirm the hypotheses.

Because the operations of formal thought are the basis for scientific reasoning, the possible accomplishments of the adolescent period can lay the groundwork for scientific thought. Does Piaget mean that human intellectual prowess reaches a peak or even a permanent plateau at adolescence? Not at all. Throughout life the organism can acquire through its experience new data to be classified, new classifications for the refinement of the ordering schemes, and new operations for the treatment of propositions. Consider, for example, the effects on a fifty-year-old adult of being introduced to an academic discipline (chemistry, let us say). As the adult assimilates the new experience, structures are reorganized and new ones formed. He

acquires an abundance of new classificatory systems and of new propositions and hypotheses.

Flavell uses poetic metaphor to give the essence of change and development in the preoperational, the concrete, and the formal operational periods.

> What could be the archetypes for the three postinfantile eras? The preoperational child is the child of wonder; his cognition appears to us naïve, impression bound, and poorly organized. There is an essential lawlessness about his world without, of course, this fact in any way entering his awareness to inhibit the zest and flights of fancy with which he approaches new situations. Anything is possible because nothing is subject to lawful constraints. The child of concrete operations can be caricatured as a sober and bookkeeperish organizer of the real and a distruster of the subtle, the elusive, and the hypothetical. The adolescent has something of both: the seven-eleven-year-old's zeal for order and pattern coupled with a much more sophisticated version of the younger child's conceptual daring and uninhibitedness. Unlike the concrete-operational child, he can soar; but also unlike the preoperational child, it is controlled and planned soaring, solidly grounded in a bedrock of careful analysis and painstaking accommodation to detail.[17]

Piaget and his colleagues have given the world the most comprehensive and systematic theory about development. It is theory and not hypothesis because its general depiction of the overall contours of intellectual growth has been confirmed. There are some gaps; some periods have been more thoroughly studied than others; some points are open to question (for instance, the precise transitional age from period to period). Perhaps the time will come when an entirely fresh approach will displace this theory or at least make fundamental alterations. Until that uncertain time this is the best —indeed, the only—systematic explanation of how, from infant to man, that unique achievement, human consciousness, is biosocially created.

Until educators know Piaget as something more than a name— and it would be safe to say that the majority of persons in American education have never heard of him (in 1960 it would have been safe to place the estimate at 90 percent)—until that time, education will remain fixed at a "preoperational" stage, responding now to this stimulus (reading machines), now to that one (the whole child) or

that one (adjustment classes). At that level it will be as shifting and unstable as the thought of the preoperational child who has not yet acquired enough of a systematic conception of the world.

The educational enterprise must have systematic conceptions to provide consistent guidance. Without it, like the child under seven, the schools are like ships without compasses; without even the stars in the heavens to show them the way. Theory provides direction, and there is no substitute. In its absence faddism is in charge. Even good ideas like the Head Start program and good technological devices like teaching machines and closed-circuit television, which in the broad context of sound theory would be useful to the schools, are vitiated by exaggerated hopes and claims in the vain search for panaceas. The preparation of all professionals who are to be involved with education in any capacity should emphasize the theory from Piaget's Geneva school, for the following purposes:

1. To understand the components of human thought. Cognition is not mysterious. A function of a highly specialized mass of protoplasm, the brain, it arises and develops as a result of the organism's social experience. It passes through periods, and each has its unique quality about which there is much concrete and particularized knowledge. Teachers ought to know what constitutes thought.

2. To understand the developmental process and especially the form that thought takes in any particular period, so that expectations and content may be attuned to the appropriate cognitive form. By observation adults know that children cannot engage in profound philosophical argumentation, and by practice such activity is not incorporated in the class work. Yet how often teachers will miss the mark, disappointed that children fail to understand some concept or relationship or, on the other hand, infantilizing the children by failing to challenge them with ideas they are becoming able to handle.

3. To reexamine the total program of instruction, reorganizing and realigning it in accordance with insights gleaned from the theory. Subject matter should be organized in such a fashion that it corresponds to the evolving capacities of the pupils. Piaget cites the inappropriate placement and content of geometry in the curriculum in Geneva and in France,[18] where it is offered at age eleven while arithmetic is first offered at seven. Yet the child constructs spatial

operations at about the same time as the numerical, and the first geometrical structures developed are topological, whereas they are the last to be taught in the course. Commenting about the relationship between school learning and the child's spontaneous development, he said, "Yet it should be clear that to my mind it is not the child that should be blamed for the eventual conflicts, but the school, unaware as it is of the use it could make of the child's spontaneous development, which it should reinforce by adequate methods instead of inhibiting it as it often does."[19]

This calls for the reexamination of every field of knowledge, such as mathematics and social studies; for the review of every subject or grade within each field, such as algebra and fourth-grade social studies; for the careful analysis of each unit within each subject, such as binomial equations and the discovery of America. Each should be studied in terms of adequate presentation and appropriate placement and sequence in light of the child's period of development.

4. To examine critically the procedures and methods of instruction to insure that they contribute to the acquisition of the concrete and formal operations that constitute intelligence, and at the very least that they do not conflict with this growth process. Most of the teaching methods now in use were accumulated from experience over the centuries and have been transmitted from generation to generation of educators. Some were created or reformulated as a result of the influence of Freud, Dewey, and Thorndike. Only in the past decade have classroom practices—and few at that—been subjected to rigorous evaluation. Usually the criterion of success employed is the grade earned or the facts learned in a course. That will no longer suffice. Education that fails to contribute to the development of operations has failed the child. If, in addition, it has not added to his conception of the world, then his schooling has been worse than wasteful; it has discouraged looking and listening and reading and learning. Piaget comments:

> In some cases, what is transmitted by instruction is well assimilated by the child because it represents in fact an extension of some spontaneous constructions of his own. In such cases, his development is accelerated. But in other cases, the gifts of instruction are presented too soon or too late, or in a manner that precludes

> assimilation because it does not fit in with the child's spontaneous constructions. Then the child's development is impeded, or even deflected into barrenness, as so often happens in the teaching of the exact sciences. Therefore I do not believe . . . that new concepts, even at school level, are always acquired through adult didactic intervention. This may occur, but there is a much more productive form of instruction: the so-called "active" schools endeavor to create situations that, while not "spontaneous" in themselves, evoke spontaneous elaboration on the part of the child, if one manages both to spark his interest and to present the problem in such a way that it corresponds to the structures he had already formed himself.[20]

5. To redirect and "retool" educational research so that it will encompass the areas reflected in 3 and 4, above—revision of the curriculum and of instructional methods consistent with the process of mental development—and some others as well. Not all the prerequisites for optimal development during the preschool years (covering all of the sensory-motor and part of the preoperational period) are known, but the necessity for certain conditions is incontrovertible: a mother whose health has been good from childhood; a stable, successful, and full-term pregnancy; a safe, uncomplicated delivery; freedom from accident and serious illness during infancy; satisfaction of the six basic needs; freedom to explore and manipulate the environment. These conditions call for enormous change, because for vast numbers of children some—even most—of them are lacking. Concerted efforts to correct the fundamental social and economic ills that give rise to these conditions need to be accompanied by planned experiences with the social and physical environment, which are most productive during the preschool years. For example, preliminary study suggests that children from deprived groups are handicapped by a tendency toward impulsiveness in problem-solving; they will answer a question more quickly than middle-class children and too quickly for adequate thought.[21] Such a tendency, which is probably due to lack of experience in disciplined thought, calls for some preschool experience that will instill the habit of momentary reflection before responding to the equivalent of a test question.

Research is urgently needed in the preparation of diagnostic devices to identify deficiencies in sensory-motor coordinations and

preoperational actions. One of the greatest challenges now is how to identify the child's deficiencies when he starts to school and how to remedy them. A recent study by a guidance specialist, Linda de Bottari, shows that third-grade achievement is a moderately good predictor of success in completing high school,[22] and the finding is not surprising. So long as educators do not intervene in the process of mental development by isolating and coping with intellectual inadequacies, there is every reason to expect that those who are ineffectual learners in grade three (or one) will remain so for the rest of their formal education. Some work has been done in inventing instruments that can be used to diagnose developmental lacunae.[23] Their use thus far has been largely experimental, and it cannot be productive until the notion about the overriding import of experiences especially selected by teachers to be used in the development of intelligence is generally recognized. One important aspect of the future of psychological testing lies in this diagnostic role.

The values of the school that call for a certain kind of class discipline and general school climate must also be examined, since they have a direct bearing on learning. In particular, the kind of behavior that teachers are expected to require partly determines whether or not children will have the conditions for growth, whether they will overcome that great barrier to learning, the persistence of egocentric thought. Delay in passing on to higher-order cognition affects interpersonal relationships as well as scholastic learning. It makes discipline problems, yet, ironically, insistence on quiet and conformity can cause these very delays. As the need for certain kinds of arguments and disagreements—for challenges to growing minds—in the metamorphosis from one period to another is recognized, it will threaten those principals and teachers—and Americans at large—who favor consensus and accord at the price of freedom of inquiry.

Writing about the Genevan view of social interaction, Flavell says:

> One of Piaget's firmest beliefs, repeated over and over in scores of publications, is that thought becomes aware of itself, able to justify itself, and in general able to adhere to logical-social norms of noncontradiction, coherence, etc., and that all these things and more can emerge only from repeated interpersonal interactions (and especially those involving arguments and disagreements) in

> which the child is actually forced again and again to take cognizance of the role of the other. It is social interaction which gives the ultimate *coup de grâce* to childish egocentrism.[24]

Again and again Piaget stresses the role of experience, and, of course, especially social experience, as one of the essential ingredients in the developmental process. Adults and only adults determine what those experiences shall be, and thereby what the intelligence of infants shall become.

In 1965, Leon Eisenberg, then professor of child psychiatry at Johns Hopkins University, and a colleague studied the effects of six weeks of preschool education (Head Start) on over four hundred children in Baltimore, Maryland, comparing them with controls who were to enter kindergarten with them in September but were not included in the summer preschool program. The controls were in the same social classes and the same neighborhoods. The Peabody Picture Vocabulary Test and the Draw a Person Test were used. The differences between the Head Start children's scores at the beginning and the end of the summer experience are highly significant, rising from a score of about 33 to 40 (standard, 50) on the Peabody Test, and from 7.7 to 9.8 on the Draw a Person Test (standard, 15.2). The differences between the Head Start children in September and the control children were exactly as great, and the magnitude of the differences "cannot be explained away by test repetition or . . . by initial asymmetry in comparison groups." The investigators wrote:

> What must be considered remarkable is that these gains were obtained by a six-week program conducted by elementary school teachers without extensive training and experience with preschoolers. How much more might we not anticipate from year long thoroughly planned and pedagogically more sophisticated programs of preschool enrichment!
>
> We are, however, far from convinced that these gains will endure, given the overcrowding, educational impoverishment, and generally negative attitudes toward the poor that characterize inner-city elementary schools. We would not, after all, anticipate that a good diet at age five would protect a child against malnutrition at age six. The mind, like the brain, requires alimentation, biochemical, physiological, and cognitive, at every stage of its development. The durable gains from Head Start will be measured less by our test findings, however significant, than by the demonstration that a national effort could be mounted, by the experience

offered teachers in working with classes of 15 instead of 40, by the firsthand knowledge gained by volunteers, many of whom for the first time confronted the ugly face of poverty.[25]

Those who believe that such changes are possible only with the young should be reminded of the success of the Special Training Units operated by the army during the Second World War. By use of an eight-week course, about 85 percent of the enrollees, all identified as illiterates, were able to attain the minimum essentials of literacy, that is, fourth-grade reading level.[26]

The success of such ventures depends very greatly upon the teacher's expectations for the student. Many years ago an old social worker in an institution for orphans said to young assistants: "It's what the children see in your eyes that counts. It's what you tell them that way about what you think of them—what you think they can do and what they can be." She meant, in her professionally untutored but wonderfully insightful way, that children responded to the expectations they sensed. She might have added that our expectations of children also shape our behavior with them.

That was the wisdom of a deeply sensitive woman, unforgettable to those who experienced it personally, but lacking in the controlled observations essential to convince a profession of its significance. Very recently some of the objective evidence has been made available, evidence that begins to lay bare the mechanisms of teachers' expectations for children.

In a study by Harvard psychologist R. Rosenthal, about 20 percent of the children in each of eighteen classrooms in an elementary school were assigned to their classes in an unusual way. Though the students had been selected randomly (and hence were presumably not different in ability from the student body as a whole) the teachers were told that their scores on an IQ "test for intellectual blooming" indicated these particular children "would show unusual intellectual gains during the academic year." Thus these children differed from others only in that they had been identified "to their teachers as children who would show unusual intellectual gains."

And they did! Eight months later all the children were retested and those in the first and second grades (though not the upper grades) who had been falsely identified as highly promising on the IQ test showed dramatic gains on the retest in comparison with the other

children. For example, though the control group of first-graders gained a substantial 12 IQ points during this period, the experimental first-graders gained over 27 points.[27] The fact that the younger children showed substantial gains as a result of teacher expectancy and the older did not is consistent with other studies which show greater change in the young.

It appears clear that teacher expectancies operate upon young children to promote and facilitate their learning and their intellectual development. How does this happen? In an ingenious study involving seven first-grade classes, Ira Goldenberg, a Yale psychologist, compared the amount of time the teachers spent with each of their four reading groups. (The children were grouped homogeneously on the basis of standardized testing and observation.) He also observed whether the groups were given "prime time" (early-morning time when teacher and children were fresh) or least prime time (before lunch) or "neither prime nor least prime time." The results were unequivocal: "The teachers tended to spend more and 'better' time with their higher-ranked groups than with their less advanced students." That is, their expectancy is for higher achievement from these children and the teachers perform in such ways as to have this prophecy fulfilled. Professor Goldenberg interpreted the findings in terms of self-fulfilling prophecy: Unwittingly for the most part, teachers behave in ways that create the conditions that achieve the anticipated outcomes.[28] Perhaps the children play a part too, responding with the kind of performance that is expected of them as they see it "in the eyes of their teacher."

Several foreign psychologists (Israeli and Soviet) in a break with standard procedures have used the test-teach-test method of diagnosis. If a child does not know certain concepts ("horizontal" and "vertical," for example), the task of the examiner-instructor is to teach them and to observe the child's success and speed in mastering them. The assumption of Israeli psychologist Reuven Feuerstein and his colleagues is that the low-social-class North African background of many Israeli children has not enabled them to acquire the operations that are necessary for effective learning and for successful performance on standard tests. Unlike the typical psychologist, the examiner-teacher does not sit as a neutral judge but engages the child in a learning experience that may occupy a full day or more. The purpose

of this time-consuming activity is not to classify the child but to determine the defects in his functioning ability and to identify the kind of instructional help he will need.

To one accustomed to the traditional psychologist's role of dispassionate neutrality, Feuerstein's method is somewhat disconcerting. Humor, sensitivity, warmth, encouragement—all may be combined to capture the child's interest in learning what he does not know. The niceties of testing are disregarded; the child knows the concept of triangular or not, and if he does not the psychologist sets about the task of teaching it. By that procedure he can determine the child's operating level and the educational experiences he needs. Assessment of learning potential is followed by what is known as instrumental enrichment, a series of steps to develop the necessary attitudinal set and to provide the missing perceptual and cognitive functions. Specially designed exercises are used for that purpose. The testing and the teaching are inseparable in this process, as they must be if they are to be worthwhile.[29]

Man makes illiteracy, ignorance, and stupidity. He can change them. Here the social and educational determinants are inextricably bound. Society's will for change calls for actions like vast expenditure of funds for universal free nursery and kindergarten education, higher salaries, smaller classes; it also calls for the modification of the ideology of its intellectuals and professionals. It sends them in search of theory to inform and guide their practice. Valid theory incorporates the educational determinants of educability: the curriculum and the instructional methods follow the developmental process; they nurture, stimulate, and extend knowledge of the world to help in building a stable conception of a dynamic universe; and they help construct the concrete and formal operations of thought, in part by encouraging argument and disagreement.

There are no panaceas in education, but if we adhere to the emerging laws of human development, we are likely to achieve the improvements we want. Our "mental classification" system could be replaced by an active system of intervention to facilitate the growth process. School life could one day become an exciting, adventurous experience for both teacher and students. It has all the ingredients for the enjoyment of learning the arts and sciences and of exploring the uses that the human mind can put them to. The games teachers

and students play to make the best of things could be abandoned for an encounter with the substance of education rather than the trimmings. Under those conditions the creative and the nonconformist thinker, and the disadvantaged child who never learned to play the game and has, because of the little help he has gotten, better reason to engage in subterfuge, could be expected to involve themselves in the schoolwork.

One great hope for the active transformation of American education lies in the use it can make of a comprehensive theory of the origin and development of intelligence. Until another scientist produces a better one, Piaget's can serve us well.

THE OUTLOOK

PART 3

9

CAPACITY FOR CHANGE

If America is to struggle successfully with today's educational problems, it must not be handicapped by a lopsided view of the nature of man. Technological and even theoretical sophistication is no guarantee against error so long as the hypotheses to be tested are drawn only from current observations of man's behavior. Study of man in the past is protection against a narrow view dictated only by the present, and any contemporary theory worth its salt ought to be able to explain man's past as well as current behavior.

Psychologists are well aware of the necessity for a historical approach in studying the problems of an individual. They understand that to know the causes of a behavioral problem they must trace it to its roots. This principle is indispensable in the diagnosis of social and educational problems: The study of contemporary man will not suffice in providing the knowledge necessary for the solution of his problems. The searchlight must be beamed on his past as well, to isolate both continuities and discontinuities and to evolve explanatory principles for the changes that history will reveal in his intellect, personality, and motivation.

Biology thrived when Darwin provided the sciences with a natural history of man. The behavioral sciences that purport to explain human behavior are likely to flourish when they derive or adapt from available sources a comparable psychological history of man. Such a history would be a record of the evolution of man's consciousness. Aside from the fact that it would profit the sciences, the

times demand it. A valid conception of man as a changing species, as a learning, thinking organism that responds to the present—and to the past only as it inheres in the present—requires it.

The need for a conscious effort to add a historical focus to investigation in the behavioral sciences is made strikingly evident by the recent statement of a distinguished psychologist. Jerome S. Bruner has played a leading role in directing scientists' attention to the pressing problems of human learning and teaching. Commenting on the adjustments in education necessary to prepare for the rapid changes in the world, especially the accelerating rate of knowledge accumulation, he writes, "We are bound to move toward instruction in the sciences of behavior and away from the study of history." This will occur, he suggests, because of the unprecedented growth in the store of knowledge. "One would surely not dwell then with such loving care over the details of Brumaire or the Long Parliament or the Louisiana Purchase." There is an even more compelling reason to shift emphasis from history to the social or behavioral sciences, he says. "It has to do with the need for studying the possible rather than the achieved—a necessary step if we are to adapt to change. It is the behavioral sciences and their generality with respect to variations in the human condition that must be central to our presentation of man, not the particularities of his history."[1]

Such a characterization of history as the study of the "achieved" and of the "particularities" of man's past may well reflect the quality of instruction in that field today. Voltaire, with his customary use of strong language, described history as "a collection of crimes, follies, and misfortunes among which we have now and then met with a few virtues, and some happy times."[2]

History is much more than a "collection" and more indeed than a record of the "achieved." The present is incomprehensible except as the past provides laws for the meaningful interpretation of current phenomena. Henri Bergson oversells the role of the past in his famous sentence, but at least he provides a corrective to its neglect: "The present contains nothing more than the past, and what is found in the effect was already in the cause."[3] The present is something more than the past just because new conditions are impinging upon and altering our view of the past. The current movement for integra-

tion and civil rights is incomprehensible except in the context of the history of slavery, its role in the economic development of America, and the political and social consequences. Bruner is right that the particularities are *per se* of little value; but they are of enormous value when the major issues of the day are seen as the leaves on a great oak, and history is treated as the limbs and trunk and roots and the environment itself that create—and give meaning to—the leaves.

History, in Hegel's words, "presents us with a rational process."[4] It is subject to error, and historians must fight, said Lord Acton, against many temptations, including those of country, class, church, and party.[5] We can acknowledge the fact that historians err, that they fail to provide systematizing interpretation, and that history teachers stress particularities, without concluding that we ought to abandon history as a subject for study. We would be more rational to make history functional, directing it to the solution of problems of our time.

An ahistorical approach to any social phenomenon, including education, deprives the observer of a longitudinal view of man's development, and inevitably gives to our twentieth-century behavior the character of permanence and universality that is belied by historical facts. This is the stuff from which stunted theories are made. The truth is that the qualitative difference between man and the other forms of animal life can be accounted for by man's capacity to accumulate and transmit wisdom through teaching and learning. Each new generation can profit from the benefits of the past. The other forms of life must pass on their "wisdom" primarily through the slow process of biological evolution. The difference between the two explains man's vulnerability to change and the necessity for a historical perspective of his behavior.

Biological evolution is a slow process; it plods along on turtle feet. Wearing modern clothes, the ancient Greek or Roman would be indistinguishable from others on our city streets. Even the humans who preceded them by two or five thousand or as many as five hundred thousand years would pass unnoticed, for in appearance and physical behavior they would be no different from modern man.

Social evolution, by contrast, moves with the speed of birds. As a case at point, the position of college students as a dynamic force in American life has been transformed in less than a decade. In a

few years they have achieved more power and influence than during the preceding three centuries since Harvard was established as America's first college. Indeed, the life of every man born in America since the beginning of the Colonial period has coincided with vast social change. Some of the change has been epitomized by cataclysmic events like the Revolutionary War, the Civil War, and the Great Depression of the 1930's, but much of it occurred during periods of relative tranquility. Each historical turning point was preceded by steadily changing conditions that led to the eruption, and each was followed by a chain of events which affected the nation and often the rest of the world.

The sudden appearance of new social relationships can be wrongly interpreted as springing entirely from contemporary forces. The recent unprecedented actions of black and white people to undo the results of American slavery can give the impression that we are witnessing a transformation that was set off in recent times and was brought about largely because of the conditions imposed upon Negroes and largely because they, with other Americans, were determined to correct the inequities. The facts are very different. Opposition to and revolt against slavery began three centuries ago. Furthermore, changing conditions in the economic structure in the South are in no small measure contributory factors to the so-called Negro revolution. Primarily, the South has lost the need for massive numbers of farm laborers. In 1910, when 90 percent of all Negroes lived in the South, more than 80 percent of them lived on farms.[6] Fifty years later, when 60 percent were in the South, only 13 percent lived on farms.[7] The plantations had gone; mechanized equipment had replaced most of the unskilled farm hands; fewer Negroes were needed, even to be exploited. Industrial developments in the urban South were not extensive enough to absorb them. On the other hand, demand for labor in the North and West during the Second World War drew large numbers, and others moved there after the war because their own region offered them no employment. The point is that the explosive movement for equality has its origin in part, at least, in an economic change that has developed quietly, never once achieving the newsworthiness of a headline.

The same cannot be said about changes in sexual behavior in the United States. Headlines aplenty have characterized the country's

preoccupation with sex, which has witnessed a vastly increased permissiveness to write about and display (on stage and film) sexual relations. According to one investigator, I. L. Reiss, most of the radical changes in sexual behavior occurred between about 1900 and 1920, after which "a consolidation and acceptance" of the new sexual attitudes has taken place. Rates of premarital coitus may have increased moderately and "milder forms of premarital sexual behavior have increased," but the significant change has been in the wider acceptance of behavior that was already practiced by the 1920's. "What was done by a female in 1925 acting as a rebel and a deviant can be done by a female in 1965 as a conformist. This is a significant change."[8]

The manifold causes of the Negro revolution and of the sexual revolution precipitated changes in human thought. Changed behavior is accompanied by changed consciousness. Negroes have different conceptions of their problems and undoubtedly different concepts of themselves. The concepts of masculinity and femininity have likewise undergone modification.

In these and many other spheres of activity man has been "becoming" different. He has been modifying himself. The characteristic of social evolution that is absent from biological evolution is simply: Changing circumstances lead to altered consciousness. The swift responsiveness of the mind to new conditions of life and new ideas of relationships between people has no parallel in the biological history of the species. The biological scientist can and frequently does study natural life without reference to the evolution of the species he is investigating. His counterpart in the behavioral sciences cannot disregard the evolution of consciousness and the social as well as biological factors that have influenced it, without doing irreparable damage to his conceptions.

Man can control the determinants of his educability to so great a degree that it is difficult to imagine the level of functioning of "average man" one or two centuries hence. The possibilities are staggering. The species *homo* need not wait out those centuries to initiate dramatic developments. What is more, he is not waiting.

Certainly in his desire for education he is waiting very impatiently. America is astir with activity to improve its schools. Money is appropriated as never before in support of new programs in

institutions that range from the nursery school to the university. "Excellence" is the magic word, and though "goodness" would be a realistic aspiration for schools in urban centers in the next decade, the thrust of activity—the conferences and committees, new programs and new personnel, revised curricula and enriched offerings—is intended to achieve some mythical static state of excellence.

The pity is that most of the hubbub is for nought and will continue so unless certain essential conditions are met. One of them is the widespread acceptance of an open-ended conception of educability. Not all the money in America, not all the sophisticated theory and research, not the expensive technology, nor the new programs and the study committees, nor White House conferences—not all of these together will produce a significant change in education in urban America so long as the classroom teacher looking into the face of the child before her explains his current functioning in terms of a predictable "potential." So long as children's poor performance is followed by a quick recourse to, "But we've got to consider their low ability," failure will be attributed to the children rather than to the educator and his continued lack of ingenuity; to the nonlearning students rather than to the nonlearning educators who have been slow in finding solutions to learning problems, slow in making learning exciting, meaningful, and relevant for all children, not only for those whose positive attributes of learning are acquired at home.

Let us make no mistake about it: Society must assume ultimate responsibility for the performance of children who fail in school or who drop out. The community is no less responsible for scholastic failures than for malnutrition, high infant mortality, and racism. It is reassuring and convenient to attribute academic shortcomings to some qualities inherent in the child, such as a low IQ or depressed motivation. But both of these are so largely social products that educators must come to learn that when they look upon them they are looking into a mirror, seeing a social reflection. IQ's and motivations are not born, they are made. We make them, we the society, by many things we do—including what we do in the making of parents and teachers.

At one time men believed that the earth was the center of the

universe; that this planet was flat, and precipitous at its edges; that man himself was a species apart from all other creations and surely not the end-product of an evolutionary process. Retrospectively we wonder with some amusement that our ancestors could have been so naïve. One day our descendants will react in similar fashion to the antediluvian conception of intelligence of the twentieth century, and their historians and social critics will note that of all these misconceptions about man and nature, misunderstanding of mental ability was by far the costliest to humanity. For it is a fact that if educators must be possessed of some myth, it would be better if it were about astronomy or geography or even evolution. But not intelligence.

But not intelligence. For when it was reported in the spring of 1967 that the reading scores of children in New York City public schools showed one out of every three pupils a year or more behind in reading, many people were bewildered. Ten years ago there would have been a straightforward explanation: "It's the Negroes and Puerto Ricans. Look at their IQ's. They just don't have it." Today, as a mark of genuine if insufficient progress, most people do not express such views even if they have them, except among those who are known to be *simpático*. But on the other hand, the national effort to enrich and upgrade is thoroughly confusing. Teachers are thereby informed that something can be done to narrow the gap. But what? Either the IQ's are valid or they are not. If they are valid, what can really change? (Or, teachers wonder, are we witnessing a great big political hoax?) If they are not valid for deprived urban children, then maybe they are not valid for other children. Such thoughts shake the foundations of our school systems. They fly in the face of all the teacher has learned about intelligence and individual differences. More profoundly than that, they disturb the delicately balanced conception of man that teacher, educator, and layman alike have acquired and which they use to give meaning to their perception of individual men. Their image of men, no matter how clearly or poorly formulated, whether explicit or implicit, is jeopardized by the suggestion that there is a fundamentally different way to view species *homo* and that, in fact, this other way may be the more valid one.

This—man's ability—is the fundamental issue in America's

educational problems. Not class size, nor curricula, nor proper books, nor any other on the almost endless list of deficiencies, but this one, for the others to a considerable degree are a function of it. If you start with the assumption that the child's capacity to learn is unknown and may, in fact, be infinite, your educational strategies, experimental though they may be and compounded with failure as they may become, flow from this correct assumption.

How many years ago was it (post–Second World War) that educators were still declaring that only 15 or 20 percent of our youth could profit from higher education! How recent history has begun to belie them with increased college enrollments! More than 53 percent of the 1965 high-school graduates entered college, and they represented almost 40 percent of their age group.[9] To those who assert that many of the new crop of college students are not benefiting, the answer is twofold. How many, one must ask in response, even of the elite families of America "profited" from their education twenty, thirty, and forty years ago? More affirmatively, one must point to the claims of that awakening giant, the educationally conscious college student body, that the college and university are failing the student, drowning him in irrelevancies, stultifying him with formalism and disciplines that remain immaculately removed from the harsh realities of a dying, addicted, sex-obsessed, hypocritical world bent on destroying its youth in war and its principles in continued deprivation of dignity and equality for millions of its citizens. "If we are not learning what you teach," they say to the adults, "consider it your failure, not ours." And if only 9.1 percent of the population twenty-five years old and older (in 1964) has completed four or more years of college[10] when it suffers from such shortcomings, imagine to what heights the figure might soar if education in the elementary and secondary schools as well as the colleges improved to meet the needs of contemporary life.

Who can be educated? *Everyman.* There is no known reason to set a lower estimate. For the immediate future the outlook for those who suffer from serious brain or other central neurological defects is not favorable, but on a long-term basis the current proportion of such defective newborns (about ½ to 1 percent) can be greatly reduced through social change and medical advances. It is possible, too, that a combination of medical and educational intervention

will activate and elevate the learning processes of those who cannot now be helped. In any event, for all the rest of our children, there is no known reason to believe that they will be unable to do the work of an academic high school and of a college. That is to say, as a given society is fearless enough to welcome and encourage the emancipation of the mind, it will facilitate the heightening of man's consciousness. It will nurture every child's natural curiosity and cherish his openness to ideas. It will struggle against the forces that censor and inhibit, that make school learning a sterile chore. Research and experimentation, administration and teaching, curricula and textbooks will be directed toward that end, but not in a diffuse, anarchic fashion as now, and, far more important, not in search of some abstract good-teaching formula as if in the hope of discovering the secret to turning out models of an urban, modern-day Mr. Chips. Education will be the powerful arm of a society whose mission is to create optimal conditions for the nurturing of the fetus and the birth and growth of the infant, to facilitate the development of the child, and to solve the problems that are most relevant to man, those that distress his mind and undermine his stability.

To say that all humans, with the exceptions mentioned above, possess the wherewithal to be well educated is not to say that this possibility can be achieved tomorrow, but the sooner a society really wishes it and decides to become a society that plans for it, the sooner it can be realized. Let us not imagine that we are on that road now, nor that some Great Society legislation can put us on that road. For its beginning point is not a budgetary matter, nor a school matter. The mission or purpose for which a society exists is a broad social matter that cannot be settled by an act of Congress enlarging appropriations nor by a decision of our school systems to add "head starts" or to modify curricula or hire teacher aids. A decision to allow, enable, and encourage all people to be intelligent is a far-reaching one. It is profound in that it goes to the roots of power and control. It answers the question: Who shall be informed and be capable of asking and answering basic questions about control? Injustice, inequity, corruption, mismanagement, exploitation could not long survive in a society that really meant to actualize human intelligence.

The choice today is not between the current implicit and limited objectives of education which are not succeeding and the grand ones just described. The objectives have been and will continue to be those that the people of America can articulate and demand. Change has come about only in that way. The schools are changing today—still in relatively minor ways—because some segments of the population have demanded change. What those segments want and what they are being given are for the moment, at least, two different things. For what they insist upon calls for an educational system far different from any that America has known, and one that would abolish ignorance in all the population. In the Negro movement, the most vocal of these segments, there are, of course, different voices. Some leaders would settle for an equivalent distribution of the good things, including good education. Such an outcome is impossible, for the great bulk of Negroes are at the same time members of a race and members of the low social classes. To raise them from that class requires a social commitment that would affect all in the class, black and white. It would mean a commitment by those in control of power to give up the benefits they get from partial ignorance in large numbers of the lower social classes. The militant black leaders who will not settle for a quota of middle-class people believe that those in the seats of power will not easily give up the advantages of ignorance in part of the population, will not pay the taxes to support such a commitment, nor reduce the military expenditures that drain the country's wealth just as the military efforts drain its energy. At least they believe those in power will not yield except as they are confronted by greater power.

An honest recognition of this state of affairs is important today, not only to avoid self-deception but in particular to avoid one consequence of it. The immediate future holds the unwelcome but understandable promise of failure of some if not many of the experimental programs now underway in the country. Only those who understand that patchwork is not enough and that the educational enterprise needs a thorough revamping will look upon the failures neither as catastrophes nor as vindications of racial-inferiority theories.

Experimental projects in education are foredoomed to failure if they are based on the old conceptions or if they tackle only a

fragment of the educational experience. Even the richest of nursery-school experiences will show little if any benefit three years later if in the meantime the child's interests and aspirations have been dulled in a class taught by a bewildered young teacher in a school headed by a bureaucrat who does it all "by the book."[11]

What will convince man that his mind's potentialities are relatively unexplored and largely unknown? What will convince him that an interpretation of its limits as open-ended does no violence whatsoever to truth and the canons of science, while the scientific validity of the finite-potential theory is highly suspect? What will convince him that the former opens the vistas to exploration while the latter, in its typically static character, writes *finis* to the species' intellectual development?

Consider the so-called normal-curve distribution of fixed intelligence, a theory which has been implicitly accepted ever since Galton's time. If, as Galton believed, mental ability is similar to height in the way it is distributed in the population, we would find in a random sample a few extremely dull and a few extremely bright people (but these two categories would be about equal in number); the categories of dull (but not dullest) and bright (but not brightest) would be next largest in number and about equal; and so on until the middle category or average intelligence was reached. This would be the largest in number.

At this point it is worth noting that even so strictly material a human characteristic as height can show a decided change as a result of environmental changes. There are still the tall, the short, and the average, but all of these have moved upward in affluent nations. What about intelligence, even as measured by this theory? Can the whole distribution move upward? If so, how far? For though it would not necessarily be practicable for man's height to exceed a particular average, it would be of indescribable benefit for his average intelligence to reach unimagined heights.

These are not Utopian dreams. Facts themselves are persuasive.

If humans are to be able to do the work of an academic high school and college, they will need to function at an intellectual level that can be identified with a moderate degree of accuracy. For example, it has been estimated that with an IQ of 105 a student

has a 50–50 chance of passing in an academic high-school curriculum. With an IQ of 110 he has a 50–50 chance of graduating from college. The average IQ of college graduates is 120, which means that many graduates have IQ's of less than 120. The average IQ of persons receiving the Ph.D. is 130, which means that many have IQ's of less than that, and, in fact, some have had high-school IQ's of less than 110.[12]

If there are to be very significant changes in educability, they will occur as a result of considerable increases in the percent of the population functioning at the levels represented by an IQ of 105 to 120 and above. To examine the facts and estimate the possibilities of change, consider a group of 100 as representing the entire population of the United States. Figure I shows a theoretical distribution of IQ's. Each square represents one of the 100 persons. Starting at the midpoint, we note that the theoretical distribution is symmetrical. Between 90 and 110, 48 percent of all scores are found with 24 on each side of the 100. Between 110 and 120, and 80 and 90, there are

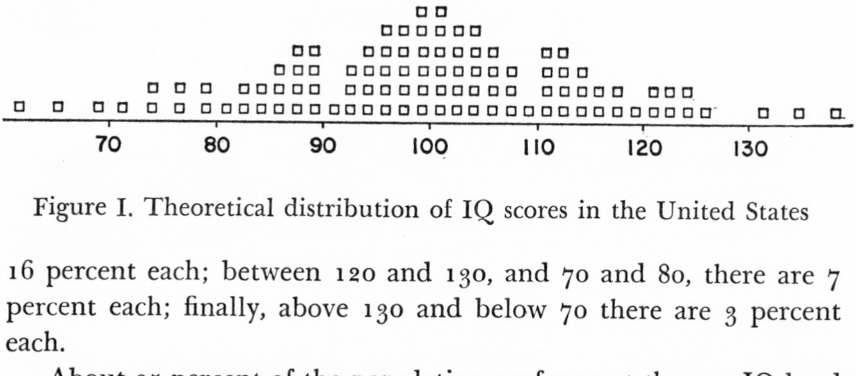

Figure I. Theoretical distribution of IQ scores in the United States

16 percent each; between 120 and 130, and 70 and 80, there are 7 percent each; finally, above 130 and below 70 there are 3 percent each.

About 35 percent of the population performs at the 105 IQ level or higher. Now let us consider the possibility of raising the intellectual level of each of the groups under the 105 score.

In 1964, in a brilliant analysis of human change possibilities, Benjamin Bloom, a psychologist at the University of Chicago, reviewed the many studies on environmental influence on the IQ. He concluded that a fair estimate of the differences produced by abundant and deprived environments was 20 IQ points. The difference estimates between deprived and normal environments and between

normal and abundant environments were 10 each. Half of the difference on the development of intelligence is registered, he hypothesized, between birth and age four, 30 percent between four and eight, and 20 percent between eight and seventeen.[13]

What Bloom means by abundant environment is that the child's conditions of life provide good models of language usage and the encouragement of good language development; opportunity to acquire general knowledge about the world; opportunities and encouragement to solve problems and to think logically; parents who encourage interaction and communication, have aspirations for and expectations of intellectual achievement in the child, and provide assistance and circumstances for the fulfillment of aspirations. We know that statistically—in spite of many exceptions created by devoted parents against great odds—a close relationship exists between social-class status and these conditions and between economic deprivation and intellectual deprivation.

To apply Bloom's estimate of the effects of deprivation, a further estimate must be made of the number of Americans who experience deprivation. Let us use Lampman's proposal that a reasonable range is 16 to 36 percent of the population. We will take the midpoint, 26 percent.

Examining the distribution of the IQ scores in Figure I, we must decide which twenty-six of the one hundred are the deprived "other Americans." Projecting the possibility of social changes whereby children will be provided an abundant environment, we will credit them with 20 additional IQ points. While there is general agreement that "the relationship of IQ to socioeconomic level is one of the best documented facts in mental history,"[14] there are no clear-cut guides as to the representation of the social classes in the IQ categories in the normally curved distribution of scores. Drawing upon clues in various research and theoretical works[15] and adjusting them for the general population (because in some the percentage of nonwhites was far below that in the nation), we emerge with our own guide. Admittedly it is a rough estimate, but it is precise enough to test on an empirical basis the validity of a key assumption about human ability. The table below shows the percent of each IQ category that is assumed to be in the deprived group and the number that are

to receive an increment of 20 IQ points as a consequence of projected change to an environment of abundance:

IQ RANGE	NUMBER OF 100 IN THE RANGE	PERCENT DEPRIVED	NUMBER DEPRIVED
under 70	3	50	1
70–79	7	60	4
80–89	16	45	7
90–99	24	35	9
100–109	24	15	4
110–119	16	5 }	
120–129	7	0.5 }	1
130 and over	3	0.1 }	

Each of those in the deprived category is to be given 20 additional IQ points. The resultant changes yield Figure II, very different

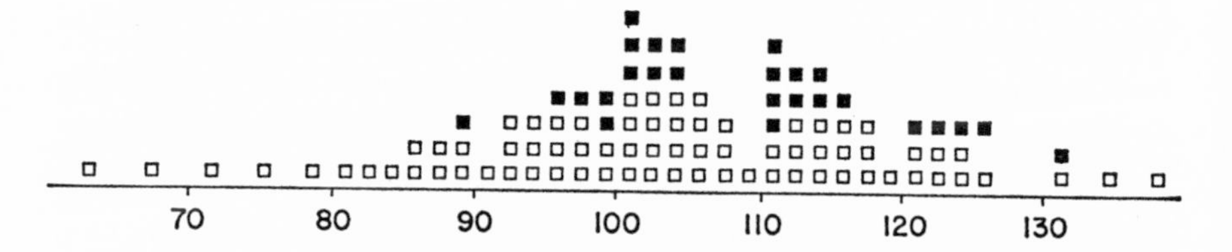

Figure II. Distribution of IQ scores after correction for deprived environment

from the normal or bell-shaped curve representing the generally accepted view about intelligence in the nation and, in fact, in nature. The squares or cells (each representing one out of a hundred individuals) that are darkened are those that have been shifted.

The next stage in projecting change requires an estimate of the percentage of Americans who grow up in a *normal* as against an *abundant* environment. In his study Bloom judged that the difference between these two accounts for about 10 IQ points.

In the absence of criteria even as reliable as those for determining the deprived environment, a rough but highly conservative estimate of 50 percent will be used. Since the figure of 26 percent was used for the deprived, and now 50 for the normal, we are left with 24 percent as representing the incidence of current abundant en-

vironments. This appears to be a gross exaggeration, but in a discussion like this it is better to make an error of underestimation.

The distribution of 50 percent that will receive an IQ increment of 10 points is shown in this table:

IQ RANGE	NUMBER OF 100 IN THE RANGE	PERCENT NORMAL	NUMBER NORMAL
under 70	3	25	1
70–79	7	30	2
80–89	16	45	7
90–99	24	60	14
100–109	24	70	17
110–119	16	50	8
120–129	7	20	1
130 and over	3	5	0

Applying these increments to the data of Figure II, we now have a new distribution (Figure III). The shaded squares represent movement from the normal to the abundant environment.

When environments of abundance are provided, the distribution of level of functioning intelligence can be dramatically altered. Now more than two-thirds of the population has an IQ of 105 or higher. The current static conception that the distribution forms a normal curve closely approximating the theoretical one, and with a mean IQ of 100, turns out to be a myth—serious and costly, but a myth. Of course, pyschologists intent on having our tests produce such a distri-

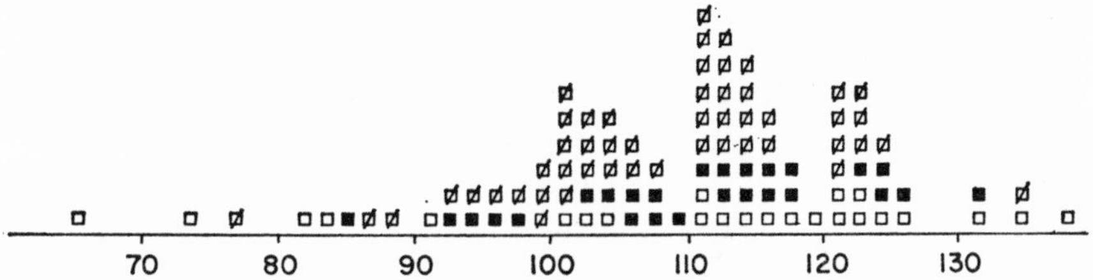

70 80 90 100 110 120 130

Figure III. Distribution of IQ scores after correction for deprived and normal environment

bution could easily do so by developing more difficult tests, but that would not salvage the false static theory. The distribution would look "normal" once again with the mean IQ back down to 100 after

having moved up above 110, but this statistical operation could only conceal, not diminish, the advance in the functioning intelligence of the population. The fact is that educability is not a finite quality; its limits are unknown.

Use of the concept of the abundant environment does not mean that a change in living conditions automatically makes a child better able to learn. Moving a child from a slum tenement to clean public housing could have no positive and even a negative effect on his performance, if, for example, he and his family felt cut off from friends. The theory espoused in this book is neither strictly environmental nor biological but interactionist: A socio-biological organism interacts with a social and material environment and develops as he himself participates in controlling the environment. The abundant environment Bloom suggested would surely be found to be associated with at least the middle-class physical environment, but its striking and developmentally significant characteristics are the quality of relationships and intellectual functioning of the parents and other important persons in the life of the child, which are by no means synonymous with middle-class life.

It is a further fact that our analysis has not exhausted the possibilities for change in IQ in the population. For one thing, Bloom's concept of the abundant environment specifically excludes the schools. In his view more than half of all intellectual development occurs by the age of four and even more by the time the child enters kindergarten. That leaves some 40 percent of development to be subject to influence by the formal educational experience and considerably more if schooling begins before kindergarten. Every child is affected by his experiences in the classroom, even the child whose home provides considerable opportunities for stimulation, interaction, and exploration. During the three and later the six or seven hours he spends in school, he is in one kind of real environment or another—a normal or abundant one; perhaps in some instances a deprived one. It is difficult to estimate the shift in the IQ distribution that would follow if we transformed all our schools into institutions in tune with the enormous capacity of children to be curious, excited, and involved in learning. Surely the effect would be substantial.

To use another example of possible change, our analysis has not

considered the effects of future social changes on premature birth and birth accidents. The lowest 3 percent of our IQ distribution consists of three different groups of subnormal people. The severely defective (who are totally dependent) compose about one-tenth of 1 percent of the country's population, the moderately retarded about three-tenths of 1 percent, and the mildly retarded make up the rest of the 3 percent.[16] Some among these three groups are brain-damaged children whose condition was caused by birth injury or postnatal accidents. These are usually associated with poverty and with inadequate medical and parental care respectively. Social change can prevent most of these cases. Other cases are caused by kernicterus, a disease of the birth period caused by excessive amounts of bilirubin in the blood stream. Recent understanding of its etiology and the development of treatment methods (exchange transfusions) "have reduced the incidence of this condition almost to the vanishing point in certain clinics."[17]

Other cases are caused by such prenatal factors as infections—congenital syphilis, for instance, which is clearly a social problem subject to a great degree of control and prevention. Other prenatal factors are genetic in origin, due most often to single mutant genes. Recent advances in knowledge about the "mechanisms by which the respective metabolic disorder injures the brain or interferes with its growth and function" give promise of some prevention of the manifestation of the genetic factor. Already two types seem to be yielding to control.[18]

We have seen that investigators believe many of the 8 percent of the population prematurely born suffer effects that interfere with optimal vision, hearing, and coordination. Except for a few who are noticeably damaged, the others are not distinguishable from their classmates, and their defects can be inferred only from their performance. The possibility of dramatically reducing the incidence of prematurity is great. Such action would further elevate the IQ's of perhaps 5 percent of our population, some ten million people.

Nor has our analysis so far taken into consideration the opportunities for facilitating intellectual development by improving the mental health of the total community; or by using drugs and chemicals to facilitate cognitive development in special types of cases;

or by simply improving the human diet, which we know would dramatically improve mental health and general development.

To sum up, the estimated shift in mental functioning as between Figures I and III is not only conservative; it also represents only that which is now concretely possible as soon as our nation wills the changes. Other possibilities of equal or perhaps greater import to cognitive development may well emerge in another half-century or so. Poverty is a relative matter, as anyone comparing India with America readily notes. The same is true of abundance, especially when it is defined in intellectual and spiritual as well as material terms. In family life, parent-child relations, the processes of education, we are a long way from knowledge of what represents their most advanced forms, and we are even further from mastery in implementing what we know. Most important, as always, is the mobilized power of people who want these changes to occur. This kind of group learning is similar to that of the individual: The most important stage in the developmental process is that at which the child takes over his own learning and consciously seeks understanding and mastery of his environment. As in the past, the people of America will continue to recognize new intellectual heights within the power of their children and will demand the conditions necessary for the fulfillment of their wish. Imagine, then, the advances in intellective functioning as the people of America—and the world—conquer each new height.

And that will not be the end, nor is it likely ever to come, for man makes himself. His power to change himself is beyond any limits conceivable today. Until an open-ended concept of his intellectual powers is accepted, one that concedes ignorance about the possible limits of mental development under varying conditions, our system of education will be in bondage to a mythical formulation.

The term "crisis" is so hackneyed that we have become inured to it. Yet sometimes its use is justified, and one of those times is now. For the country faces a crisis of confidence in the decisions that are being made to solve its educational problems. The time is fast approaching when current experimental programs will be found to yield pitifully little, when hopes will be dashed, and when the

hardware of modern technology will stand as a monument to well-intentioned but woefully misguided beliefs about why people do not learn.

Miscalculations are inevitable in the process of evolving new theories and forms. Ehrlich had to try 606 times before he discovered the drug to destroy the syphilis organism. The only condition science imposes on experiments that fail is that the experimenters analyze and evaluate the causes of failure. Unless this is carried to the level of theory, the consequences may be grave. Unless the behavioral scientists and educational researchers come to recognize that late-twentieth-century aspirations cannot be fulfilled under the guidance of nineteenth-century conceptions of man, not even if the ideology masquerades in sophisticated twentieth-century statistical design and is analyzed by means of near-twenty-first-century data processing equipment—unless they recognize these facts, they and the readers of their reports are likely to reach false conclusions.

Experimenters must recognize that the outcomes can be no better than the ideas from which they are derived. Unless this is understood and accepted, leading to a critical review of the prevailing ideas, there is the serious danger that professionals and the public will conclude, as large segments of both have done from the start, that the inferior academic achievement of the disadvantaged is due not to their disadvantage—for look at all our efforts and all for nought—but to their nature. The word will pass once more that there really are innate racial and ethnic differences in intelligence. And the pressures to make that interpretation will increase, for the alternatives involving significant social as well as educational changes are not easy ones. Unabashedly to admit the depth of the social crime of the past centuries, its continued existence today, and the deep wounds in the children and in those yet unborn which we have caused—to admit this is more than some can bear. Even to yield the short-term benefits of keeping the disadvantaged "in their place" is more than some of the general public are willing to do. They will not give up their restricted housing practices or their segregated schools, or pay higher school taxes for other children. To reject a habitual way of comprehending human behavior (to many, the basis of their expertise) or even to question its tenability is more than some in the social and behavioral sciences and in education

can tolerate. Together, by protecting the hoary myths about educability, diverse groups, including some of the wealthy, the influential, and the intellectuals, serve each other's interest.

The course of events in the near future is likely to bring a higher percentage of Negroes into the middle class, including an increased percent of college students and graduates. These events, deliberately planned through intense recruitment, compensatory programs, scholarships, will serve to give a "better share" of the fruits than before; they will not materially alter the conflict-producing circumstances of the disadvantaged, who are and will continue to include a large percentage of our Negro, Indian, Puerto Rican, Mexican, and lower-class white populations. They will continue to be disadvantaged. They will organize and protest. Scientists and educators will be compelled to choose between the two explanations: These people are inferior by nature; we continue to keep them in a state of inferiority.

The battle over theory (a battle over strategy too) is not unique, nor is it limited only to those phenomena that are patently social. Writing about the structure of scientific revolutions, Thomas Kuhn, a Princeton professor, remarked that the scientific community "often suppresses fundamental novelties because they are necessarily subversive of its basic commitments." But at some point anomalies arise as normal science—the activity that involves most of the members of the scientific community—fails to solve problems. Others arise as a piece of equipment (read, "an experimental educational project") "fails to perform in the anticipated manner, revealing an anomaly that cannot, despite repeated effort, be aligned with professional expectation." When the profession "can no longer evade anomalies that subvert the existing tradition of scientific practice—then begin the extraordinary investigations that lead the profession at last to a new set of commitments, a new basis for the practice of science."[19]

Necessity produces change. When this occurs, "time-honored scientific theory" is rejected as new theory which solves the contemporary problems replaces the old. The ensuing change, as Kuhn stresses, is not simply the addition of new knowledge to an accumulation of old but rather a fundamental transformation. The assimila-

tion of the new "requires the reconstruction of prior theory and the re-evaluation of prior fact."[20]

Necessity will produce fundamental changes in the theory of the behavioral sciences. When it does, behavioral sciences will experience their own scientific revolution, and, as "time-honored theories" are rejected, new concepts will be formulated that will serve mankind better in the never ending effort to solve problems. And such new ideas, providing deeper insight into human development, learning, and teaching, will enable the schools to serve the children better. But we need not assume that progress must wait upon these changes.

10

SOME QUESTIONS, SOME ANSWERS

Conditions in the city schools have become so desperate that Edgar Z. Friedenberg, sociologist and articulate critic of the schools, published an article late in 1967 entitled "Requiem for the Urban School." To him and to others, including some city superintendents in moments of unguarded candor, the situation is almost hopeless because the cities have neither the budgets, the personnel, nor the facilities to cope with the accumulated problems caused by years of neglect.[1] The schools with able students have been supported while those attended by many students classified as dull and backward have been largely ignored, as if their education could yield only marginal returns. Now with the crisis at hand, educational leaders charged to deal with it can bring to bear only the same theories that misguided them in the past.

"Brutal pessimism" was Binet's succinct description of the belief that intelligence is a fixed quantity. How discouraging it is sixty years later to find expressions of the same "brutal pessimism" by those with major responsibilities to improve the schools.

Plato's spirit lives on, and his conception of human ability and special education for an elite shows itself in many forms. In the late 1950's the Rockefeller Brothers Fund, Inc., sponsored the publication of a report on the problems in the nation's schools. More than forty leading Americans—among them John W. Gardner, who later became Secretary of Health, Education and Welfare, were involved in the preparation or review of the report, which was published in

1958 under the title *The Pursuit of Excellence.* The schools, it said, are creating inequalities by insisting that all children have the same exposure to education, regardless of differences in interest and capacity. Equality of opportunity, an essential in a democracy, is not equivalent to uniformity of treatment, which is a disservice to the more able who are thereby deprived of more challenging work. The American system of education has evolved into a lock step in which all start off at age six and move forward together one grade at a time. The report concluded that the ablest students are often exposed to programs that are too thin and unchallenging because some educators reject the idea of ability grouping.

The history of education reveals certain persistent characteristics of the differential system of education. They are all there in this report. Native ability is not "the sole ingredient in superior performance," for excellence is "a product of ability and motivation and character." Many with ability fail to go beyond high school, and while the problem for some is financial, for many it is "that their family and neighborhood environment have not provided them with the motivations and values which produce educational ambition." How clearly the authors of this report have stated a modern-day version of Platonic ideas about education: Mediocrity is the fault of the individual; lack of motivation is the fault of the family and neighborhood environment. After hearing this same dirge for so many centuries, isn't it finally time to ask where, in the assignment of responsibility for adequate motivations and appropriate values, are the society at large, and the forces of societal power for which these Americans were a voice?

The question would be futile. Later the report declares, "Any educational system is, among other things, a great sorting-out process." The sorting is done to identify and guide the able and to challenge each student to develop his capacities to the utmost. The sorting out should be done "mercifully and generously, rather than ruthlessly, rigidly or mechanically." The general academic capacity should be "at least tentatively identified by the eighth grade . . ." The school personnel are given a special charge in respect to those who are able. "Within the framework of concern for all, guidance should give particular attention to able students." The guidance counselors should help insure that each student has the kind of

program that will develop to the full the gifts he possesses. This means attention to individual differences and sensible experimentation with various kinds of flexibility in the curriculum to satisfy the varying needs of students. "And especially it means providing unusually able boys and girls with rigorous and challenging experiences."[2]

The authors of the report express no doubt whatever about individuals having a fixed ability level or about the availability of the measuring instruments to identify that level. Furthermore, as their own statements indicate, they believe that able students need "particular attention" more than less able students, and that unusually able students need "rigorous and challenging experiences" more than ordinary able students or just plain average students. Yet our analysis of the determinants of educability is clear on the point that the origin and development of intelligence depends to a substantial—but unknown—degree upon the attention the child gets, the stimulation, the challenge, and the rigor of the planned experiences that make up a curriculum from prekindergarten through at least the high-school level.

This 1958 report was written by key persons in American society, some of them now in even more influential posts. The chairman of the overall study project, which yielded reports on military security, foreign economic policy and other areas in addition to that of education, was New York Governor Nelson A. Rockefeller. Others included Mr. Gardner, Dean Rusk, Charles H. Percy, David Sarnoff of Radio Corporation of America, physicist Edward Teller, psychiatrist Dana L. Farnsworth, economist Eli Ginzberg, sociologist David Riesman, as well as Dael Wolfle, executive officer of the American Association for the Advancement of Science, Fred M. Hechinger, now education editor for the *New York Times,* presidents of several leading universities, and leading publishers, editors, and bankers.

These distinguished Americans concluded that the less able were deterring the education of the more able, despite the tenuous evidence at the time about the merits of ability grouping for able students. More recently, as we have seen, the evidence is substantial that such grouping does not improve the achievement of any group.

More significant than the proposal on grouping is the fact that so many leading people would diagnose an alleged conflict between

quality and equality as one of the major ills of the schools. The year 1958 was, it must be noted, only four years after the historic Supreme Court decision of *Brown v. Board of Education,* May 17, 1954, outlawing racial segregation in the schools and declaring separate education to be unequal. It was little more than a decade after the largest migrations to urban centers began. It was a period of stress for the schools, a time of high tide in the movement to the suburbs, to new communities and newly created schools with newly selected faculty, including many young teachers on their first job. It was a year after Sputnik, too soon as yet for the schools to have benefited from federal largess "for defense" and following a period of budget cutting and other attacks on public education. It was early in a period during which scientists and scholars from the universities ventured forth into the public schools (facetiously called slumming) to modernize and revitalize the science and mathematics curricula, and later other programs of study. This was the time when teachers, tired of their position as "headless horsemen" or second-class citizens, of a TV image of a good-hearted boob as played by Eve Arden, and tired especially of low salaries and a muted voice if any in school policy making, were developing stronger, more militant teacher organizations. It was a time, too, when students in colleges and universities declared themselves against segregation and risked their interests and sometimes their safety by their action.

To paraphrase Charles Dickens, these were the best of times in education, and these were the worst of times—the worst because of the many complex problems that new conditions had generated, but the best because these same new conditions offered the hope of a great future. Major modifications in social and educational institutions generally are accomplished, like childbirth, only with risk and pain. Yet those who participated in preparing the report responded to the times by seeing in universal high-school education a threat to the welfare of the talented rather than the great promise of more talent and more personal fulfillment.

In reflecting on the report one cannot help but wonder how familiar the authors themselves were with the schools. In 1961 Mr. Gardner, in his popular book, *Excellence,* supplied some answers. Commenting that differences in educational opportunity will never be eradicated, he went on to make the following incredible state-

ment: "But it would be wrong to leave the impression that stratification of educational opportunity is still a dominant feature of our system. It is not." At another point he observed: "Even the most casual glance at our education system will reveal our great reluctance to put labels on individual differences in general capacity."[3] One is tempted to wonder if the glances were not too casual, for neither of these observations seems remotely related to the reality of our schools, where stratification is maintained even within a single school building by the device of ability grouping, and where the lowest group is labeled by the students if not by the teachers as "the dummies." One can only hope that Mr. Gardner's experience as Secretary of Health, Education and Welfare gave him a different perspective.

The *Pursuit of Excellence* report plays a prominent role in the concluding chapter of a recent interesting book on twentieth-century American education, *Schools in an Age of Mass Culture,* by Willis Rudy. The author, a historian, considers the ultimate value of democratic education as it has developed in this country in this century. To what extent, he asks, is "man in the mass improvable, even educable? Can the school build a new social order which will produce a 'new man,' or must there *first* be the 'new man'?" In answer to these questions he turns to the opinions of Edward L. Thorndike, whose studies on learning during the first quarter of the century we have already noted. This pioneer American psychologist was a strong advocate of free public education but he had little faith in its ability to transform mankind and he ridiculed the "educational evangelists" who promised that the right education would make people healthy, wealthy, and wise. Instead he placed reliance upon a eugenics program of selective breeding to increase the productivity of intellectually and morally good stock, for he believed that the child's potential for educational and vocational achievement was determined by heredity. The function of education was twofold: for the intellectually elite, to prepare them for leadership to improve the lot of all; for the rest of mankind, who have really not appreciated and made best use of their good leaders, an education to prepare them for intelligent followership.[4]

After presenting Thorndike's views Rudy referred to an article published in 1920 by Professor R. M. Harper of the University of

Alabama, who asserted that the progress of civilization in any society depended upon one ten-thousandth of the population.[5] Rudy then cited the *Pursuit of Excellence* report to support the thesis that leading Americans were becoming convinced that "the actual survival of American democracy depended, first, on the cultivation of such a creative segment and, second, on the development of an appreciation among the masses of the people of the vital contributions such talents were capable of making."[6] The author was careful to point out that the appreciation of excellence in a democracy is different from the ancient concept of differential education for a tiny elite, and for slaves, serfs, and artisans.

These, of course, are old arguments wrapped in an up-to-date package, and offered to the public by leading Americans. Before the nation has had an opportunity to test the possibilities of secondary and even higher education on a universal basis, leaders reach the conclusion that there is a most talented group that will be handicapped if educated with the less talented, and that each group must have a different kind of education. And the fate of the American people hinges on a solution to this problem, according to the Rockefeller report! The ideology of the leaders is transmitted to teachers in textbooks like Rudy's.

Why are such conclusions reached *before* the inequities are eliminated, and *before* the nation uses its great intellectual and material resources to overcome the schools' inadequacies? Why is the Platonic concept of an intellectual elite perpetuated when the country is approaching the time when it can become a laboratory to test the effects of universal education and to determine the percent of its population that can perform at a high level? One answer to questions like these was given by a leading pioneer in the psychoanalytic movement, Alfred Adler, who was as cognizant of social as of biological determinants of behavior. In 1927, in *Understanding Human Nature,* he wrote: "The real reason for assuming that character is inherited lies elsewhere. This evasion enables anyone who has the task of education to escape his responsibilities by the simple gesture of blaming heredity for the pupil's failures." Those who now support the view expressed in the report on excellence are prejudging the capacities for learning of the great mass of the people and evading their responsibility to work indefatigably at improving

the very school systems whose shortcomings they have been at pains to point out.

In all the years that men have discussed quality education they have talked of an elite student body. Generally they have created one: whether in Plato's Greece or Thorndike's America, the children who are given the best education—the best teachers, the richest programs, and usually the best facilities—are those who by and large come from the upper social groups. What would happen if all these components of the best education were to be applied to a different student body? What would happen if the faculty of the Bronx High School of Science, often cited as one of the country's best, were to be transferred willingly to one of the ghetto schools?

Equality, the mechanics of Philadelphia predicted in 1830, would be an empty shadow until "the means of equal instruction shall be equa-secured to all . . ." The means of equal instruction have still not been "equa-secured" to all, and the steps we are taking in our country today are too small to justify a forecast that it will be achieved in the foreseeable future. Yet experts today make judgments as if they knew what human performance would be like under conditions of equal instruction. They make them at a time when in the schools of the nation's capital "many children classified as retarded by the schools simply need glasses or hearing aids," and the assistant principal of a junior high school cautions a shocked young teacher on her first day of school, "Don't expect too much from these kids. . . . Just keep them moving along as best you can, and don't break your heart over how stupid they are." And in the same system the former superintendent, who did not mean to absolve teachers of the responsibility of poor teaching, once said that "the greatest problem the schools face is that large numbers of children are entering school uneducable."[7]

The difficult conditions in the schools are no cause for "brutal pessimism" about intelligence but a challenge to the intelligence of those in a position to influence the future shape of education. And they can be sure their intelligence is going to be tested in that fashion because the intelligence of the common man, raw and unrefined as it may be, leads him as it did the mechanics of Philadelphia to press and press further for the education of his children.

Desperate as the present conditions of our city school systems are,

they are not beyond our ability to repair. Changes do not depend upon new knowledge; we know enough now to bring about some dramatic improvements. Here are some steps that can be taken.

1. We need a clear mandate to make the schools first-rate, and this mandate must include money. Those who wish to estimate the cost might take the per capita expenditure for all purposes, including buildings, in the best school systems in the country, add a small amount (perhaps 10 or 20 percent) for compensatory purposes, and multiply this by the number of children in the schools. Our country has the necessary financial resources to do all of this and more; what we need is the desire to use them for these purposes.

In the *New York Times* annual education review of January 12, 1968, Fred M. Hechinger writes that education gets more money than ever but "not nearly enough to do the vast job." The total expenditure is $52 billion, almost 7 percent of the gross national product. Over $18 billion goes to higher education, leaving less than $34 billion for all public and private education from preschool through high school. If the public schools were to have the class size of the academically successful private elementary and secondary schools, they would need classes half the present size, which means twice the number of teachers.

According to the recent *Report of the National Advisory Commission on Civil Disorders,* the financial need of the cities is great and neither state nor federal government is satisfying it. In Detroit alone, to bring the teacher-pupil ratio in line with the average ratio in the state of Michigan would call for almost 17,000 additional teachers at an annual cost of about $13,000,000.

When will the people advocate the expenditure of the necessary money? What will bring it about? How much worse will the situation become before the community awakens sufficiently to the need to demand the funds from the state and federal treasuries?

2. The second urgent need is for a change in the composition of the local school board. Unless it is representative of all segments of the population, and particularly of that segment that has been represented meagerly if at all, the lowest social class, the board may as in the past use such additional resources as it obtains for the benefit of the advantaged groups only.

The local school boards have ultimate responsibility for the

success or failure of the public schools in the community. They select the superintendent and are responsible for policy in the hiring and promoting of teachers. Salary scales, building programs, and even curriculum matters come under their purview. The way they do their job is of major consequence to the health of the system.

In the late 1950's Neal Gross, Harvard professor of education, studied a group of officials who "run the schools." The subjects were 508 board members and 105 school superintendents in Massachusetts. Asked what they considered the major obstacle to doing their job in a professional way, nearly one in five superintendents picked his school board. Some board members "felt their jobs were political-patronage posts and many of them sought election to the board to represent special segments of the community."[8] Gross recommended state legislation forbidding malpractices in such areas as business and personnel patronage and to guard against conflicts of interest.

In neighborhoods or communities with predominantly lower-class children, the board members should come predominantly from that group. If the area is largely Negro, then so should the membership be. Those who assert that the low level of education of the adults disqualifies them would do well to remember in the first instance that boards with well-educated members have done a hopelessly poor job in the cities, and, in the second, that it was the uneducated working men who played the major role in winning previous campaigns for free public education. Their participation is essential if the parents and the children themselves are to be convinced that the schools are really theirs and are in operation to educate them with as much devotion and enthusiasm as any other children. An old slogan can be appropriately adapted to the compelling need of all disadvantaged groups to have the chief responsibility in shaping the policy of the schools their children attend: No education without representation.

If the boards of education were responsive to the needs of the children, they would say to the people at large and to political leaders at every level of government: The schools are in desperate condition. Unless you give us the funds, you will be responsible for their continued and accelerated deterioration, and for the terrible social consequences when the patience of the people is exhausted.

Will the quality of board members be improved? Will their

composition be changed so that they will be in fact representative of all school children and will demand whatever is necessary to see that all the children are properly educated? What actions will be necessary to bring about these changes?

3. Our third need is for educational leaders with convictions about the educability of children and the courage to carry out thoroughgoing changes in the entire system. Let the cities hire management specialists to handle the business affairs of the system, but not to serve as superintendents and principals. Only those persons should be selected who recognize that we have hardly begun to tap the intellectual resources of the population and are prepared to give teachers this orientation. These administrators must also be strong enough to stand up to the economy-minded and to other enemies of public education.

School administrators, especially superintendents and principals, find themselves at a crossroads today as the teacher organizations alter the power balance in the system. Formerly the administrator made recommendations to the policy-making board of education and carried out those policies with little or no consultation with the faculty. He cannot do that now, not at least in the major urban centers and in many of the smaller cities and towns. As a result, he is faced with these choices: a bullheaded determination to carry on as before which can only lead to failure; a quiet retreat and uninvolvement which can only lead to chaos; a democratic relationship with his faculty which can only lead to the infusion of ideas and an invigoration of the schools. Unless they want to end up as errand boys for boards of education that engage in a running battle with organized teachers, they will see themselves as first-among-teachers, as leaders of the Horace Mann type who have the courage to find out what the schools need and to say it even at the displeasure of some in the community. In other words, they would do well to win and hold the respect of their teachers as intelligent educators who are pleased to get ideas from their faculty and share ideas with them. Such administrators do not permit the kind of deadening faculty meetings that are empty of substance and clearly calculated to avoid controversy. They seek to develop systems for the continuing involvement of teachers in the process of evaluation and improvement of education and in the formulation of school policy.

In a sociological study of staff leadership in the public schools, Gross and Herriott were interested in what they called "executive professional leadership." An administrator has such leadership ability if his role definition stresses improvement in the quality of performance of members of his faculty and staff. For example, a principal with this ability will tend to have constructive suggestions for teachers in connection with their problems; he will give them the feeling that they can make important contributions to raising the performance of students; he will make faculty meetings valuable educational experiences.

The investigators found that the higher the principals' ratings in executive professional leadership, the higher the morale of teachers. The teachers feel pride and enjoyment in their work, loyalty to the school, respect for the judgment of the administrators, acceptance of the philosophy underlying the curriculum, and, of great importance, they work cooperatively. Specifically, the classroom performance is better, they use more creative methods of individualizing instruction, and, as one would expect of a phenomenon that improves *teaching,* the children's *learning* seems to improve. Various indices of pupil performance like achievement test scores are higher in schools in which the principal is a better leader. These results are not and cannot be as conclusive as one would like, because a school system that selects able principals usually has other features that make it a better system than others, and it is difficult to pinpoint beyond any doubt the cause of higher morale or improved performance. The study by Gross and Herriott, nonetheless, gives convincing evidence.

Among the conditions that stand in the way of a principal's serving as leader of his professional staff, they found the following: Some principals are quite unwilling to allow teachers to participate in decision making about central school issues. In contrast are the principals who encourage teachers to become involved in evaluation of the school, or in establishing policies about supervision or discipline or performance levels. Another obstacle to effective leadership is the principal's stress on a distinction in status; that is, some of the poorer principals insist upon maintaining a bureaucratic and remote relationship to the teachers. This contrasts with the behavior of the more effective principals, who tend, for example,

to be informally friendly with members of their faculty. The less effective principals are unwilling or unable to work at cultivating an easy relationship with teachers and a "we-feeling" in the faculty. They tend to be inconsistent in decision making and in other activities that should provide good managerial support for the staff. Finally, they fail to stand behind teachers when their authority is questioned.

One very important implication of this study is that many school systems are using the wrong criteria in selecting principals. Apparently there is no need to call for a particular kind or amount of teaching experience in candidates for principalships, nor even for experience as an assistant or vice-principal. Those with experience often become inured to the defects of the system and are less likely to recognize or change faulty practices. The number of undergraduate and graduate courses in education and even in educational administration also seems to be irrelevant; so are the sex and marital status of the candidate. On the other hand, Gross and Herriott report, the characteristics that should be preferred in selecting candidates for the principalship are: "A high level of academic performance and knowledge, a high order of interpersonal skill, a motive for service, the willingness to commit off-duty time to their work, and relatively little seniority as teachers."[9]

The two investigators urged that the universities and schools collaborate in helping the new principal by offering specially prepared summer courses after his or her first year or two. These courses would provide an opportunity for reflection, discussion, and the consideration of methods for solving the real-life problems of the principal. It is interesting that their investigation has led them to recommend for principals what other studies and many observations have recommended for teachers—that a most important need during the first few years is for both support and supervisory help from a source outside the school, perhaps in the form of a collaborative arrangement between school and university.

Are there administrators who could give such leadership? Are there some who would insist on community participation in policy making, demand the necessary budget, and innervate the instructional program? Indeed there are, and a few of them have already demonstrated that kind of leadership in isolated slum schools. There

are many more who will function that way when the communities select boards of education that want high quality for all and get the money to do the job of transforming the schools.

We have already asked the relevant question: When will the communities select the kinds of boards that would appoint such superintendents and principals?

4. A fourth need is improvement in teaching. There is much to be desired in the quality of American teaching (although we would be hard put to find a profession or other occupational group which could not be criticized with equal fairness).

Scapegoating is the way out for some at any time of crisis: "Blame it on the teachers." That is why we need to see that our teachers did not ask the society in general and the colleges and universities in particular to give them a poor education and an invalid and pessimistic conception of human ability, and it is just as important to recognize that the low value that many teachers put upon the intellect is pervasive in our society, even as education is highly valued as a commodity that possesses purchasing power.

John Holt, author of *How Children Fail* and *How Children Learn,* in a recent review of two books about the Boston schools in the *New York Review of Books,* blames the teacher for the low quality of instruction in the city schools. To be exciting or at least interesting, he points out, teachers themselves must be excited by and interested in learning. They must find in the pursuit of knowledge the satisfaction of their own curiosity and a fulfillment of needs that no other activity could provide so well. Only under such circumstances is teaching something more than a job, a job no different from one in the post office, except perhaps that it offers more status and sometimes more pay. According to Holt, the teachers in the city schools come from predominantly nonintellectual or even anti-intellectual lower-middle-class families. They did not go into education because they had a love for learning or believed in its importance or even because there was anything in particular they wanted to teach. They went into it because it was a position that did not take much in the way of ability, training, or connections to get into and it was secure if they did what they were told. It was a safe, respectable way to rise a few rungs up the socio-economic ladder. For someone who likes learning and teaching and

is fortunate enough to be assigned to a school where the children are if not eager at least docile, and where the administrators give some freedom and respect if not understanding—even for such a person teaching is difficult and demanding. For the individual who chooses teaching simply as the best of several types of secure occupations available to him, it is an entirely different experience. Holt states it well when he says:

> For someone to whom it is only a job, not a calling—obliged, most of the time, to do exactly what he is told, forbidden, even if he wanted, to use more than a tiny part of his initiative or intelligence or imagination, compelled to play in his classes only the roles of taskmaster, policeman, and judge, harassed and hampered with an infinity of paperwork and petty administrative duties, faced with large classes of bored or hostile children, neither well paid nor highly esteemed, by society or even his own "profession," in which he is all too often looked on and treated like the lowest factory laborer or foot-soldier—for such a person, teaching must be, at best, drudgery and, at worst, a nightmare.[10]

Such people have never had freedom and do not have it now. They are very much at home in the conformity-ridden city school system, where there is very little encouragement of, little more support for, and a great deal of hostility toward a free exchange of ideas, challenge, dissent, and controversy. Because they grew up in it, they are comfortable in this kind of bland scholastic atmosphere in which orthodoxy is rewarded.

Although the ideology of many of our teachers is incompatible with good education, they are not some strange breed. They seem to be what the public wants them to be, and they seem to have been this way for some time. In a 1957 article in the *Nation,* Arnold A. Rogow declared that the American public is not interested in intellectual things or nonconforming ideas, and that it does not want the schools to be questioning institutions and values. Its teachers should be unquestioning and noncritical, accepting community customs and mores, and reading *Reader's Digest* and *Life.*[11] When the controlling voices of the public want teachers to be independent and unorthodox in their thinking, and when the teachers themselves want that, the teachers will be so.

Constraints upon the teacher do not have to take the form of punitive action or even the threat of it. Many of those who are in

teaching, and especially those who take positions in the more provincial communities, have no desire to conduct themselves in a way that conflicts with the norms. Sociologist W. B. Brookover says that many teachers have "so completely internalized the desires and beliefs of the controlling group that these attitudes are clearly their own."[12] This occurs as a result of interaction and identification with those in the schools who hold such values and beliefs, and as a result of the desire for the security, status, and approval which those in control are in a position to give or withhold. Teachers respond to the expectations of those in power.

Now, however, the locus of power is changing. As long ago as 1957 H. G. Grobman and V. A. Hines pointed out that the overt constraints are loosening as a result of teacher shortage and changes in cultural standards. The progressive urbanization of the nation should be added as a factor, because life in a big city does not permit control over the private life of the teacher and contributes to loosening his internal constraints.[13] Some internal controls are of course essential if teaching is to be more than just a job, and one new source of them is the teacher organization. Active and vigorous organizations are beginning to breathe new life into the profession and into the schools themselves. They are demanding higher salaries and better working conditions, both of which are conducive to the improvement of education, the former to attract and hold able people and to obviate the need for "moonlighting"; the latter to free the teacher from time-consuming clerical and custodial tasks.

The teachers' greater degree of control over their position is remarkable progress, considering that a majority of the eighteenth-century schoolteachers of the Middle Atlantic region "had come into Philadelphia or Baltimore from England as indentured servants to be sold to the highest bidder. Significantly, a schoolteacher did not bring as high a price as a shoemaker, a cooper, a mason, a carpenter, or a barber."[14] No more than thirty years ago some teachers worked under contracts that prohibited them from having company on week nights or even riding in an automobile, not to mention smoking and drinking, or even marriage in the case of women. Adults who teach children ought to have a sense of pride and self-respect, personal qualities that are difficult to maintain when one works in a servile position. The teacher organizations have made it possible to change

all that, but they will not succeed so long as teachers remain servile to ideas either in their subject field or about learning and teaching. For then the organizations will serve only as an instrument to raise salaries, an important but insufficient function of a professional organization or a union.

It remains to be seen how active the organizations will be in changing the norms of the profession, and in setting high-quality instruction for all children as the appropriate aspiration for people in the profession. If they succeed they will help attract and retain able people for whom the pressures for conformity and the nonintellectual climate of many schools now create serious conflicts. W. W. Charters described such a conflict as an "occupational disadvantage, driving more competent persons out of the ranks of teaching and leaving behind those who are the most compliant and submissive or, perhaps, those who are most able to tolerate ambiguity and cope with conflict."[15]

If any educational or professional agency is to have an effect on teachers already in the schools, it is their own organization, and it would be well for such organizations to actively help uproot the ingrown tendency to place blame for failure upon the students' inherent weaknesses. It is interesting that this habit of thought seems to become established through experience in the school system. In a study of the effects of three years of experience in New York schools upon graduates of the four colleges of the City University of New York, the investigators found as one change "a decline in the tendency to attribute pupil misbehavior or academic difficulty to the teacher or the school."[16] With each passing year the teachers seem increasingly to lose confidence in the schools' and their own capabilities to alter children's functioning. Some force must be activated to counter this pessimism and defeatism.

Will teachers be given better education? Will the public demand, at least desire, or even just tolerate active intellects, independent and unorthodox thinkers? Will the teacher organizations work as hard at raising standards as at increasing wages, in particular at changing the conception of ability and expectations for student achievement?

5. A fifth need is improvement of teachers' education. Their undergraduate program consists first of general education (humani-

ties, physical and social sciences), then of a major field of study (such as biology or English literature), and only thereafter of the professional aspect of teaching (such as educational psychology, methods of teaching, and a supervised teaching experience). The last of these three aspects of their undergraduate program makes up only about 18 to 30 percent of the total course work, and in some instances even less. Many leaders in government and the universities find an outlet for their frustration over general urban conditions by scapegoating teachers and *their* teachers in departments of education, forgetting that 70 to 82 percent and sometimes even more of the teacher-education curriculum is in the liberal arts.

Since there are few ways in which the effectiveness of colleges can be evaluated, and since the success of their teacher graduates is one of these ways, the inadequacy of many working teachers suggests that the colleges and universities are failing in the education of their students. *They* are failing, and students who are not apathetically going along with the game of doing whatever is necessary to earn a diploma and a good job are protesting.

To be sure, the teacher-education sequence in the universities is to be faulted for excessive superficiality, duplication, and unrelatedness to life in the schools, but the primary fault in the education of teachers is a weakness inherent in undergraduate study in general at the universities. Every subject taught in the general education of the college student (usually in his first two years and constituting almost half of his total program) is potentially relevant to the crucial issues of the human condition that interest most students. Instructors who think that introducing relevance is pandering to low taste and unbecoming the role of the college teacher have a peculiar notion of the purposes of general education and are abjectly ignorant of the values of adolescents. They are, furthermore, carrying out the conservative role of the intelligentsia that Mannheim wrote about in his *Ideology and Utopia* and that Thorstein Veblen early in the century described in his devastating attack upon the universities. That is, the professors are teaching in such a way as to keep things in the society unchanged, offering "preprocessed gospel" dressed up in the respectable terminology of scholarship but generally with no reference to controversy, no matter how critical the matter under discussion.

Clearly there are differences among institutions of higher learning in respect to orthodoxy and conformity versus independence and dissent. Some are more likely than others to produce those quiet and respectable young teachers, so much appreciated by many school systems, who cannot be accused of ever entertaining an unorthodox idea—that is, one not officially sanctioned by one teacher or another —and who, in fact, can quite safely be declared innocent of ever having an idea of their own, about teaching or anything else.

In *The Academic Mind,* the pioneer study published in 1958, investigators rated the permissiveness of social-science faculties at different types of colleges, all of which are educating teachers. Permissiveness was defined as tolerance of controversy, dissenting ideas, and nonconforming faculty and students. Among the large private colleges (Harvard and Yale, for example) 57 percent were "clearly permissive"; in the very large public institutions (California and Michigan) 55 percent were so rated; in the small public colleges (Texas Southern University), 23 percent; the teachers' colleges (Ball State Teachers, Muncie, Indiana), 27 percent; the Protestant colleges (Baylor University, Waco, Texas), 32 percent; and finally the large Catholic institutions (Notre Dame), 12 percent, and the small Catholic colleges (Holy Cross), 3 percent. There have probably been changes in the intellectual climate in some of these categories, especially the Catholic institutions, which have been the beneficiaries of the new ecumenical spirit in the Roman Catholic Church. Some of the institutions labeled teachers' colleges in 1958 are now liberal arts colleges, but some of them would in all probability fit in the category of the small public college whose rating on permissiveness was even lower.[17] Nonetheless, the point that emerges is that the student who attends a private university, large or small, or a very large public university, is much more likely to be exposed in the humanities and the physical sciences as well as the social sciences to the values we need in the public schools. But even in the best of the institutions, 43 percent of the professors were not clearly permissive, were not clearly tolerant of controversy, dissenting ideas, and nonconforming faculty and students.

In the decade since *The Academic Mind* was published many colleges have opened their classroom doors somewhat wider, if not to controversy in the respective disciplines then to the conflicts on

the streets, in the slums, on foreign battlefields, and on the campus itself. But while they have gained in one way they have lost in another, for at the same time many of the instructors, figuratively at least, have slipped out of the classroom. It is a regrettable fact that the objectives of some professors could be more easily met if there were no students to occupy their time. Research is often blamed for this, but contributes to it no more than the frequent coming and going of professors who lecture and consult and manage the affairs of their professional and scientific organizations. Scholarship and research are essential to the vitality of an institution, and the other activities often do provide important services, but they have come to displace teaching and to depress it to a very low rank in the hierarchy of values. In Madison Avenue style the universities are rewarding with money and status those who engage in the flashy, publicity-making activities, even if they do not teach a single class; and the instructor dedicated to teaching and devoted to his students goes unnoticed except as he may be appreciated as the workhorse of a department, especially in private institutions dependent upon tuition income.

One of the best safeguards against irrelevance in the curriculum and alienation of the students is their active participation in the review and modification of courses of study. This may take many different forms, ranging from service on a student advisory committee to a dean of instruction, to full and equal membership on the curriculum committee of the institution, to membership on a student committee that offers a duly recognized program of courses that are taught by instructors whom the students select and that parallel courses established by the regular faculty committee. At a minimum each of these approaches provides opportunity for students to make their views about their education known to the administrators and faculty.[18]

Along with the problems of higher education in general go those of teacher education in particular. In the most essential sense the problems are identical: Courses in the so-called foundations—the history, philosophy, psychology, and sociology of education—have been taught in traditional ways with little relevance to the life and the work of the teacher. Partly this is so because the professors ape their counterparts in the arts and sciences departments in their dis-

dain for the schools, and partly because they have not stepped into one for years except perhaps as a parent.

The courses have the same weaknesses as others in the university: they are simply irrelevant, unimportant, unexciting. Yet any one of these foundation subjects is inherently vital and dramatic enough to arouse the interest of even the most sophisticated. The history of education, for example, is one approach to the social history of man. Far from being a dry tale about dead theories of pedagogy, the struggles for free education are exciting chapters in American history, and educational theories of the past seen in the context of their time can be helpful in evaluating and developing contemporary theory. Courses on curriculum and on methods of teaching can be as lively and practical as any in the university bulletin. The curriculum is that portion of the accumulated knowledge of man that children and adolescents study. How it is to be organized and in what form students are to engage themselves with it are important questions worthy of serious thought. Courses on the methods of teaching are widely scorned, yet no one would choose to undergo surgery with a physician who had not been taught to use scalpel and suture or to be defended by a lawyer untrained in courtroom practice. How the teacher teaches, in what sequence he presents concepts, the encounters he arranges for a child as an introduction to new ideas, the procedures he uses to get a group to work together constructively—these are the proper and challenging subject matter of a methods course.

Student teaching is the crowning experience. Usually too much time is given to teaching too many classes with too little close supervision. Students need more time for reflection on their experience and more help in coping with problems that are first apprehended only when they face thirty pupils. To protect them against knuckling under to old-guard teachers and administrators who tell them it is all pretty hopeless, they need support, as they also need it during the first few years of regular full-time teaching.

The education of teachers and of teachers of teachers will be improved as universities and school systems establish close working relationships rather than affairs of convenience. The medical school–hospital collaboration serves as an example of how to safeguard education from irrelevance and detachment, how to give the professor

a continual feedback on the effectiveness of his instructional efforts. As closer collaborators, the universities could then take a more responsible and informed part in the struggle to improve the schools. Nonetheless, as the medical model also shows, it does not automatically follow that the university and the teachers they educate will be inclined to serve the schools most in need of improvement, and the people most in need of excellence in teaching. That will take independent thought and realistic cooperation in both the public schools and the colleges and universities.

6. A sixth need is for a new approach to instruction built on an open-ended conception of educability. The overall design of this new orientation is obvious: Assessment and teaching would go hand in hand, the former indicating the necessary concepts the child has not assimilated and the latter directed to mastery of the concepts through carefully planned learning experiences. In contrast with current test practice, evaluation devices would be used on a continual basis, and for the sole purpose of organizing instruction to teach what is assumed to be learnable by the child. He is expected to learn, and his failure challenges the school staff and the educational researcher to find better ways to help him master the concepts.

Assessment and teaching should begin early in the life of the child, as early as the first year. Nobody who values life and health questions the desirability of regular medical examinations beginning in early infancy. Increasingly we also appreciate the need for periodic evaluations of the emotional-social development of the child, though little enough of this is done in a systematic fashion, and the job of early detection of problems is left to the alert parent, pediatrician, or teacher. Now the time has come for infants and children to have careful attention given to their mental development on a regular schedule. Normal growth of the intellect is obviously as important as that of the body.

It follows from this that substantial funds are necessary to enable the school system to perform the essential functions of evaluation and instruction. Under the new conditions teachers, curriculum specialists, and psychologists would construct two general types of assessment devices. The first, used for periodic checkups, would be designed to evaluate the child's stage of mental development and to identify areas where help is needed. An instrument like Feuerstein's

Learning Potential Assessment Device involving teaching and testing is a prototype. The second type would be used by the teacher as an integral part of instruction in specific subject fields. These would be used to diagnose deficiencies in concept (in arithmetic, for example, this might be the child's failure to grasp the meaning of zero), in skill (such as multiplication of fractions), and furthermore in those basic concepts that undergird all thought (such as reversibility: 5 plus 4 is 9, so 9 minus 5 is 4; *do, re, mi* is up the musical scale, so *mi, re, do* is down).

Some current activity in the United States can be helpful in this big job of recasting concepts and changing diagnostic and teaching methods. Perhaps the major figure among the many investigators and authors is Professor Jerome Bruner, whose publications include the popular little volume *The Process of Education,* and whose most recent work, *Studies in Cognitive Growth,* a collaborative effort, is dedicated to Piaget, "Friend and mentor, whose brilliant insights have given new and powerful form to the study of cognitive growth." Bruner is himself giving new and powerful form to the study of mental growth, and his work has been conducted with much more of an eye toward instruction than Piaget's, another recent book being *Toward a Theory of Instruction.* No brutal pessimist, he has in fact been called an optimist by Piaget, who thinks he is unduly hopeful about the acceleration of learning. The new insights coming from him and others influenced by his work will in time be useful in the transformation of instruction.[19]

The past few years, especially the past two, have seen the publication of many books and articles concerned with the instruction of disadvantaged children. In addition to Gordon and Wilkerson's book,[20] which evaluates compensatory education programs and finds them wanting, some, like Martin Deutsch's, report on studies of the social and psychological factors in slum children's learning,[21] and others concentrate on teaching and general problems of education in the urban school.[22]

Books like these not only add to our insights about children, they also compel the attention of educators and teachers to the effects of long deprivation. The problem, however, is not ignorance about how to teach deprived children but unwillingness to offer them a good education. Their stages of mental development are essentially like

those of other children; stimulating and exciting classes appeal to them as to others; they too respond to teachers whose personal interest in their welfare is apparent. Systematic and cohesive work like Piaget's and Bruner's developing theories applies no less to them and can only lead to better instruction for *all children.* Such new knowledge is to be welcomed wholeheartedly, but at the same time we should remember that we have the competence *now,* without further research, to give all children vastly better schooling than they are getting.

Is integration going to be a necessary condition for the improvement of education? The 1966 report, *Equality of Educational Opportunity*—known as the Coleman report after the Johns Hopkins sociologist who headed the study—suggests that it is. The finding was that a child from a home without much educational strength put with schoolmates with strong educational backgrounds is likely to show increased achievement. On the other hand, children with strong backgrounds do not suffer academically if 10 to 30 percent of weaker students are added (as the White Plains, New York, experience has shown), nor do they suffer if they are clearly in the minority (as Coleman reported).

These findings argue against segregation by ability or by race. But since many of the big cities have exceedingly large black populations (91 percent of all elementary-school enrollment in Washington, D.C., was Negro in 1965–66), integration will be impossible until school districts are set up across city lines, embracing city and suburban children. It seems unlikely that the middle-class suburban groups will permit this at the same time that militant black groups are insisting on separate schools in which they can have the decisive voice. While we strive to change the housing patterns that prevent integration, educators can concentrate on the task of improving the quality of instruction. They can use to advantage the knowledge gained from these studies by insisting on intermingling the abler students with the rest in an effort to raise expectations and to stimulate greater intellectual engagement.

7. We need a dramatically broadened concept of the school. The new community-school idea—in some aspects a very old one in America—is being tried in Chicago, Flint, Michigan, and a few other cities. The community school aims to meet the educational needs of

the whole community. It is meant to be an institution of the people, run by the people, for the people. Its policy board directly represents the citizens in the area it serves, and the members support programs to suit the interests and needs of people of all ages—health, social, psychological, vocational, recreational, and cultural needs as well as educational ones. Open seven days and nights each week, it becomes the center of community life. Because its programs are developed in response to varied interests, it will attract varied kinds of people, including some of those who are now most resistant to school and school people.

Early assessment and teaching would require this educational arm of the community to become part of a child's life shortly after he is born. At the other end of the life span the community school adapts for itself the fine adult-education programs now available in some affluent communities, except that the people who do not frequent such programs now will have more of a voice in saying what they want.

The concept of the community school is very much in the American tradition. If it takes hold and is realized on a large scale it will be a most appropriate culmination to a history of public education that has seen the common man play a major role. The Philadelphia workingmen who demanded public elementary schools for their children would be pleased to know that almost a hundred and forty years later the working people in some sections of America are establishing policy in the schools their children attend. They would be pleased to know too that some cities are providing free education for children under five and higher education for those who are high-school graduates.

8. Education in America needs the attention of more concerned parents rather than fewer. The many lower-class parents who have felt alienated from the schools as a result of their own unhappy experience, and have avoided P.-T.A. meetings and contacts with teachers and principals, would do the community and their children a service by becoming involved. Adults do not need a high-school diploma themselves to know whether their children are interested and are learning. If there are some among the lower-class parents who accept as truth a child's distorted version of an episode in class, teachers will testify to the fact that their counterparts may be found

in every middle-class school. In these times, when many principals and teachers are making a genuine effort to improve the schools, parents can help by distinguishing between good and bad schools, then cooperating with the good and working to improve the bad.

Parents in deprived and disadvantaged groups have long carried especially heavy burdens in trying to achieve good education for their children, as most of them well know. These parents have lately made great progress in voicing their discontent in a few urban areas. More protest, and more constructive action toward change—cooperation with good educators, merciless war against those who are failing the children—is necessary and inevitable.

Parents who seek to intervene actively in their children's education will have to change and probably many will want to if the schools become centers for the cultivation of the intellect. Mothers and fathers have heard their children groan about boring classes and meaningless work, and if they have questioned and listened carefully they have often had to agree with the criticisms. Realizing that the teachers are after all doing what they think the community pays them for—"to get the kids into college" (or trained for a job, whether it exists or not)—parents will say in unmistakable terms that this is not their sole aim for their children.

The schooling of their children could be much more pleasurable for parents if they placed more emphasis on learning and personal development than on the vocational significance of education. But parents should know in advance that there are risks in change if they are frightened by inquiring minds and shocked to find their adolescent children questioning their most cherished ideas.

Families can profitably discuss the new knowledge and new ideas that children bring home with them rather than question them about grades and behavior. It is true that children want to know their parents are interested in the quality of their performance, but if they are to value learning in itself they must see it valued by their parents. The growing mind flourishes in an atmosphere of stimulated interaction with the physical and social environment. Parents who are open-minded and who encourage exploration and who find delight in any or all of the media of expression such as language, mathematics, art, and music, are giving the child what he needs. They must also give him a full measure of freedom to utilize these

in his own way. He should not be pushed to value something merely because they value it. They provide structure enough in the security of a home and in the satisfaction of his needs for love and esteem. The latter need regrettably is sometimes neglected. Children must have the respect of their parents as well as of their teachers; that is, their rights to be individuals and to be different must be secure, a condition which in no way interferes with the parental role. The parent-child relationship is not that of two peers, and the adult must provide the structure and limits that the child requires.

The child's world is a fascinating one but different from that of adults. Whether or not adults enjoy the fresh candor and the delightful fantasies of children, they ought not to laugh at them and certainly not inhibit them. If they wish to understand some of the workings of their child's mind, they will engage in frank and honest conversation about these ideas.

Perhaps the major problem of parenthood is in determining how much freedom to permit and how much constraint to exercise. Often it is not a matter of choice but a reflex-like tendency to be the kind of parent one experienced as a child, or, equally disastrous, to be exactly the opposite. Hence a first task is to emancipate oneself as much as possible from past conditioning and to construct a pattern of behavior consistent with the needs of both child and parents and compatible with what we know about human development and upbringing.

Children require a large degree of freedom. They need freedom to move their limbs, to turn and twist, to creep and crawl; freedom to look, hear, touch, taste, and smell; freedom to experiment and freedom to inquire. Through these opportunities and others like them, and only through these, do they create their intelligence. Such freedom may be denied because adults regard the child as a being so fragile that it must be protected from life itself. Pity the child, for it will grow up to be a helpless adult. Some mothers reveal their overprotectiveness even while carrying the fetus. While few pregnant women have to be advised to avoid daredeviltry on a motorcycle or stunt parachuting, they should not behave as if they were ill.

The problem of some parents is their own fear. They become fearful when their children tread where they have dreaded (or sometimes secretly wished) to go. How will they react if their child brings

home a friend who is identified with a group different from their own? And when his ideas about people, life, politics, or the arts are different from theirs, will they respect him, rationally discussing the differences, or will they shut the door on freedom? Openness to people and openness to ideas are the most frightening of all. The parental defense for those who become overanxious is resistance to change and insistence that the children be an imitation of themselves, with only those changes that will satisfy their own unfulfilled aspirations.

Freedom for infant and child means providing an environment rich in stimuli and in the opportunity to explore them. The stimuli should exercise all the senses. Of course, the child should not be overwhelmed, and it is not necessary to have a Picasso hanging on his wall and the Beethoven Ninth blaring from his own little phonograph, with a stream of "My Sin" perfume released every hour. With a diversity of stimuli he will use all the senses and still be free to pursue the experiences he wants to repeat or to explore at greater depth.

In a description of his version of the ideal learning environment for adolescents, James S. Coleman, the Johns Hopkins sociologist, emphasizes both freedom and responsibility. The environment must be so structured that the student has the opportunity to carry out his own actions and to make mistakes. He should be allowed, in fact compelled, to feel the consequences of his actions, including his mistakes, for the chance to escape them gives encouragement to irresponsibility. Coleman's ideas can be applied in many different forms—in student surveys in the school or the neighborhood, in experiments, role-playing, problem-solving in any and all subjects offered by the school.[23]

Freedom is the key word. There are no political or philosophical connotations in the usage here. Its prominence is earned on empirical grounds. Does that mean that constraint is out? Not at all. The human thrives on freedom, but he can use it only as it is bounded by restrictions.

The infant needs restrictions to ensure his survival. Therefore there are cribs and playpens. Eating feces is not a healthful practice, so the parent pins the diapers firmly and arranges to time rediapering to the infant's bowel schedule. The child must be ready for

school on time. For social experience as well as reasonable parental convenience, he must eat his meals with the family, not haphazardly. When there is homework, he has a given place and a given time for it, and his parents work with him, at the beginning at least, until he masters the controls and know-how necessary to perform his assignments. By experiencing structure and order he is able to discipline his own actions, control his own freedom.

Freedom without discipline is like imagination without structure: the great artist who never puts oil on canvas; the great poet who never shares his verse. Discipline without freedom is like structure or content without imagination: it creates pedants. Important as discipline is, freedom is the key when it is equated with openness of opportunity to know the environment, the precursor to mastering and changing it.

What can parents do to foster the developing intelligence of their child? We cannot say with certainty, but probably they ought to be people who value learning for its own sake—which does not necessarily mean those who are the best educated themselves. They appreciate the satisfaction of curiosity, the desire to understand the world and to have some power in controlling it. Probably they are trying to create a home in which there is a large measure of freedom, with the freedom increasing as the child ages, and, along with the freedom, a substantial measure of control, with the control declining as he ages. There is much social stimulation. People talk and listen and respect each other's view—even those of a child (who is a person, not a cute little thing)—even as they differ with each other. The world the parents open up to the child is truly the world—not just their own racial, ethnic, and social-class group, but others in this country and elsewhere. They help him acquire a sense of and respect for the differences between peoples. They help him develop a sense of history—of past and present and the relationship between the two. They help him appreciate and experience the beauty of language and music and the other arts. And as the supreme achievement of intellectual development, they help him use higher-order forms of conceptualization. They do this by what they are, the way they think and talk. They observe, analyze, sort, and classify. They solve problems and generalize. They encourage him to solve problems.

Regrettably, there is no formula for parenthood. The only way to be sure of a perfect outcome is to be the compleat person. Since such a person can be found only in fiction if at all, the best we can do in our efforts at good parenthood is to strive to make ourselves "compleat," a never ending process but an exhilarating one that can go on to the final breath.

Parents aiming at such an ideal will find themselves in conflict. They will want the best possible education for their own children but will not want it at a cost to other children in the community. They will know that ignorance, like an epidemic, has consequences which go beyond the threshold of the original victim. In all likelihood they will come to understand that their child will benefit from their own involvement in the struggle to improve the schools for all children. They will know that hoarding advantages for themselves or their own social class or group arouses guilt that will find its defense in one way or another. At the moment, guilt and would-be self-defense most often take the form of questions like, "We made it on our own, why can't they?" Aside from the fact that this argument teaches a child both to hate and to resort to rationalizations, the argument itself is inaccurate. From the Pilgrims onward, the generations of Americans who have "made it" have not made it alone. To take just one example, we have seen how many of the services that benefit all children today were "compensatory" at the beginning of the century for children from families with little or no school-going tradition. People tempted to use this argument need only examine history to discover the struggles their own ethnic or national or social group had and the bad name it acquired in the process. They will find also that their group too used some form of power to reach a level of equality in the society.

Will each group concerned with schools and the children in them play its part in introducing new modes of instruction and new forms of school organization? In making the schools the center of community activity in the intellectual and cultural life of the people? In creating the day-to-day social, political, and economic pressures that generate change?

These major needs must be met if we are to cope with the crisis in education. If we ask how and when they will be met, history

gives us some approximate answers. People will declare that token changes are not enough and will demand real change with such force that increasingly their demands will be heeded. More money will be appropriated, the composition of school boards will slowly change until the now unrepresented groups will have a powerful voice, educational leaders will be hired expressly to initiate changes of substance, institutions of higher learning will respond simultaneously by creating new types of experiences for their students as they evolve new conceptions of their role in public education, and teachers will thrive intellectually in this new ferment of ideas. From this ferment and from the strong, active concern of organized parents will come real community schools.

As to when this will come about, history's tentative answer is not a pleasant one. It will come after much travail and many wasted years, after more of what we have witnessed in the past few years in exacerbated form. But it does not have to be this way, if we resolve to learn from history as we create it. And no matter what the delays, *one day it will come*. As Ernest Hemingway said, "Man is not made for defeat."

NOTES & INDEX

NOTES

CHAPTER 1

1. Warner, W. Lloyd, Robert J. Havighurst, and Martin B. Loeb. *Who Shall Be Educated? The Challenge of Unequal Opportunities.* New York: Harper, 1944.

2. "The Rich Get Richer & the Poor Get Poorer . . . Schools." *Carnegie Quarterly,* Carnegie Corporation of New York, 1966, 14, pp. 1–3.

3. *Ibid.,* p. 1.

4. *Ibid.,* p. 2.

5. *Ibid.*

6. "Racial Studies: Academy States Position on Call for New Research." *Science,* 1967, 158, p. 892. See also the symposium on "Race and Science" in *The Columbia University Forum,* 1967, 10, pp. 5–12.

7. Pointed out by Edward B. Fry, professor at Rutgers University. In the fall of 1966 when the country's population was under two hundred million, estimated total enrollment (school and university) was 55,900,000, and teachers at all levels, 2,511,000. *Digest of Educational Statistics,* U.S. Office of Education. Washington: U.S. Government Printing Office, 1966, pp. 2, 5.

8. Boffey, Philip M. "Health Crisis: LBJ Panel Calls for Reshaping American Medicine." *Science,* 1967, 158, p. 1160.

9. Greene, Mary F., and Orletta Ryan. *The Schoolchildren, Growing Up in the Slums.* New York: New American Library, 1967.

10. *Ibid.,* p. 15.

11. *Ibid.,* p. 16.

12. Kozol, Jonathan. *Death at an Early Age: The Destruction of the Hearts and Minds of Negro Children in the Boston Public Schools.* Boston: Houghton Mifflin, 1967.

13. *Ibid.,* pp. 1–7.

14. *Ibid.,* p. 10.

15. *Ibid.,* p. 9.

16. *Ibid.,* p. 207.

17. Kohl, Herbert. *36 Children.* New York: New American Library, 1967, p. 187.

18. *Ibid.,* p. 177.

19. *Ibid.,* p. 188.

20. *Ibid.,* p. 178.

21. *Ibid.*

22. Hechinger, Fred M. "Foreword." In Miel, Alice, *The Shortchanged Children of Suburbia.* New York: Institute of Human Relations Press, 1967.

23. Pines, Maya. *Revolution in Learning.* New York: Harper, 1966.

24. *Ibid.,* p. 231.

CHAPTER 2

1. Rogers, Arthur K. *Student's History of Philosophy.* New York: Macmillan, 1929, p. 67.

2. Popper, Karl R. *The Open Society and Its Enemies.* London: Routledge and Kegan Paul, 1957.

3. Kazamias, Andreas M., and Byron G. Massialas. *Tradition and Change in Education.* Englewood Cliffs, New Jersey: Prentice-Hall, 1965, p. 27.

4. Aristotle. *Politics,* Book V, Chap. 3, p. 224. New York: Macmillan, 1888 edition. In Smith, W.O.L. *Education.* Harmondsworth, England: Penguin, 1957.

5. Butts, R. F. *A Cultural History of Education.* New York: McGraw-Hill, 1947, p. 196.

6. Atkinson, Carroll, and Eugene T. Maleska. *The Story of Education.* Philadelphia: Chilton Co., 1962, pp. 45–47.

7. Locke, John. *Essay Concerning Human Understanding,* Book I, Chap. 2, p. 1 (1690). In Smith, T.V., and M. Grene (eds.). *From Descartes to Kant.* Chicago: University of Chicago Press, 1940, p. 389.

8. Godwin, William. *Enquiry Concerning Political Justice and Its In-*

fluence on Morals and Happiness (3rd edn., 1798), Book I, Chap. 4, pp. 43–44. Quoted in Simon, Brian. *Studies in the History of Education, 1780–1870.* London: Lawrence and Wishart, 1960, p. 49.

9. Smith, Adam. Quoted *ibid.,* p. 50.

10. Mill, James. *Analysis of the Phenomena of the Human Mind* (1829). Quoted *ibid.,* p. 145.

11. Dahlke, H. Otto. *Values in Culture and Classroom.* New York: Harper, 1958, pp. 72–73.

12. *Ibid.,* p. 73.

13. Doughton, I. *Modern Public Education: Its Philosophy and Background.* New York: Appleton-Century, 1935, p. 60.

14. *Ibid.,* p. 399.

15. *Ibid.*

16. Galton, Francis. *Hereditary Genius.* London: Macmillan and Co., 1892, p. 330.

17. *Ibid.,* p. 328.

18. *Ibid.,* p. xxvi. Italics added.

19. Boring, Edwin G. *History of Experimental Psychology.* New York: Appleton-Century-Crofts, 1950, p. 483.

20. Lippmann, Walter. "A Future for the Tests." *New Republic,* Nov. 29, 1922, p. 9.

21. Dahlke, *op cit.,* pp. 73–74.

22. King, Edmund J. *Other Schools and Ours.* New York: Holt, Rinehart and Winston, 1958, p. 85.

23. Walsh, John. "Education Reform: Britain Tries It Top to Bottom." *Science,* 1967, 158, pp. 1162–1165.

24. Kazamias and Massialas, *op. cit.,* p. 45.

25. "Education in France." *World Survey of Education.* Paris: UNESCO, 1955, p. 3.

26. Butts, R. F., *op. cit.,* p. 421.

27. *Ibid.*

28. "Education in France," *op. cit.,* p. 10.

29. Kazamias and Massialas, *op. cit.,* pp. 45–47.

30. Atkinson and Maleska, *op. cit.,* pp. 166–172.

31. Kazamias and Massialas, *op. cit.,* pp. 47–49.

32. *Ibid.,* p. 49.

33. *Ibid.,* p. 50.

34. Hechinger, Fred M. "Soviet Education System at the Crossroads." *The New York Times,* Oct. 5, 1967, p. 1. Other statements by Hechinger in this chapter are drawn from the same article.

35. Mulhern, James. *A History of Education.* New York: Ronald Press, 1959, pp. 708–709.

36. Atkinson and Maleska, *op. cit.,* p. 179.

CHAPTER 3

1. Knox, Samuel. "An Essay on the Best System of Liberal Education Adapted to the Genius of the Government of the United States." (Baltimore, 1799.) In Vassar, Rena L. *Social History of American Education,* Vol. I: *Colonial Times to 1860.* Chicago: Rand McNally, 1965, pp. 135–136.

2. Vassar, *ibid.,* p. 165.

3. *Ibid.,* pp. 245–247.

4. *Ibid.,* p. 158.

5. *Report of the Committee of Ten on Secondary School Studies.* New York: American Book Co., 1894, p. 51.

6. "The High School Question." *Report of the Commissioner of Education for the Year 1877.* Washington: U.S. Government Printing Office, 1879. In Vassar, *op. cit.,* Vol II: *1860 to the Present,* p. 16.

7. *Digest of Educational Statistics.* U.S. Office of Education. Washington: U.S. Government Printing Office, 1966, p. 12.

8. *Biennial Survey of Education, 1928–1930.* U.S. Office of Education. Washington: U.S. Government Printing Office. Vol. 2, p. 7. See also *Statistical Abstract of the United States, 1967.* Washington: U.S. Bureau of the Census, 1967, p. 131.

9. Wayland, Sloane R. "Old Problems, New Faces, and New Standards." In Passow, A. H. (ed.) *Education in Depressed Areas.* New York: Bureau of Publications, Teachers College, Columbia University, 1963.

10. Haubrich, Vernon F. "Teachers for Big-City Schools." In Passow, *ibid.*

11. Harrington, Michael. *The Other America.* Baltimore: Penguin, 1963.

12. *Statistical Abstract of the United States.* Washington: U.S. Bureau of the Census, 1966, p. 340.

13. *Ibid.,* p. 55.

14. "Negroes' Health Is Found Lagging." *New York Times,* March 14,

1967. Drawn from papers presented by two public health specialists of New York City, J. G. Haughton and P. M. Densen, at conference at Howard University.

15. *Statistical Abstract of the United States, op. cit.*, p. 340.

16. *Ibid.*, p. 336.

17. Handlin, Oscar. *The Newcomers.* Cambridge, Massachusetts: Harvard University Press, 1959. Handlin, Oscar. *The Uprooted.* New York: Grosset and Dunlap, 1951. Wayland, Sloane R., *op. cit.*

18. Snygg, D. E. "Learning: An Aspect of Personality Development." In *Learning Theory, Personality Theory, and Clinical Research.* New York: Wiley, 1954.

19. Thorndike, E. L. *Educational Psychology* (1903) and *The Psychology of Learning* (1913).

20. Cattell, J. McK., and G. S. Fullerton. *On the Perception of Small Differences* (1892).

21. Freud, Sigmund. *The Interpretation of Dreams* (1900; English translation, 1914).

22. Binet, Alfred, and Theodore Simon. "Méthodes Nouvelles pour le Diagnostic du Niveau Intellectuel des Anormaux." *L'année Psychologie,* 1905, 11, pp. 191–336.

23. Terman, Lewis M. *The Measurement of Intelligence.* New York: Houghton Mifflin, 1916.

24. Bingham, Walter V., and M. Freyd. *Procedures in Employment Psychology.* New York: McGraw-Hill, 1926. Otis, A. S. "An Absolute Point Scale for the Measurement of Intelligence." *Journal of Educational Psychology,* 1918, 9, pp. 239–261, 333–348.

25. Parsons, Frank. *Choosing a Vocation.* Cambridge, Massachusetts: The Riverside Press, 1909.

26. Dewey, John. *The School and Society.* Chicago: University of Chicago Press, 1899.

27. Cremin, Lawrence A. *The Transformation of the School.* New York: Knopf, 1961.

28. Hilgard, Ernest R. *Theories of Learning.* New York: Appleton-Century-Crofts, 1956.

29. Snygg, *op. cit.*

30. Binet, Alfred. *Les Idées Modernes sur les Enfants.* Paris: Flammarion, 1909. Cited in Hunt, J. McV. *Intelligence and Experience.* New York: Ronald Press, 1961, p. 13.

31. The *proportion* of private school graduates in *Who's Who in America* is six times as great as that of public school graduates. Larson, Cedric A. *Sixty Years of American Eminence.* New York: McDowell, Obolensky, 1958.

32. Brigham, C. C. *A Study of American Intelligence.* Princeton: Princeton University Press, 1923.

33. Tuddenham, R. D. "Soldiers' Intelligence in World Wars I and II." *American Psychologist,* 1948, 3, pp. 54–56.

34. *The Intelligence of Scottish Children.* London: University of London Press, 1939. *The Trend of Scottish Intelligence.* London: University of London Press, 1949.

35. Lippmann, Walter. "The Abuse of the Tests." *New Republic,* Nov. 15, 1922, p. 297.

36. Lippmann, Walter. "The Mental Age of America." *New Republic,* Oct. 25, 1922, p. 213.

37. Lippmann, Walter. "The Mystery of the 'A' Men." *New Republic,* Nov. 1, 1922, p. 248.

38. Lippmann, Walter. "The Abuse of the Tests." *New Republic,* Nov. 15, 1922, p. 297.

39. Lippmann, Walter. "A Future for the Tests." *New Republic,* Nov. 29, 1922, p. 9.

40. Terman, Lewis M. "The Great Conspiracy or The Impulse Imperious of Intelligence Testers, Psychoanalyzed and Exposed by Mr. Lippmann." *New Republic,* Dec. 27, 1922, pp. 116–120.

41. *Ibid.,* p. 120.

42. Toynbee, Arnold. "Conclusions." In Myers, E. D. (ed.) *Education in the Perspective of History.* New York: Harper, 1960, p. 270.

43. Kilpatrick, Wm. H. (ed.) *The Educational Frontier.* New York: Century Co., 1933.

44. Rudy, Willis. *Schools in an Age of Mass Culture.* Englewood Cliffs, New Jersey: Prentice-Hall, 1965, pp. 312–313.

45. Cremin, L., *op. cit.,* p. 324.

46. Cantril, Hadley. Letter on Eric Larrabee's article, "Scientists in Collision." *Harper's,* October, 1963, p. 14.

47. Mannheim, Karl. *Ideology and Utopia.* New York: Harcourt, Brace and Co., 1936.

48. Burt, Cyril. *Intelligence and Fertility.* London: Cassell and Co., 1952, p. 5.

49. Terman, Lewis M. In *Intelligence: Its Nature and Nurture*, 39th yearbook. Chicago: National Society for the Study of Education, 1940. Vol. I, pp. 460–461.

50. Stoddard, George D. *The Meaning of Intelligence*. New York: Macmillan, 1943, p. 68.

51. Brigham, *op. cit.*, p. 210.

52. Stoddard, *op. cit.*, pp. 321, 336, 481.

CHAPTER 4

1. *Educational Testing Service Annual Report, 1965–1966*. Princeton: Educational Testing Service, 1967, pp. 55–58.

2. *Manual of Directions for Alpha Test*. Otis Quick Scoring Mental Ability Tests. Yonkers, New York: World Book Co., 1939.

3. *Examiner's Manual*. The Henmon-Nelson Tests of Mental Ability. Boston: Houghton Mifflin, 1957.

4. *Examiner's Manual*. SRA Primary Mental Abilities, Primary Form. Chicago: Science Research Associates, 1948, p. 5.

5. Freeman, Frank S. *Theory and Practice of Psychological Testing*. New York: Henry Holt and Co., 1951, p. 487.

6. Thorndike, Robert L., and Elizabeth Hagen. *Measurement and Evaluation in Psychology and Education*. New York: Wiley, 1955, p. 239.

7. Super, Donald E., and John O. Crites. *Appraising Vocational Fitness*. New York: Harper, 1962, p. 84.

8. Remmers, H. H., and N. Gage. *Educational Measurement and Evaluation*. New York: Harper, 1955, pp. 214–215.

9. Binet, Alfred. *Les Idées Modernes sur les Enfants*. Paris: Flammarion, 1909, p. 118.

10. Terman, Lewis M. *The Measurement of Intelligence*. Boston: Houghton Mifflin, 1916, p. 116.

11. "Cities Reporting the Use of Homogeneous Grouping, the Winnetka Technique and the Dalton Plan." *City School Leaflet*, No. 22. Washington: U.S. Bureau of Education, December, 1926.

12. "Trends in City-School Organization, 1938–1948." *Research Bulletin*, Vol. 27, No. 1. Washington: National Education Association, February, 1949.

13. "Ability Grouping." *Research Memo*, No. 54, NEA Research Division. Washington: National Education Association, 1960.

14. Otto, Henry J. *Elementary School Organization and Administration.* New York: Appleton-Century, 1954 (3rd edn.), p. 151.

15. Caswell, H. L., and A. W. Foshay. *Education in the Elementary School.* New York: American Book Co., 1957, pp. 339–340.

16. Douglass, H. R. (ed.) *The High School Curriculum.* New York: Ronald Press, 1956 (2nd edn.).

17. Carlsen, G. R. Quoted *ibid.,* pp. 390–408.

18. Tiegs, Ernest W. *Tests and Measurements in the Improvement of Learning.* Boston: Houghton Mifflin, 1939.

19. Anastasi, Anne. "Practice and Variability: A Study in Psychological Method." *Psychological Monographs,* 1934, 45, pp. 1–55.

20. Cook, W. W. "Individual Trait Differences in Public Schools, with Implications for School Organization and Curriculum Development." *Teachers College Journal,* 1947, 19, pp. 56–57.

21. Otto, *op. cit.,* p. 201.

22. Thorndike and Hagen, *op. cit.,* pp. 237–238.

23. *Ibid.,* p. 237. The study cited is: Justman, Joseph A. *Comparison of the Functioning of Intellectually Gifted Children Enrolled in Special Progress Classes in the Junior High School.* Unpublished doctoral dissertation, Columbia University, 1953.

24. Wilhelms, Fred T., and Dorothy Westby-Gibson. "Grouping: Research Offers Leads." *Educational Leadership,* 1961, 18, pp. 410–413.

25. Goldberg, M. L., A. H. Passow, and J. Justman. *The Effects of Ability Grouping.* New York: Teachers College Press, 1966, p. 25.

26. *Ibid.,* p. 167. (A careful reading of Chapter 3 suggests that the authors have been more generous in their appraisal of grouping in their statement of conclusions than their own data and their own chapter summary (pp. 69–71) would justify.)

27. Heathers, Glen. *Organizing Schools Through the Dual Progress Plan.* Danville, Illinois: The Interstate, 1967.

CHAPTER 5

1. Thorndike, E. L. *Educational Psychology* (1903) and *The Psychology of Learning* (1913).

2. Hilgard, Ernest R. *Theories of Learning.* New York: Appleton-Century-Crofts, 1956 (2nd edn.), p. 481.

3. Pasamanick, B., and H. Knobloch. "Epidemiologic Studies in the Complications of Pregnancy and Birth Process." In Caplon, G. (ed.) *Preven-*

tion of Mental Disorders in Childhood. New York: Basic Books, 1961, Chap. 4.

4. Masland, Richard L. In Masland, Richard L., Seymour R. Sarason, and Thomas Gladwin. *Mental Subnormality.* New York: Basic Books, 1958, p. 11. The studies referred to in the text are in Benda, C. E. "The Familial Imbecile or Oligocephaly as a Morbid Entity." *American Journal of Mental Deficiency,* 1944, 49, p. 32.

5. Chauchard, Paul. *The Brain.* New York: Grove Press, 1962, p. 44.

6. Luria, A. R. "An Objective Approach to the Study of the Abnormal Child." *American Journal of Orthopsychiatry,* 1961, 31, pp. 1–16.

7. Crowell, D. "Sensory Defects" In Louttit, C. M. *Clinical Psychology of Exceptional Children.* New York: Harper, 1957.

8. *Characteristics of Persons with Impaired Hearing.* National Center for Health Statistics Series 10, No. 35. Washington: U.S. Dept. of Health, Education and Welfare, April, 1967, p. 21.

9. *Ibid.,* p. 22.

10. *Ibid.,* p. 39.

11. Gustafson, Sarah R. (ed.) *The Pediatric Patient, 1966.* Philadelphia: J. B. Lippincott, 1966, p. 155.

12. Sexton, Patricia. *Education and Income.* New York: Viking Press, 1961.

13. Kephart, Newell C. "Reading Readiness in the Brain-Injured." In Figurel, J. A. (ed.) *New Frontiers in Reading.* Conference Proceedings, International Reading Association. Vol. 5. New York: Scholastic Magazine, 1960. Kephart, Newell C. *The Slow Learner in the Classroom.* Columbus, Ohio: Merrill, 1960.

14. Delecato, Carl H. *Treatment and Prevention of Reading Problems.* Springfield, Illinois: Chas. Thomas, 1959. Also *The Diagnosis and Treatment of Speech and Reading Problems* (1963) and *Neurological Organization and Reading* (1966).

15. Glass, Gene V., and M. P. Robbins. "A Critique of Experiments on the Role of Neurological Organization in Reading Performances." *Reading Research Quarterly,* 1967, 3, pp. 5–51.

16. Harden, D. G. "The Chromosomes." In Penrose, L. S. (ed.) *Recent Advances in Human Genetics.* Boston: Little, Brown, 1961. The original report was by Tjio, J. H., and A. Levan. "The Chromosome Number of Man." *Hereditas,* 1956, 42, p. 1.

17. Clark, C. A. *Genetics for the Clinician.* Philadelphia: F. A. Davis, 1964 (2nd edn.), p. 27.

18. Yannet, Herman. "Classification and Etiological Factors in Mental Retardation," In Rothstein, J. H. (ed.) *Mental Retardation.* New York: Holt, Rinehart and Winston, 1961, p. 41.

19. Crome, L. "Causes of Mental Defect." In Hilliard, L. T., and Brian H. Kirman. *Mental Deficiency.* Boston: Little, Brown, 1965, pp. 134–135.

20. Gustafson, *op. cit.,* p. 143.

21. Gustafson, *op. cit.,* p. 63.

22. Darke, R. A. "Late Effects of Severe Asphyxia Neonatorum." *Journal of Pediatrics,* 1944, 24, p. 148.

23. Thurston, D. L., J. N. Middelkamp, and E. Mason. "The Late Effects of Lead Poisoning." *Journal of Pediatrics,* 1955, 47, pp. 413–423.

24. Report from Bureau of Preventable Diseases. New York City Dept. of Health. June, 1967.

25. Masland, Sarason, and Gladwin, *op. cit.,* p. 15. This book was the source of some of the citations that follow.

26. Antonov, A. N. "Children Born During the Siege of Leningrad in 1942." *Journal of Pediatrics,* 1947, 30, p. 250.

27. MacMahon, B., R. G. Record, and T. McKeown. "Secular Changes in the Incidence of Malformations of the Central Nervous System." *British Journal of Social Medicine,* 1951, 5, p. 254.

28. Eichmann, E., and H. Gesenius. "Die Missgeburtenzunahme in Berlin und Umgebung in den Nachkriegsjahren." *Arch. Gynäk,* 1952, 181, p. 168.

29. Stearns, G., and I. G. Macy. *Maternal Nutrition and Child Health: An Interpretive Review.* Washington: National Research Council, 1950. Bulletin 123.

30. Dieckmann, W. J., D. F. Turner, E. J. Meiller, M. T. Straube, and L. J. Savage. "Observations on Protein Intake and the Health of the Mother and Baby: II. Food Intake." *Journal of American Dietetic Association,* 1951, 27, p. 1053.

31. Jeans, P. C., M. B. Smith, and G. Stearns. "Incidence of Prematurity in Relation to Maternal Nutrition." *Journal of American Dietetic Association,* 1955, 31, p. 576.

32. Harrell, R. F., E. Woodyyard, and A. I. Gates. *The Effect of Mothers' Diets on the Intelligence of Offspring: A Study of the Influence of Vitamin Supplementation of the Diets of Pregnant and Lactating Women on the Intelligence of Their Children.* New York: Bureau of Publications, Teachers College, Columbia University, 1955.

33. Masland, *op. cit.,* p. 66.

34. Baird, D., and R. Ulsey. "Environment and Childbearing." *Proceedings, Royal Society of Medicine,* 1953, 46, p. 53.

35. MacFarlane, W. V., P. R. Pennycuik, and E. Thrift. "Resorption and Loss of Foetuses in Rats Living at 35° C." *Journal of Physiology,* 1957, 135, p. 451.

36. Knobloch, Hilda, and Benjamin Pasamanick. "Seasonal Variations in the Births of the Mentally Deficient." *American Journal of Public Health,* 1958, 48, pp. 1201–1208.

37. Wiener, Gerald. "Psychologic Correlates of Premature Birth: A Review." *Journal of Nervous and Mental Diseases,* 1962, 134, p. 142.

38. Pasamanick, Benjamin, and Hilda Knobloch. "Retrospective Studies on the Epidemiology of Reproductive Casualty: Old and New." *Merrill-Palmer Quarterly of Behavior and Development,* 1966, 12, pp. 7–26,

39. *Ibid.,* p. 7.

40. *Ibid.,* p. 12.

41. *Ibid.,* p. 13.

42. Freedman, Alfred M., M. Braine, C. B. Heimer, M. Kowlessor, W. J. O'Connor, H. Wortis, and B. Goodman. "The Influence of Hyperbilirubinemia on the Early Development of the Premature." *Psychiatric Research Records,* 1960, 13, pp. 108–123.

43. Pasamanick and Knobloch, *op. cit.,* pp. 18–19. Two investigators at the University of Florida, James D. Harmeling and Marshal B. Jones, report very interesting findings on the birth weight of high-school dropouts. Comparing thirty-nine dropouts from an all-Negro high school who were matched with their former classmates still in school as normal learners or slow learners, they found that the average birth weight of the dropouts was the lowest, the slow learners next, and the normals the highest. The dropout group included six prematures, the slow learners five, and the normals none. Apparently the low birth weight reflects malnutrition *in utero,* with prematurity, brain damage, and reduced mental functioning as the result. "Birth Weights of High School Dropouts." *American Journal of Orthopsychiatry,* 1968, 38, pp. 63–66.

44. Culliton, Barbara J. "Vaccine Conquers Baby-Killer." *Science News,* 1967, 92, pp. 520–521.

45. Gustafson, *op. cit.,* pp. 86–102.

46. Culliton, *op. cit.*

47. Gustafson, *op. cit.,* p. 140.

48. *Ibid.*, pp. 142–152.

49. John, E. Roy. "The Brain and How It Changes." *Bulletin of Atomic Scientists,* 1965, 21, pp. 12–14.

50. Masland, *op. cit.*, p. 40.

51. Kirman, Brian H. "Metabolic Syndromes." In Hilliard, L. T., and B. H. Kirman. *Mental Deficiency.* Boston: Little, Brown, 1965, pp. 134–135.

52. John, *op. cit.*

53. Stratton, L. O., and L. Petrinovich. "Post-trial Injections of an Anticholinesterase Drug and Maze Learning in Two Strains of Rats." *Psychopharmacologia,* 1963, 5, pp. 47–54. For more recent studies and discussion see the significant new book by E. Roy John, *Mechanisms of Memory.* New York: Academy Press, 1967.

CHAPTER 6

1. Boring, Ernest G. *A History of Experimental Psychology.* New York: Appleton-Century-Crofts, 1950 (2nd edn.), p. 560.

2. Ruch, Floyd L. *Psychology and Life.* Chicago: Scott Foresman, 1948 (3rd edn.).

3. Hilgard, Ernest R. *Theories of Learning.* New York: Appleton-Century-Crofts, 1956 (2nd edn.).

4. Lindgren, Henry C. *Educational Psychology in the Classroom.* New York: Wiley, 1956. Skinner, Charles E. (ed.) *Essentials of Educational Psychology.* Englewood Cliffs, New Jersey: Prentice-Hall, 1958.

5. Shaffer, Laurance F., and E. J. L. Shoben. *The Psychology of Adjustment.* Boston: Houghton Mifflin, 1956.

6. Piaget, Jean. *The Moral Judgment of the Child.* London: Kegan Paul, 1932; New York: Free Press, 1965. The material on Piaget's system was taken from his book, *The Origins of Intelligence in Children.* New York: International Universities Press, 1952. For a concise statement on Piaget's ideas see an article by his associate, Bärbel Inhelder, "Some Aspects of Piaget's Genetic Approach to Cognition." In Kessen, William, and Clementina Kuhlman (eds.). *Thought in the Young Child.* Monograph of the Society for Research in Child Development, 1962, 83. The other papers represent an attempt by American psychologists to understand and evaluate Piaget's work.

7. Hilgard, *op. cit.*, pp. 457–458.

8. Snygg, D. "Learning: An Aspect of Personality Development." In

Learning Theory, Personality Theory and Clinical Research (the Kentucky Symposium). New York: Wiley, 1954.

9. Brearley, M., and E. Hitchfield. *A Teacher's Guide to Reading Piaget.* London: Routledge and Kegan Paul, 1966.

10. Flavell, John H. *The Developmental Psychology of Jean Piaget.* Princeton, New Jersey: Van Nostrand, 1963, p. 43.

11. Maslow, Abraham H. *Motivation and Personality.* New York: Harper, 1954.

12. Escalona, S. K. "Children and the Threat of Nuclear War." See also Milton Schwebel, "Nuclear Cold War: Student Opinions and Professional Responsibility." In Schwebel, Milton (ed.). *Behavioral Science and Human Survival.* Palo Alto: Science and Behavior Books, 1965.

13. Freud, Anna, and Dorothy Burlingham. *War and Children.* New York: New York Medical Books, 1943, p. 37.

14. Schwebel, *op. cit.*

15. Linton, Ralph. Quoted by Hill, Reuben, and Donald A. Hansen. "Families in Disaster." In Baker, George W., and Dwight W. Chapman (eds.) . *Man and Society in Disaster.* New York: Basic Books, 1962, p. 221.

16. Skeels, Harold M., and H. B. Dye. "A Study of the Effects of Differential Stimulation on Mentally Retarded Children." *Proceedings of the American Association of Mental Deficiency,* 1939, 44, pp. 114–136.

17. Kirk, Samuel A. "The Challenge of Individual Differences." In Tumin, Melvin M., and M. Bressler (eds.). *Proceedings of Conference on "Quality and Equality of Education."* Princeton: Princeton University Press, 1966.

18. For an excellent review of the studies and an analysis of the problem see Yarrow, Leon J. "Separation from Parents During Early Childhood." In Hoffman, Martin L., and Lois W. Hoffman (eds.). *Review of Child Development Research.* New York: Russell Sage Foundation, 1964.

19. Bernard, Viola W., Perry Ottenberg, and Fritz Redl. "Dehumanization: A Composite Psychological Defense in Relation to Modern War." In Schwebel, *op. cit.*

20. Various sections of the remainder of the chapter are drawn from a monograph: Schwebel, Milton. *Resistance to Learning.* New York: Early Childhood Education Council of New York, 1963.

21. Hollinshead, August B. *Elmtown's Youth.* New York: Wiley, 1949. Havighurst, Robert J., Paul H. Bowman, Gordon P. Liddle, Charles V. Matthews, James J. Pierce. *Growing Up in River City.* New York: Wiley,

1962. Passow, A. Harry (ed.). *Education in Depressed Areas.* New York: Bureau of Publications, Teachers College, Columbia University, 1963.

22. Charters, W. W., Jr. "The Social Background of Teaching." In Gage, N. L. (ed.) *Handbook of Research on Teaching.* Chicago: Rand McNally, 1963, pp. 739–745.

23. Sherif, Muzafer, and Hadley Cantril. *Psychology of Ego-Involvements.* New York: Wiley, 1947.

24. Clark, Kenneth B. *Prejudice and Your Child.* Boston: Beacon, 1955.

25. Thomas, Alexander, Stella Chess, Herbert G. Birch, Margaret Hertzig, and Samuel Korn. *Behavioral Individuality in Early Childhood.* New York: New York University Press, 1963. Also personal conversation with Dr. Thomas.

26. Riesman, David. *Constraint and Variety in American Education.* Garden City, New York: Doubleday, 1958, p. 127.

27. Lazarsfeld, Paul F., and Wagner Thielens, Jr. *The Academic Mind.* Glencoe, Ill.: Free Press, 1958.

28. Friedan, Betty. *The Feminine Mystique.* New York: Norton, 1963.

29. Tannenbaum, Abraham J. *Adolescent Attitudes Toward Academic Brilliance.* New York: Bureau of Publications, Teachers College, Columbia University, 1962.

30. Harris, I. *Emotional Blocks to Learning.* Glencoe, Ill.: Free Press, 1959.

31. Rogers, Carl R. *On Becoming a Person.* Boston: Houghton Mifflin, 1961.

32. Sontag, Lester W., Charles T. Baker, and Virginia L. Nelson. *Mental Growth and Personality Development: A Longitudinal Study.* Monograph of the Society for Research in Child Development, 1958, 23.

33. Du Bois, W. E. B. "Of Our Spiritual Strivings." From *The Souls of Black Folk.* Fawcett World Library. In Josephson, Eric and Mary (eds.). *Man Alone.* New York: Dell, 1962, pp. 343–344.

CHAPTER 7

1. Snell, Bruno. *The Discovery of the Mind: The Greek Origins of European Thought.* New York: Harper, 1960.

2. *Ibid.,* p. 21.

3. *Ibid.,* p. 53.

4. *Ibid.,* p. 53.

5. Barbu, Zevedei. *Problems of Historical Psychology*. New York: Grove Press, 1960.

6. Bateson, Gregory. "Cultural Determinants of Personality." Chap. 23 in Hunt, J. McV. *Personality and the Behavior Disorders*. New York: Ronald Press, 1944.

7. Mead, Margaret. *Coming of Age in Samoa*. New York: Morrow, 1928.

8. Gladwin, Thomas, and S. B. Sarason. *Truk: Man in Paradise*. Quoted in Masland, R. L., S. B. Sarason, and T. Gladwin, *op. cit.*, Chap. 15.

9. Davis, A., and Robert J. Havighurst. "Social Class and Color Differences in Child-Rearing." *American Sociological Review*, 1946, 11, pp. 698–710.

10. Rosen, B. C. "The Achievement Motive and Value Systems of Selected Ethnic Groups." Paper read before the American Sociological Association, Washington, D.C., 1957. Cited in Masland, Sarason, and Gladwin, *op. cit.*, p. 221.

11. Malinowski, Bronislaw. *Sex and Repression in Savage Society*. New York: Harcourt, Brace, 1927.

12. Goddard, H. H. *The Kallikak Family: A Study of the Heredity of Feeblemindedness*. New York: Macmillan, 1912.

13. Masland, *op. cit.*, p. 64.

14. Klineberg, Otto. *Negro Intelligence and Selective Migration*. New York: Columbia University Press, 1935. Lee, E. J. "Negro Intelligence and Selective Migration: A Philadelphia Test of the Klineberg Hypothesis." *American Sociological Review*, 1951, 16, pp. 227–233. Long, Herman H. "The Intelligence of Colored Elementary Pupils in Washington, D.C." *Journal of Negro Education*, 1934, 3, pp. 205–222. McAlpin, A. S. "Changes in the Intelligence Quotients of Negro Children." *Journal of Negro Education*, 1932, 1, pp. 44–48.

15. Pasamanick, Benjamin. "A Comparative Study of the Behavioral Development of Negro Infants." *Journal of Psychology*, 1953, 83, pp. 137–157.

16. Anastasi, Anne, and Rita D'Angelo. "Comparison of Negro and White Preschool Children in Language Development and Goodenough Draw-a-Man I.Q." *Journal of Genetic Psychology*, 1952, 81, pp. 147–165.

17. Dreger, Ralph M., and Kent S. Miller. "Comparative Psychological Studies of Negroes and Whites in the United States." *Psychological Bulletin*, 1960, 57, pp. 361–402.

18. Shuey, Audrey M. *The Testing of Negro Intelligence.* Lynchburg, Va.: J. P. Bell Co., 1958.

19. Osborne, R. Travis. "Racial Difference in Mental Growth and School Achievement: A Longitudinal Study." *Psychological Reports,* 1960, 13, pp. 233–239.

20. Klineberg, *op. cit.*

21. Lee, *op. cit.*

22. Fishman, Leo (ed.). *Poverty Amid Affluence.* New Haven: Yale University Press, 1965, pp. 58–59.

23. Riesman, *op. cit.,* p. 127.

24. Henry, Jules. *Culture Against Man.* New York: Random House, 1963.

25. Bernal, J. D. *Science in History.* London: Watts, 1957, p. 30.

26. *Ibid.,* p. 528.

27. Handlin, Oscar. "Textbooks That Don't Teach." *Atlantic,* December, 1957, pp. 110–113.

CHAPTER 8

1. Bestor, Arthur. *The Restoration of Learning.* New York: Knopf, 1955.

2. Rickover, Hyman G. *Education and Freedom.* New York: E. P. Dutton, 1959, p. 154.

3. Hutchins, Robert. *Conflict in Education in a Democratic Society.* New York: Harper, 1953.

4. Adler, Irving. *What We Want of Our Schools.* New York: John Day, 1957, p. 163.

5. *Ibid.,* p. 168.

6. Conant, James B. *The Revolutionary Transformation of the American High School.* Cambridge: Harvard University Press, 1959, p. 27.

7. Bestor, *op. cit.,* p. 112.

8. Koerner, James D. (ed.) *The Case for Basic Education.* Boston: Little, Brown, 1959, p. xii.

9. Hutchins, Robert. *Some Observations on American Education.* New York: Cambridge University Press, 1956, p. 45.

10. Zeigler, H. *The Political World of the High School Teacher.* Eugene, Oregon: Center for Advanced Study of Educational Administration, 1967.

11. Miel, Alice, with E. Kester, Jr. *The Shortchanged Children of Suburbia.* New York: Institute of Human Relations Press, 1967, pp. 52–56.

12. Piaget, Jean. *The Origins of Intelligence in Children.* New York: International Universities Press, 1952, p. 267.

13. *Ibid.*, p. 338.

14. Flavell, John H. *The Developmental Psychology of Jean Piaget.* Princeton, New Jersey: Van Nostrand, 1963, p. 166.

15. *Ibid.*, p. 204.

16. *Ibid.*

17. *Ibid.*, p. 211.

18. Piaget, Jean. *Comments on Vygotsky's Critical Remarks.* Cambridge: M. I. T. Press, 1962, p. 10.

19. *Ibid.*, p. 11.

20. *Ibid.*

21. Schwebel, Andrew. "Effects of Impulsivity on Performance of Verbal Tasks in Middle- and Lower-Class Children." *American Journal of Orthopsychiatry,* 1966, 36, pp. 13–21.

22. de Bottari, Linda. "Primary School Correlates of Secondary School Achievement." Unpublished Ph.D. dissertation. New York University, 1966.

23. Laurendeau, Monique, and Adrien Pinard. *Causal Thinking in the Child, A Genetic and Experimental Approach.* New York: International Universities Press, 1963.

24. Flavell, *op. cit.*, pp. 156–157.

25. Eisenberg, Leon, and C. Keith Conners. "The Effect of Head Start on Developmental Processes." In Jervis, George (ed.). *Kennedy Foundation Symposium on Mental Retardation, 1966.* Springfield, Ill.: Chas. Thomas (in press).

26. Bradley, G. H. "A Review of Educational Problems Based on Military Selection and Classification Data in World War II." *Journal of Educational Research,* 1949, 43, pp. 161–174.

27. Rosenthal, Robert, and L. Jacobson. "Teachers' Expectancies: Determinants of Pupils' IQ Gains." *Psychological Reports,* 1966, 19, pp. 115–118.

28. Goldenberg, Ira. "Reading Groups and Some Aspects of Teacher Behavior." Preliminary draft of research report provided by Professor Goldenberg, Dept. of Psychology, Yale University.

29. Feuerstein, Reuven. "Problems of Assessment and Evaluation of the Mentally Retarded and the Culturally Deprived." Proceedings of the First International Congress on Mental Retardation. Montpelier, France, September, 1967. *Excerpta Medica* (in press).

CHAPTER 9

1. Bruner, Jerome S. "Education as Social Invention." *Journal of Social Issues,* 1964, 20, p. 31.

2. Voltaire. *Essay on the Morals and the Spirit of Nations.*

3. Bergson, Henri. *Creative Evolution.* New York: Modern Library, 1944.

4. Hegel, G. W. F. *Philosophy of History.* New York: Dover, 1956.

5. Acton, (Lord) J. E. E. D. *Historical Essays and Studies.* London: Macmillan, 1907.

6. Thompson, D. C. "The New South." In Reissman, Leonard, and Thomas Ktsanes (eds.). "Social Change in the South." *Journal of Social Issues,* 1966, 22, p. 11.

7. Killian, Leonard, and C. Grigg. "Race Relations in an Urbanized South." *Ibid.,* pp. 20–21.

8. Reiss, Ira L. "The Sexual Renaissance: A Summary and Analysis." In Reiss, I. L. (ed.) "The Sexual Renaissance in America." *Journal of Social Issues,* 1966, 22, p. 126.

9. "Facts on American Education." *Research Bulletin.* Washington: National Education Association, 1966, p. 37.

10. *Ibid.,* p. 39.

11. Hentoff, Nat. "Educators as Dropouts: New York City's Public Schools." *Evergreen Review,* October, 1966, p. 19.

12. Strauss, Samuel. "High School Backgrounds of Ph.D.'s," *Science Education,* 1960, 44, pp. 45–51.

13. Bloom, Benjamin S. *Stability and Change in Human Characteristics.* New York: Wiley, 1964.

14. Tyler, Leona E. *The Psychology of Human Differences.* New York: Appleton-Century-Crofts, 1956 (2nd edn.).

15. Havighurst, *op. cit.* See also Miller, S. M. "The American Lower Classes: A Typological Approach." In Shostak, Arthur B., and William Gomberg (eds.). *New Perspectives on Poverty.* Englewood Cliffs, New Jersey: Prentice-Hall, 1965.

16. Rothstein, Jerome H. "General Considerations." In Rothstein, J. H. (ed.). *Mental Retardation.* New York: Holt, Rinehart and Winston, 1961, p. 2.

17. Yannet, Herman. "Classification and Etiological Factors in Mental Retardation." *Ibid.,* p. 39.

18. *Ibid.*, p. 37.

19. Kuhn, Thomas. *The Structure of Scientific Revolutions.* Chicago: University of Chicago Press, 1962, p. 5.

20. *Ibid.*, pp. 6–7.

CHAPTER 10

1. Friedenberg, Edgar Z. "Requiem for the Urban School." *Saturday Review,* Nov. 18, 1967, p. 77.

2. *The Pursuit of Excellence.* Rockefeller Brothers Fund, Inc. Garden City, New York: Doubleday, 1958, pp. 17, 19, 29, 30, 31.

3. Gardner, John W. *Excellence.* New York: Harper, 1961, pp. 41, 66.

4. Rudy, Willis. *Schools in an Age of Mass Culture.* Englewood Cliffs, New Jersey: Prentice-Hall, 1965.

5. Harper, R. M. "Graphic Methods of Measuring Civilization." *Scientific Monthly,* 1920, 10, pp. 292–305.

6. Rudy, *op. cit.*, p. 353.

7. Jacoby, Susan L. "National Monument to Failure." *Saturday Review,* Nov. 18, 1967, pp. 71–73, 89–90.

8. Gross, Neal. *Who Runs Our Schools?* New York: Wiley, 1958, p. 136.

9. Gross, Neal, and R. E. Herriott, *Staff Leadership in Public Schools: A Sociological Inquiry.* New York: Wiley, 1965, p. 157.

10. Holt, John. Review in *New York Review of Books,* Dec. 21, 1967, p. 5.

11. Rogow, Arnold A. "The Educational Malaise." *Nation,* Jan. 26, 1957, pp. 71–74.

12. Brookover, William B. *A Sociology of Education.* New York: American Book Co., 1955, p. 69.

13. Grobman, Hulda G., and V. A. Hines. "Private Life of the Teacher." In Stiles, L. J. (ed.) *The Teacher's Role in American Society.* New York: Harper, 1957, pp. 132–145.

14. Gummere, R. M., Jr. "Prestige and the Teacher." *School and Society,* 1960, 88, pp. 117–118.

15. Charters, W. W., Jr. "The Social Background of Teaching." In Gage, N. L. (ed.) *Handbook of Research on Teaching.* Chicago: Rand McNally, 1963, p. 777.

16. Rabinowitz, W., and Rosenbaum, I. "Teaching Experience and Teachers' Attitude." *Elementary School Journal,* 1960, 60, p. 317.

17. Lazarsfeld, Paul F., and Wagner Thielens, Jr. *The Academic Mind.* Glencoe, Ill.: Free Press, 1958, p. 128.

18. Schwebel, Robert. "Wakening Our Sleepy Universities: Student Involvement in Curriculum Change." *Teachers College Record* (in press).

19. Bruner, Jerome S. *The Process of Education.* Cambridge: Harvard University Press, 1961. *Toward a Theory of Instruction.* Cambridge: Harvard University Press, 1966. *Studies in Cognitive Growth.* New York: Wiley, 1966.

20. Gordon, Edmund W., and Doxey A. Wilkerson. *Compensatory Education for the Disadvantaged.* New York: College Entrance Examination Board, 1966.

21. Deutsch, Martin, and Associates. *The Disadvantaged Child.* New York: Basic Books, 1967. Witty, Paul A. (ed.) *The Educationally Retarded and Disadvantaged.* The 66th Yearbook of the National Society for the Study of Education. Chicago: National Society for the Study of Education, 1967.

22. Beck, John M., and Richard W. Saxe (eds.). *Teaching the Culturally Disadvantaged Pupil.* Springfield, Illinois: Chas. C. Thomas, 1965. Kerber, August, and Barbara Bommarito (eds.). *The Schools and the Urban Crisis.* New York: Holt, Rinehart and Winston, 1965. Loretan, Joseph O., and Shelley Umans. *Teaching the Disadvantaged.* New York: Teachers College Press, Columbia University, 1966. Strom, Robert D. *Teaching in the Slum Schools.* Columbus, Ohio: Charles E. Merrill Books, 1965. One of the most striking is Bereiter, Carl, and Siegfried Engelmann. *Teaching Disadvantaged Children in the Preschool.* Englewood Cliffs, New Jersey: Prentice-Hall, 1966. The authors report their own very successful experiment with fifteen severely deprivd four-year-olds over a nine-month period. Starting with fifteen very specific learning objectives (for example, the ability to recognize and name the vowels and at least fifteen consonants), they used old-fashioned methods of direct instruction. Lessons were carefully planned and involved demonstration, drill, exercises, and problems; children were rewarded or punished depending upon their effort and success. The children progressed from the status of over a year's retardation in language ability to normal level in language test scores and IQ, and to second-grade level in arithmetic and first-grade in reading. Carefully planned direct instruction had given them mastery over the conceptual tools they needed for learning in school.

23. Coleman, James S. *Adolescents and the Schools.* New York: Basic Books, 1965, p. 108.

INDEX

ABOUT THE AUTHOR

Milton Schwebel, Dean of the Graduate School of Education at Rutgers University, has a background in public education and work with children which uniquely fits him for the writing of *Who Can Be Educated?* He has taught in city, town, and rural schools, at elementary, high-school, and college levels. He has also worked with the National Youth Administration; helped to organize NAACP chapters in upstate New York; served as "house father" in an orphanage; and for many years maintained a private practice as a child psychologist.

A native of Troy, New York, Dr. Schwebel earned his B.A. at Union College, his master's degree and teacher certification at New York State College for Teachers in Albany, and his Ph.D. at Columbia University. Before joining the Rutgers faculty, he was Associate Dean of the School of Education at New York University. Dr. Schwebel is a psychoanalytic psychotherapist certified by the Postgraduate Center of Mental Health; a diplomate of the American Board of Examiners in Professional Psychology; editorial board member of the *American Journal of Orthopsychiatry,* the *Journal of Social Issues,* and the *Journal of Counseling Psychology;* a fellow of the American Psychological Association and the American Orthopsychiatric Association; and a member of the American Association for the Advancement of Science and the New York Academy of Science. He has been a consultant to universities, school systems, and government agencies.